A Conceptual Guide
to *Finnegans Wake*

edited by

Michael H. Begnal

and Fritz Senn

The Pennsylvania State University Press

University Park and London

Library of Congress Catalog Card Number: 73-13219
International Standard Book Number: 0-271-01132-7
Copyright © 1974 The Pennsylvania State University
All rights Reserved
Printed in the United States of America
Designed by Glenn Ruby

KNIGHT-CAPRON LIBRARY
LYNCHBURG COLLEGE
LYNCHBURG, VIRGINIA 24501

A Conceptual Guide to *Finnegans Wake*

Contents

Notes on Contributors   vii

Introduction
    Michael H. Begnal   ix

1
Where Terms Begin / Book I, chapter i   1
    J. Mitchell Morse

2
Recipis for the Price
of the Coffin / Book I, chapters ii–iv   18
    Roland McHugh

3
Concerning Lost Historeve / Book I, chapter v   33
    Bernard Benstock

4
The Turning Point / Book I, chapter vi   56
    E. L. Epstein

5
Portrait of the Artist
as Balzacian Wilde Ass / Book I, chapters vii–viii   71
    Robert Boyle

6
Music and the Mime
of Mick, Nick, and the Maggies / Book II, chapter i   83
    Matthew Hodgart

7
Night Lessons on Language / Book II, chapter ii   93
    Ronald E. Buckalew

8
"but where he is eaten":
Earwicker's Tavern Feast / Book II, chapter iii   116
    Edward A. Kopper

9
Love that Dares to Speak its Name
Book II, chapter iv   139
    Michael H. Begnal

10
Shaun A / Book III, chapter i   149
    James S. Atherton

11
Growing Up Absurd in Dublin / Book III, chapters ii–iii   173
    Hugh B. Staples

12
The Porters: A Square Performance
of Three Tiers in the Round / Book III, chapter iv   201
    Margaret Solomon

13
Looking Forward to a Brightening Day   211
Book IV, chapter i
    Grace Eckley

Notes on Contributors

James S. Atherton, who lives and teaches in England, is the author of *The Books at the Wake,* as well as many articles on Joyce's final work.

Michael H. Begnal is Associate Professor of English and Comparative Literature at the Pennsylvania State University. He has published essays on Joyce and Irish literature, also the book *Joseph Sheridan LeFanu,* and his study of *Finnegans Wake* is forthcoming from Bucknell University Press.

Bernard Benstock is Professor of English at Kent State University. President of the James Joyce Foundation, his work includes, among many other productions, *Joyce-again's Wake* and the co-editing of *Approaches to Ulysses.*

Robert Boyle S. J., author of *Metaphor in Hopkins,* as well as many essays on Joyce in various journals, is Professor of English at Marquette University.

Ronald E. Buckalew specializes in English linguistics and medieval literature, and has published several essays in these fields. An editor of *General Linguistics,* he is Assistant Professor of English at the Pennsylvania State University.

Grace Eckley, Assistant Professor of English at Drake University, has published *Benedict Kiely* for the Twayne series. Her studies of Edna O'Brien and of *Finnegans Wake* are forthcoming.

Edmund L. Epstein is a former editor of *The James Joyce Review* and Advisory Editor of the *James Joyce Quarterly.* He is Associate Professor of English at Southern Illinois University and has recently published *The Ordeal of Stephen Dedalus.*

Matthew Hodgart has written about Joyce for many years, and is co-author of *Song in the Works of James Joyce.* He resides in England.

Edward A. Kopper has published widely in 20th century criticism, and his articles have appeared in such journals as the *James Joyce Quarterly*, *Wake Newslitter*, and *Analyst*. He is Professor of English at Slippery Rock State College.

Roland McHugh, a native of Sussex, England, was awarded a PhD by the University of London for research into the acoustic behavior of grasshoppers. He has published often in *A Wake Newslitter*, and is at present collaborating on a page by page set of annotations for the *Wake*.

J. Mitchell Morse, Professor of English at Temple University, is the author of *The Sympathetic Alien*, *Matters of Style*, *The Irrelevant English Teacher*, and the forthcoming *Race, Class, and Metaphor*.

Fritz Senn, one of the founders of the James Joyce Foundation and co-editor of *A Wake Newslitter*, has written numerous essays on Joyce and, most recently, edited *New Light on Joyce from the Dublin Symposium*. He lives in Zurich, Switzerland.

Margaret Solomon is Associate Professor of English at the University of Hawaii. Among her many publications is *Eternal Geomater: the Sexual Universe of Finnegans Wake*.

Hugh B. Staples is Professor of English and Comparative Literature at the University of Cincinnati. His books include studies of Robert Lowell and Sir Jonah Barrington, and he is at work on a book-length study of Joyce.

Introduction

James Joyce worked on *Finnegans Wake* for seventeen years—from 1922 to 1939—but its critical reception, both during and immediately after publication, never was very inspiring. Ezra Pound said that the book was not worth printing. Joyce's friend and patroness Harriet Shaw Weaver tried to persuade him to give it up, and even his wife Nora wondered why he did not "write sensible books that people can understand." But through it all he persevered, disappointed and confused by the poor notices since he had intended that the novel should appeal in some way to almost everyone. Just the same, the consensus of the time could probably be summed up in the comment of the critic Max Eastman, who said in 1932 that reading the *Wake* was "a good deal like chewing gum—it has some flavor at the start but you soon taste only the motion of your jaws."

Despite this less than marvelous beginning, the reading public has continued to chew for the past four decades, and *Finnegans Wake* has come to be recognized as the masterpiece it is. No student of modern literature can avoid the novel, for it stands as probably the most experimental work which has ever been attempted in prose. Employing, whether he knew it or not, Lewis Carroll's idea of combining several words to make one portmanteau word, Joyce has taken language as far as it can possibly go. He has fashioned a kind of poetic prose which transcends labels and remains inventive and uniquely itself, presenting the reader with a speech and vocabulary which not only expand the English language but also show that words can be delightful in and for themselves alone.

But along with the problem for the reader of deciphering Joyce's language goes the stumbling block of figuring out the narrative or the plot. In other words, just what is going on here? We know that Joyce was interested in Jungian archetypes, that he was influenced by the ideas of Giambattista Vico and Giordano Bruno on personality and mythology, but how are we to put all these jumbled concepts together? How many dreams or dreamers are there—one, ten, a thousand? Who are Humphrey Chimpden Earwicker, Anna Livia Plurabelle, the Willingdone, the Prankquean, and all those other amusing and frustrating characters who lend their voices to the babble of the *Wake*? Is the book moral, or is it simply an amoral reflection of all of human experience? Does the key lie in something Joyce himself once said: "One great part of every human existence is passed in a state which cannot be rendered sensible by the use of wideawake language, cutanddry grammar and goahead plot"?

Since the publication of Campbell and Robinson's *Skeleton Key* in 1944, important studies have continued to appear which begin to put *Finnegans Wake* into perspective. But, while they have been various and insightful, they illuminate aspects of the novel rather than the novel itself. Concentration on specific allusion or thematic patterns has tended to draw attention to the detail, the part rather than the whole, when what seems needed now is a work which will serve to enhance a reader's conception of Joyce's work as *novel*. Despite the steadily growing interest in Joyce's most difficult book, Fritz Senn and I noticed that actually there have been till now few serious, comprehensive attempts to come to grips with *Finnegans Wake*.

Exploration of the *Wake* has always seemed most fruitful as a group endeavor, as witnessed by Samuel Beckett and others' *An Exagmination*, which Joyce himself probably commissioned in 1929. What we wish to do here is to carry their insights several steps farther. Our contributors, most of whom are established Wakians, were each assigned an individual chapter or section of the novel and asked to deal with it from a specific angle or point of view. It was not our purpose to provide yet another pony or paraphrase, but rather we hope that each of these original essays will provide entry into a section at something deeper than the surface level—that all the essays can be tied together to comprise a unified body of work.

The differences in these approaches to the deciphering of *Wake*-ese reflect the richness and multifaceted character of the book itself. The variety of critical stances seems to be virtually essential for dealing with this many leveled novel whose scope ranges from comic strips to opera to philosophy. *Finnegans Wake* is certainly puzzling, but it is not simply a verbal puzzle. It is a structured and formed piece of work whose intricacy should finally allay the unfounded suspicion that Joyce may have lost control. He was much too meticulous to permit any loose ends.

Doubtless this book is not the final word on *Finnegans Wake*, as it is not the first, but it does make a solid statement as to where we stand right now. A few loose ends may remain, but they are ours, not Joyce's. The contributing scholars and critics from Europe and America have devoted much of their careers to Joyciana, and their interest bears fruit in this group of essays. Here we have thirteen contributors, one more than the twelve who populated the *Exagmination,* and the editors hope the questions which they answer are as stimulating and important as those they force the reader to deal with for himself.

Michael H. Begnal

1

Where Terms Begin

Book I

chapter i

J. Mitchell Morse

> ". . . the most celebrated of all battles, that of Belle Alliance . . ."
>
> Clausewitz, *On War*.

The name Kafka means Magpie; among the manuscripts that Kafka's friend Max Brod refused to burn was that of "The City Coat of Arms," a parable of the unbuilt Tower of Babel; it was published in 1931; in 1938 Joyce wrote the "Butt and Taff" episode of *Finnegans Wake*, which speaks of a future time "when the magpyre's babble towers scorching and screeching from the ravenindove" (354.27). Are we therefore to infer that Joyce was alluding to Kafka's parable? I hope not. Nothing in the context makes such an inference necessary or even plausible—especially since the Tower of Babel was not burned but merely abandoned. (For a good working definition of plausibility, very useful for us watchers at the *Wake*, see Charles Sanders Peirce, *Collected Papers* 2.661–2.) We can read "the magpyre's babble" much more plausibly as the work of Irene Kafka, a translator mentioned on p. 715 of Richard Ellmann's *James Joyce*, or as *Finnegans Wake* itself, burned in Hell, along with its author, by the Holy Ghost; but even if it isn't either of these, to infer that it is Franz Kafka's parable is to infer that Joyce threw in allusions at random, for no reason and with no design: which is to misread Joyce in the same way that Shaun misread Shem, considering a writer who was as consciously intellectual and as meticulously artful as Milton a mere undisciplined scribbler.[1]

This being the case, we cannot take seriously the suggestion that we might start reading the circular tale at any point just as well as at any other: i.e., e.g., that since I.1 is where it is by mere chance, it could just as well have been put anywhere else. "The Vico Road goes round and round, to meet where terms begin" (452.21–22). For "term" the *OED* gives twenty-three distinct but related definitions, all having to do with limits of time, space, or conditions; the three Joyce had most in mind in I.1, as I hope to demonstrate, were the philological, the academic and the military: signifying words, school sessions, and conditions for peace. Though the sly Shem tells us that the mamafesta does contain, here and there, wherever the protoparent's *ipsissima verba* are about to be quoted, a "curious warning sign . . . indicating that that the words which follow may be taken in any order desired" (121.08–13), I believe that this is because the mamafesta is (among other things) Giambattista Vico's *The New Science*, and that the warning sign is nothing more curious than the appearance of a Latin quotation, in reading which we must concentrate on the inflectional endings rather than on the word order. The sentence illustrates its own meaning. In any case, we know that Joyce himself was meticulously careful, not only to select or invent the right words, but also to put them, as he said on a well-known occasion, in "the best possible order." He was equally careful about the order of the episodes in *Finnegans Wake*. "I have the book now fairly well planned out in my head," he wrote to Harriet Weaver on May 21, 1926, and in the next sentence told her exactly where two separate future episodes would go. (*Letters*, I, 241.)

Vico's ideal history does, to be sure, go round and round; but it had an unmistakable beginning, unmistakable as a thunderclap, and it is divided into periods that begin and end; its essential argument, in fact, is that history is not a random fortuity of events but a divinely ordered pattern whose repeated sequences guarantee that in the long run there will be no progress—that the achievements of human dignity, endlessly repeated, will endlessly and forever be undone by a divine providence that cares nothing for human dignity.

In the letter from which I have quoted above, Joyce told Miss Weaver that she could gain an insight into his work in progress by reading Lewis McIntyre's *Giordano Bruno* and Vico's *The New Science*. "I would not pay overmuch attention to these theories, beyond using them for all they are worth, but they have gradually forced themselves on me through circumstances of my own life." That is to say, though not a true believer, he found some thinkers sufficiently interesting or sympathetic to suspend his disbelief, as we willingly suspend ours while reading say *The Wind in the Willows*. In *Finnegans Wake*, speaking the words of Shem with the voice of Shaun, he said of Bruno, "I will be misunderstord if understood to give an unconditional sinequam to the heroicised furibouts of the Nolanus theory" (163.23-24); and of Nicholas of Cusa, "I am not hereby giving my final endorsement to the learned ignorants of the Cusanus philosophism" (163.16-17). But he applied these and other thinkers to the problem of organizing his own experience, in the same way that he applied Aquinas. Certainly *FW* I.1 is a fine example of what we may call applied Vico. Which is not to say that Joyce believed Vico any more than he believed Aquinas.

The particular circumstance of Joyce's life that he mentioned in connection with Vico, who is said to have shared it, was his morbid fear of thunder and lightning. This is certainly significant, as we shall see; more significant, I believe, was an intellectual trait Vico shared with the other thinkers to whom Joyce was attracted, including Aquinas: a dauntless originality that caused him to be called a heretic; but most significant of all, he was, at least so it seems to me and has seemed to others, something fundamentally different: a sly dog, an enemy of all religion but particularly of Christianity, who modestly proposed, in the most reverential terms, not mere heresies but hideous blasphemies. They must have delighted Joyce's irreverence.

"I wonder where Vico got his fear of thunderstorms," Joyce wondered in that letter to Harriet Weaver. "It is almost unknown to the male Italians I have met." The statement was either disingenuous or a subtle clue or both. For Joyce knew well enough, if only intuitively, where Vico got his fear of thunderstorms. The first thunderclap in *Finnegans Wake* (3.15) begins with the first unmistakable stutter—"bababa . . ."—and occurs simultaneously with the first fall. Syntactically, the parenthetical representation of it signifies that it *is* the first fall. "The decisive event in Vico's life," say Max Harold Fisch and Thomas Goddard Bergin in the helpful introduction to their translation of his sometimes tactfully inexplicit *Autobiography,* "was his failure in the academic 'concourse' or competition of 1723," as a result of which he decided at age 55 to give up his quarter-century vain hope of academic promotion and do his own unorthodox thing. Professors Fisch and Bergin point out what Vico didn't mention: that before the competition began, the promotion that was its object had already been promised to a well-connected incompetent. Vico saw the event as a manifestation of divine providence, freeing him from worldly vanities. Or so he said. In any case, he turned inward. He wrote *The*

New Science. He revolutionized the philosophy of history and the writing of history.

Up to that point he had tried to be Shaun: he had eked out his bottom-level academic salary by writing commissioned addresses of welcome to visiting royalty, borborygmic obituary inscriptions, funeral orations, memorial tributes, epithalamia, celebrative odes, official histories, etc. But it was not in his nature to be a convincing or successful Shaun. Least of all did he convince himself. He did manage to write the authorized biography of Marshal Antonio Caraffa, as he said, "with proper honor to the subject, reverence for princes, and the justice we owe to the truth"; but the conflicts among these requirements were such that from beginning to end "he was wracked by the cruelest hypochondriac cramps in the left arm." (*Autobiography,* Fisch & Bergin trans., 1963 edition, p. 155.) He continued to perform such servile tasks from time to time for the rest of his life, because he had an invalid daughter and a criminal son and he desperately needed money; but after 1723 he no longer tried to make a career of servility. He turned in another direction. He freed his better self. Shem. He found his own purpose.

That is to say, he became conscious of it. He had been unconsciously feeling for it since childhood. The defeat of 1723 was his third fall. The second had been his failure, at age 29, to win the post of town clerk of Naples, following which he became an underpaid teacher (p. 136), who like Joyce gave private lessons on the side. The first fall had been physical. It was quite evidently the thunderclap. In the first paragraph of his *Autobiography* he tells how it changed his personality and brought about the first of three divinely ordained changes in the direction of his life:

> He was a boy of high spirits and impatient of rest; but at the age of seven [literally, in his seventh year—i.e., between the ages of six and seven] he fell head first from the top of a ladder to the floor below, and remained a good five hours without motion or consciousness. The right side of the cranium was fractured, but the skin was not broken. The fracture gave rise to a large tumor, and the child suffered much loss of blood from the many deep lancings. The surgeon, indeed, observing the broken cranium and considering the long period of unconsciousness, predicted that he would either die of it or grow up an idiot. However, by God's grace neither part of his prediction came true, but as a result

of this mischance he grew up with a melancholy and irritable temperament such as belongs to men of ingenuity and depth, who, thanks to the one, are quick as lightning in perception, and, thanks to the other, take no pleasure in verbal cleverness or falsehood. (P. 111.)

That was the fall of Finnegan from the ladder; and, as we shall see, it was the thunderous fall of HCE. Vico's choice of the phrase "by God's grace," and his insertion of it just where he did insert it, could hardly offend the most devout; but in *The New Science*—the vigilant presence of the Inquisition in conquered Naples notwithstanding—he risked a more obvious irony: so obvious as to border on sarcasm: using such terms as "pure and pious wars," "heroic slavery," etc., and attributing all human misfortunes, private and public, to divine providence. By professing that his analysis of the origins of religion applied to the pagan religions only—the Jews never having abandoned the worship of the true God and having been kept apart in order to preserve it—he was able to save the appearances and his skin. But the analogies were plain enough. He wasn't accused of heresy and atheism for nothing. (*Autobiography*, translators' introduction, pp. 44, 63, 78.) The pagan gods were born of fear, he says, and the pagan religions of credulity (*The New Science*, Fisch & Bergin trans., Section 191—and from now on I won't repeat the word "Section" or "Sections"); but throughout *The New Science* he attributes all human laws and customs, pagan, Jewish and Christian alike, however "crude, inhuman, cruel, uncivilized and monstrous" (102), to "divine providence" (146)—even trial by combat, both ancient and medieval, in which by God's will the outraged party often loses and is therefore considered guilty (27, 959–64); even the sacrifice of children to Moloch (191). All these things are necessary, says Vico, in order to raise men from savagery to full humanity through unquestioning respect for law merely because it is law: first divine secret law, interpreted and administered by priest-kings "subject to no one but God" (25, 955–8), then heroic secret law, interpreted and administered by the conquering demigods or heroes or aristocrats in their own "private interest" (38, 677, 965–73),[2] then human public law, interpreted and administered by the people and later by human monarchs in the interest of the people (29, 39, 936, 946, 974, 978, 1008). Then, with returning corruption, the whole process begins again (1108).

The first cycle had begun after the universal flood (13, 62, 301,

369–73) and ended with the fall of the Roman Empire (1047–8). Then, with "the second barbarism" or "the returned barbarism" or "the latest barbarian times" (the middle ages), the current cycle had begun, the Holy Roman Emperors being the priest-kings, the feudal nobles the heroes (1047–56, 1074–86), and the monarchs of Vico's own day the human rulers (1089–94). These large cycles have their smaller counterparts in the histories of the individual nations, Vico's purpose being "to describe . . . an ideal eternal history traversed in time by the history of every nation in its rise, progress, maturity, decline and fall" (349), ordained by "the omnipotent, wise and beneficent will of the best and greatest God" (345).

In view of Vico's vast knowledge of history, his frequent animadversions on the arrogance, avarice, cruelty, injustice, rapacity and violence of the priest-kings and aristocrats, and the lifelong injustice of his own position, he can only have been ironical in supporting his "rational civil theology of divine providence" (342) with the following "divine proofs," each of which he demonstrates in blood-dripping detail: "Since divine providence has omnipotence as its minister, it develops its orders by means as easy as the natural customs of men. Since it has infinite wisdom as counselor, whatever it establishes is order. Since it has for its end its own immeasurable goodness, whatever it ordains must be directed to a goodness always superior to that which men have proposed for themselves" (343). And since he has shown in such full detail that Christian history is as unjust and bloody as any other, he can only be ironically politic in concluding that Christianity is the only true religion because it alone leads to virtuous actions (1110), and that the purpose of *The New Science* is to promote piety (1112).

Such obeisances, which he made from time to time throughout the work, doubtless helped to get it past an ecclesiastical censor who also happened to be a personal friend. So did the dedication—to Pope Clement XII, who as Cardinal Lorenzo Corsini had consented to be its patron and had promised to pay the costs of publication, but who at the last moment had backed out. (*Autobiography*, pp. 11–17, 78, 173, 197–8, 201—the story that reveals itself in these passages is shocking and disgraceful.) Thus, though Vico knew how to stay out of prison, he hardly knew which side his bread was buttered on. He had many friends and warm admirers among the intellectuals of his time, but the patrons of letters and the dispensers of academic patronage granted him only crumbs, reserving their more generous help for safer men—men less melancholy and irritable, less ingenious and deep, less quick to perceive the way things were, and perhaps less naively blatant in praising their own genius. Vico, whose genius nobody now doubts, taught at the Royal University of Naples for 43 years without getting a raise or being granted tenure or being permitted to teach the subject on which he was a recognized authority, jurisprudence. These circumstances, along with his early brilliance as a pupil in Jesuit schools, his extensive private studies, his refusal to become a priest, and his grief over an invalid daughter, must have struck Joyce, at least as much as his fear of thunderstorms, as similar to the circumstances of his own life. (Not identical with them, of course. Joyce never undertook a writing assignment that would have given him cramps.)

One of Vico's routine duties as professor of rhetoric was to give the annual Inaugural Lecture opening the academic year. The seventh of these, which was published in 1709, was by no means a routine performance. (See Elio Gianturco's perspicuous translation and learned introduction and notes, *On the Study Methods of Our Time*, Bobbs-Merrill, 1965.) The preceding six, to judge by Vico's summaries of them, were not routine performances either: in each of them, he said, he was attempting "a theme both new and grand, to unite in one principle all knowledge human and divine." (*Autobiography*, p. 146.) But their announced topics were safe and stuffy enough to please all the Shauns among his hearers, and we can hardly avoid feeling that the speaker too was a safely routine Shaun: "That the knowledge of oneself is for each of us the greatest incentive to the compendious study of every branch of learning." "That there is no enmity more dire and dangerous than that of the fool against himself." "That the society of letters must be rid of every deceit, if you would study to be adorned with true not feigned, solid not empty, erudition." "He who would reap from the study of letters the greatest advantages, combined always with honor, let him be educated for the glory and good of the community." "That commonwealths have been most renowned for military glory and most powerful politically when letters have most flourished in them." "The knowledge of the corrupt nature of man invites us to study the complete cycle of the arts and sciences, and propounds and expounds the true, easy and unvarying order in which they are to be acquired." (Pp. 140–146.) When he returned to the theme in 1719 he was so pleased with his effort that in the summary of it he quoted a paragraph in which we can see the Vico Road going round and round and round:

> At the solemn public opening of studies in 1719 he therefore proposed this argument: "All divine and human learning has

three elements: knowledge, will and power, whose single principle is the mind, with reason for its eye, to which God brings the light of eternal truth." And he divided the argument thus: "Now as to these three elements, which we know to exist and to belong to us as certainly as we know that we ourselves live, let us explain them by that one thing of which we cannot by any means doubt, that is of course by thought. That we may the more easily do this, I divide this entire discourse into three parts. In the first of these let us demonstrate that all the principles of the sciences are from God. In the second, that the divine light or eternal truth, by the three elements above set forth, permeates all the sciences, disposes them all in an order in which they are linked by the closest ties one with another, and relates them all to God as their source. In the third, that whatever has been written or said concerning the foundations of divine and human learning, if it agrees with these principles, is true, if it disagrees is false. Three further matters concerning the knowledge of divine and human things I shall also treat: its origin, circularity, and consistency: and I shall show that the origins of all things proceed from God, that all return to God by a circle, that all have their consistency in God, and that apart from God they are all darkness and error." And he discoursed on this argument for an hour and more. (P. 156.)

For an hour and more! Such is the circularity of Shaun. Thus Vico figures in *Finnegans Wake* not only as the author of a theory of history that Joyce used for all it was worth, but also as a complex personality, a model (like Swift) for both Shem and Shaun. Several years ago I said, "Though the book begins and ends in the middle of a sentence, the second half of the sentence (3) has a style so different from that of the first half (628) that it seems not to be spoken by the same person. . . . Perhaps what we have here after all is not one sentence but fragments of two different sentences. . . . However that may be, the incomplete sentence with which the book ends is certainly spoken by Anna Livia, and the incomplete sentence with which it begins is certainly not. . . . The first narrator, who talks as if he stood with a lectern before him, a map behind him, and a pointer in his hand, is most probably Shaun." ("On Teaching *Finnegans Wake*," in *Twelve and a Tilly*, ed. by Jack P. Dalton and Clive Hart, Faber & Faber, 1966, pp. 69–70.) I now think he is most probably the Shaun in Giambattista Vico, lecturing on divine providence and the beginnings of human history, and unwittingly indicating, as Shem is aware, the difficulty of establishing the truth about the beginnings.

His performance is as farcical as his intention is solemn. *Finnegans Wake* seems to me (among other things, of course, always among other things) a burlesque—not a parody but a burlesque—of *The New Science,* somewhat in the same way that the unfinished *Pharsalia* is a burlesque of the unfinished *Aeneid:* "and none so soon either shall the pharce for the nunce come to a setdown secular phoenish" (4:16-17). *The New Science* and *Finnegans Wake* illustrate for literature Marx's remark to the effect that the great events and personages in history occur as it were twice, the first time as tragedy, the second time as farce. *FW* I.1, accordingly, is a farcical version of Vico's account of the beginnings of human history. After the flood, said Vico, the descendants of Ham and Japheth, and all the descendants of Shem except the Jews, wandered away over the soggy earth, abandoned the worship of God, and in consequence degenerated into mere animals, copulating casually and abandoning their children as soon as they were weaned. The children, wallowing in their own excrement and absorbing its nitrous salts into their bodies, grew to giant stature but lost human speech and intelligence (62, 172, 369-73). But 100 years after the flood in Mesopotamia, and 200 years everywhere else, the earth dried out enough to give off "dry exhalations, or matter igniting in the air to produce lightning." When the thunder rolled, the giants thought a big giant in the sky was trying to tell them something; they guessed correctly that he disapproved of their dirty ways and casual couplings. So the men grabbed their women of the moment and dragged them into caves out of sight of the big giant. Thus began religion, marriage, family living, burial, inheritance, classes, oppression, rebellion, wars, and all the rest of it (377 ff., 385 ff., etc., etc., etc., etc., etc., etc.). "The nature of peoples is first crude, then benign, then delicate, finally dissolute" (242).

The key word here is "peoples." Vico was the historian not of conquerors and rulers but of peoples—of the people. One of his boldest intuitions was that not only the gods and demigods but also the earliest suppositious human sages, moralists, lawgivers, conquerors, inventors, poets, etc.—e.g., Solon, Draco, Pythagoras, Homer, Aesop, Romulus, Numa, Tullus Hostilius, Tarquinus Priscus, etc.—were "poetic characters" or personifications of various talents, capacities, tendencies, schools of thought or action or behavior, to whom were attributed the anonymous achievements of many generations—i.e., of the people themselves (412–27). Thus, there is no objective evidence that a person named Solon ever existed, but it doesn't matter whether he did or not—what matters is that he is a persona, a created figure or poetic character, with or without a basis in fact, standing for certain political ideas and the laws in which they are embodied; and there is no objective evidence that a person named Homer ever existed, but it doesn't matter whether he did or not—what matters is that the *Iliad* and the *Odyssey* embody the poetic genius of the Greek peoples, who produced many poets and rhapsodes (873–9). As Croce has emphasized, Vico was painfully aware of the difficulty of discovering the truth about the earliest beginnings of anything—and as Thomas Mann also discovered, no matter how far back we go, the beginnings are already regarded as having taken place in ancient times. In any case, Vico's communal evolutionism reflects a certain skepticism about supermen, a certain faith in the capacity of the people generally, and a certain critical freedom—a freedom from awe—in the presence of human works.

"Abject discipleship," says James Feibleman, "is a betrayal of the master." (*An Introduction to Peirce's Philosophy*, Harper, 1946, p. xix); the true Aristotelians were those who, adopting Aristotle's methods, made discoveries that superseded his own; likewise Joyce, an unawed ex-hero worshipper unimpressed by Vico's romantic view of the people generally, subsumed Vico, along with Michelet, Quinet, Hegel and all other historians, in the comic poetic characters Shem and Shaun.

"The first history," said Vico, "must have been poetic" (813). That is, the first historians must have tried to recall the past not through research in non-existent or inaccessible records but through imaginative reconstructions of what poetic characters "must have" done. Vico himself supplemented his factual researches with such conjectures; *The New Science* is full of poetic evocations of the way things "must have" happened.

In *FW* I.1 Professor Shaun is himself a poetic character, the Historian. His account, endlessly garrulous, pedantically circumstantial, unconsciously pompous and unintentionally funny, subsumes all accounts, however inconsistent; and if it recounts and recounts all human history in the style of village gossip, we have no recourse, only a *ricorso:* more of the same. In I.1 he tells the story four times.

Poetically, however, in Vico's sense: through characters in dramatic situations, and starting *in medias res*. Before the thunder first spoke (3.15) there were no namable individuals and no uniquely human activities: "not yet" was there religion or war or marriage or building or brewing: the first men had to fall before they could rise into humanity. But, as Adaline Glasheen has observed (*Second Census*, p. xxvii), since they fell while building something—i.e., while "celescalating" or rapidly climbing a ladder to Heaven (5.01)—they must have fallen before. This is good Vico: for Adam's fall from grace and expulsion from Paradise took place before, therefore outside, the cycles of post-Paradisal history. HCE, "the grand old gardener" (30.13), was in fact not quite a regular human being. (Gilgamesh's hairy friend Enkidu should be in here somewhere, but I don't see him. If you find him, let me know. I think I see Shamash farther on, under the name "Sameas" (483.04).)

And what is a regular human being? That depends on which account you read or hear: the theocratic, the feudal, the civil, or the chaotic. They are not always easy to distinguish, however, for none exists in its pure form: there are always remnants of the past and germs of the future, and in every age there are people who belong by nature to other ages.

Nevertheless, the predominant quality of each age is fairly clear. In the theocratic age all wars are predominantly religious wars; in the heroic age all wars are predominantly wars for real estate; in the civil age all wars are predominantly civil or class or ideological wars; in the chaotic age there is strictly speaking no war, but a reversion to the primal struggle of each against all. The croaking of frogs in the primal swamp of the chaotic age is echoed in the civil age by a well-known chorus from Aristophanes' *The Frogs,* reflecting the clash between his and Euripides' literary values (4.02); in a later civil age the literary war is resumed by the bad partisans and the angelic enemies of Baudelaire (4.03). If this isn't Joyce mocking Vico, I don't know what mockery is; but in any case, Shaun solemnly tells us that the War in Heaven is eternal, persisting through everchanging forms on earth. Cain and Abel fought for the orthodoxy of religious ritual, Jacob and Esau for the right to the homestead; but there were elements of each struggle in the other, Cain being banished from the territory and Esau losing the blessing of God. The wars between the hunters and the ranchers, the ranchers and the farmers, the farmers and the hunters, the oystermen and the fishermen, etc., etc., go on forever: if the Ostrogoths and the Visigoths didn't actually fight each other on earth, their eternal essences did and do and always will in the abstract Heaven of Principles, where all things are as they should be. The Napoleonic wars and the Crimean War were predominantly wars between rival economic and socio-political systems—civil or class or ideological wars across national boundaries—but they too involved elements of religious hatred and territorial aggression.

In all ages metaphors of war apply to peaceful activities, especially those involving sexual rivalry and family relationships. One of the rights the plebeians won with most difficulty from the patricians, says Vico, was the right to "matrimony, the recognized source of all authority" (629), whereby they became not merely *homines,* which they had always been since the thunderclap, but also *vires*—men of *virtus,* men of some individual character and personality, men no longer absolutely interchangeable, men with some private rights of which they could not be capriciously deprived: the right to have recognized family relationships, to keep their wives inviolate, to transmit their names and property to their children (513–14, 540, 584, 598, 986). The right of marriage tended to make somewhat more nearly equal the terms of sexual competition across class lines: "Sir Tristram, violer d'amores" (*FW* 3.04), is a poetic character in Vico's sense, indicating the warlike and deeply insurrectionary character not only of courtly love but of personal love as a motive for matrimony.

All rights are won, all social and natural changes come about, by struggles to which metaphors of war are appropriate. The modern Swiss women's struggle for the right to vote and the ancient Swiss festival of *Sechseläuten* (representing the victory of Spring over Winter), both of which Fritz Senn has found throughout *FW* (*The Analyst* XIX, Dec. 1960, and *James Joyce: Aufsätze von Fritz Senn,* Zürich, 1972), are both associated with the Battle of Waterloo—or, as Clausewitz and Joyce preferred to call it, of Belle Alliance—which in turn is associated with the romance of Tristan and Iseult la Belle (7.33; cf. 144.12, 246.20, 351.30–31, 372.01, and most of the references to *Sechseläuten* listed by Clive Hart in *Structure and Motif in Finnegans Wake,* pp. 213–14). That such things go on all around the world is indicated by the repeated echoes of Robert Louis Stevenson's verse, "Ping, pang, pong, goes the Japanese gong."

Thus the story of the human race, as told by Professor Shaun in *FW* I.1, is largely a story of love and war. He is a rather rambling lecturer, afflicted like Tristram Shandy with uncontrollable associationism and compulsive circumstantiality. His account is like the conversation at a party, where the subject keeps changing and where anybody who wants to stay with the subject that is being forgotten might as well forget it; nevertheless, the intertwined themes of love and war persist through all variations.

As we all know, the first four paragraphs announce all the chief themes and motifs. The first action is that of the rise and fall of the Master Builder Finnegan, who established a family, built a tower, and fell from a ladder. After retailing this story (4.18–6.28), Professor Shaun takes us on a field trip to inspect the remains of the fallen giant (6.29–8.08), and then into the adjoining burial mound or battlefield museum, where we see relics and relicts of Belle Alliance (8.09–10.23).

"Mind your boots goan out," says Kate (10.22). Bluchers, Wellingtons and Napoleons are all boots, and since in Vico's poetics when you've seen one general you've seen them all, it may be a little hard for us to remember just who did just what. However, there is a clue. As Webster's *New International Dictionary,* Second Edition (1955), explains in more detail than the *OED,* Napoleon and Wellington are card games, in which "nap," "wellington" and "blucher" are successively higher bids. "(Bullseye! Game!)" (10.21.)

"Phew!" (10.24) Φεῦ (Woe!)

With this word Professor Shaun leads us out of the museum onto the Belle Alliance battlefield, which is poetic for all battlefields as Napoleon, Wellington and Blucher are poetic for all generals. Here we see ALP salvaging whatever is salvageable so that life can go on (10.31–12.17) and the past be preserved in the present (11.29–32). Then the professor's associationism takes us as in a dream to Dublin (13.04), where we find ourselves reading an ancient manuscript, which is Herodotus and/or the Egyptian Book of the Dead and/or a book of deeds and titles and/or *The Annals of the Four Masters* and/or Thom's Dublin Directory and/or *Ulysses* ("bluest book in baile's annals . . . *Liber Lividus*") and/or Quinet's introduction to his translation of Herder's *Ideas on the Philosophy of the History of Mankind* and/or Herder's book itself and/or Vico's and/or (as I have suggested, *JJQ* III.4, Summer 1966, 272–5) the *Peterborough Chronicle* (13.20–15.28).

Then, hopping over to England, we meet a Mousterian or Neanderthal man, whom our professor as Mutt takes to be a Jute and engages in conversation. But not only is Mutt a Norman-French scout, as Harry Levin has demonstrated; not only is he every invader mocking every native; he is also, quite concretely, an ancestor of Arthur de Gobineau: in *Histoire d'Ottar Jarl, Pirate Norvégien, Conquérant du Pays de Bray, en Normandie, et de sa Descendance* (Paris, 1879), Gobineau records a strikingly similar encounter. Unfortunately I had to go to the men's room before I had time to copy the passage or even record the page number, and when I got back the library was about to close, and what with one thing and another . . . anyhow, you can find the passage easily enough. I am convinced that Joyce read it, for Professor Shaun poeticizes Gobineau's piratical ancestor (15.18–18.16).

Next (18.17–21.04) he invites us to stoop and examine some archaeological curios. Poetic language, said Vico, involved the use of concrete names, and in its earliest stages concrete objects, to indicate such abstract concepts as birth, possession, authority, cultivation, and defense. He illustrates this point by telling how Idanthyrsus, King of Scythia, sent to Darius, King of Persia, who was about to invade his territory, a wordless message of defiance asserting that he, Idanthyrsus, was born in Scythia, lived in it, ruled it, cultivated it and would defend it—the message consisting of a frog (born of the damp earth), a mouse (a burrower in the earth), a bird (source of auguries and symbol of priestly authority), a plowshare and a bow (48, 99, 435, 488, 535, 604). Vico interprets the meanings of these objects, and introduces *The New Science* with a frontispiece showing other objects which he interprets by the same method. Likewise Professor Shaun reads the world of history and the history of the world in the "middenhide hoard of objects" (19.08) that become symbols, then words, then letters. The capacity for abstraction gradually evolves.

But our dreams reverse the process, leaping in one night back across ages of development and presenting all our fine abstractions as primal images, which in the sophisticated state of our consciousness we find unintelligible. Not that our primal ancestors found them intelligible. They were no better off than we, they were not so well off as we. They were bewildered, we are puzzled; that is an advance. Let us remember Aristotle: "The particular is unintelligible."

"The Prankquean" is a story Professor Shaun tells after he straightens up from the stoop in which he inspected the objects; it is a mythification of all our social abstractions, from Law and Order to Strict Construction to Separation of Powers. It represents a bewildered groping through the unintelligibility of particular situations toward the abstract clarity in which we now stand puzzled. We can live neither with myths nor without them. In our time, however, if we cannot yield with the ancient faith to any myth, we can inspect and enjoy it as a work of art: and this too, in terms of control over our own lives, is a gain. Not that Joyce believed that any gain is permanent.

In form, as has been observed, "The Prankquean" is a small-scale model of *Finnegans Wake:* it has three movements and a coda, all tied together by a number of recurrent motifs; its general outline is clear, and its literary allusiveness is functional: "come back to my earin" (21.23-4) and "come back with my earring" (22.10), echoing the lament of Jonson's Aeglamour for his kidnapped daughter Earine, indicate that the Prankquean is (among other things) a witch. But the Prankquean's riddle, the unrecognizably distorted expression of an inadmissible tendency as deeply suppressed as it is destructive, remains to be deciphered. In view of its many recurrences throughout *Finnegans Wake,* it would seem to justify whatever continuing analytical efforts may be necessary. I therefore offer, as supplements to such helpful analyses as those of Margaret Solomon and Bernard Benstock, the following notes.

Skeat gives etymologies for three different but related meanings of the noun "mark," designating them "Mark (1)," "Mark (2)" and "Mark (3)." One of the meanings of the verb "mark" is to observe or notice or look at or look. The grammatically confused and confusing question ". . . why do I am alook alike . . . ?" seems to be the heart of the concealment. I can make nothing of it. Reading "I am" as the Latin *iam* doesn't help, nor do any of the *OED*'s definitions of "alike," "like" and "look." "Amah," meaning wet nurse, may or may not be a clue. To "poss" is to push, shove, toss, hit or beat, and a "poss" is a stick for beating, poking, stirring, etc. It is *not* a posset or a poss-tub. In the present context it may be a phallic symbol, if that's your *shtick,* but I don't see that it points to the end of the tunnel. In connection with "porter" the meaning "push" seems most promising, especially since one of the meanings of "pease" is "peise"—weight, especially a coin of fixed weight—and one of the meanings of "Mark (2)" is a coin of fixed weight or value. It may be that the Prankquean doesn't actually kidnap the jiminies but buys them—a fact their father afterwards conceals from himself by refusing to be coherent about it: by going crazy. We need more exploration—a great deal more. Two quotations the *OED* uses to establish two meanings of "porter" are mildly intriguing: from *Piers Plowman,* "and make pees [peace] porter to pynne the gates," and from Swift's *A Further Account of Edmund Curll,* "Nursed up on grey peas, bullocks liver, and porters ale."

Finally, the *OED* says a dummy is among other things "a baby's india-rubber teat." This has all kinds of possibilities. But such vague intimations are of little or no value in the absence of further information. The guilty secret is buried very deep indeed. I suspect that we have to do not with a mere sin but with a serious crime of an outrageously anti-human kind, actual or latent. It may even be that the crime is human sacrifice, and that the dummy is one of those effigies that Frazer tells us were ultimately substituted for the victims.

After the field trip we go to a wake—or rather, since the trip was a tour of parts of the brontoichthyan form of Finn, we find ourselves at the wake. That is to say, we find ourselves reading *Finnegans Wake:* for the rest of the chapter is a babble of voices, twice interrupted by vain efforts of Finnegan to break out of the unbreakable cycle. He wants to rise, and he will rise, but only by renewing himself—not in his old form but in the form of his living sons and daughters. They insist that he die in order that they may live. It seems to me not altogether implausible to regard these vociferous wakers as (among other things) ourselves, the students of *Finnegans Wake*. That is to say, *Finnegans Wake* itself rears up from time to time and resists our formulations, but we insist on them. A great book lives in its students, however wrongheaded, or not at all. Of course Joyce knew this. When he said *Finnegans Wake* would keep the scholars busy for a thousand years he knew that it—and he—would go through everchanging forms.

So here we are back in our classroom with Professor Shaun; the mountain's head is in the stormclouds (23.21), and we talk and talk all around and all over it, alluding—always more or less appropriately—to Liam O'Flaherty (25.03) and Swift's bee and spider (25.02–08) and Jim's shuck tick in *Huckleberry Finn* (26.14–15) and Justice Holmes (26.25–26) and Hetty Green (27.11) and Booth Tarkington (28.32) and Cardinal Richelieu (29.15) and perhaps God only knows who not. In our analytical exchanges we may sometimes think we are only discussing a book, but when we look at each other we know that we are also celebrating a man; for it is Joyce himself, with all his contradictions, who will be ultimendly respunchable for the hubbub: a cyclical hubbub in which he is successively and forever a god (24.17), a hero (26.09), a decent man (27.22) and an old offender (29.30).

Such men are neither complacent nor surprised when human beings act without human dignity. They look down with sad philosophical amusement. Ironic Plato modestly proposed for human perfection a society in which he himself would have been condemned to death for irony. Erasmus wrote a mock encomium. Thoreau enjoyed village gossip, in small doses, as much as the rustling of leaves and the peeping of frogs. Joyce enjoyed also, and in large doses, the screeching of us devoted magpies. He knew we would feed on him. He played God more successfully than any other man in our time; but he was too good a student of Vico to delude himself with the notion that he would save us—even though *Finnegans Wake* is the greatest product of human ingenuity since Benjamin Franklin invented lightning.

Notes

1. There is even more temptation—and even less reason—to see the influence of Kafka's story "The Great Wall of China" in the course of wall the drunken Finnegan was erecting: "a wall of course" (13.09). The fascinating correspondences notwithstanding (cf. *The New Science,* Sections 32, 999–1003, 283–4, and *The Great Wall of China,* Schocken Books, 1970, pp. 87–8, 89, 91, 141–2), there is no positive evidence that Joyce read Kafka or that Kafka read Vico. "Dove," however, is the pronunciation of the Gaelic *dubh,* black. This does seem to me plausible as an element of "ravenindove."

2. Cf. Kafka, "The Problem of Our Laws," in *The Great Wall of China,* pp. 147–9.

Recipis for the Price of the Coffin

Book I

Roland McHugh

chapters ii–iv

If you've recently begun exposing yourself to *Finnegans Wake*, certain doubts and dissatisfactions will confront you during the first year or so. Such seemingly alien and unreasonable language will repay its debt only after much uncomprehending repetition. When you think you can follow what's happening, you become frustrated by the continual intimations that nothing really does happen. On entering a new chapter you glance about you but find only the same people and their inevitable relationship unaltered. Are you perhaps mistaken in assuming the experience of real time in this "continuous present tense integument" (186.01)? At the beginning of I.2 the king and his retainers meet Earwicker carrying a flowerpot on a pole. Now compare (194.06–10). They "have not budged a millimetre and all that has been done has yet to be done and done again."

In reconciling oneself to this strange environment one may approach all the identities and interactions under the premise that they represent components and potentialities of a sleeping mind at a single point in time. *Finnegans Wake* may also be envisaged as a template simultaneously fitting a diversity of temporal cycles—a day, a year, the lifetime of an individual or civilisation, the span of a play or musical work etc.—and making eternity of their coincidences.[1] Further, one may see it as the logical extension of the aesthetic theory of the *Portrait*, which says that the beholder of the aesthetic spectacle should be static and enthralled. If the spectacle itself is timeless and must be instantaneously taken hold of in its entirety, stasis has been brought to an ideal extreme.

These theories are all relevant, but although nothing may physically "take place" in *Finnegans Wake*, conceptual progressions definitely occur. Influences rise or fade in response to the Viconian and other foundations determining chapter arrangement. If the reader will sustain his awareness of these progressions he may find that some of his dissatisfaction has subsided. Joyce being subtle, the marks of progress will often appear in unexpected places and be lacking from obvious ones. For example, according to the letter to Miss Weaver of 24 May 1924,[2] book III contains a *via crucis* of fourteen stations. This statement has been discussed by Joyceans since the 1950's, but few stations have been convincingly identified. Had Joyce not pointed to the *via crucis* would anyone have suspected its presence?

The progression of I.2–4 is less a time sequence than an ascent through portraits of increasing remoteness and unfamiliarity, the initial one being from "the best authenticated version" (30.10). Here we are close to Earwicker; as we proceed his name, his person, his memorials and the stories about him are all subjected to attack and distortion, so that he becomes less and less accessible. A complementary progression occupying book I is the attempt of investigators to reach back to the inception of I.2, but as their research becomes more meaningful and they treat their material more objectively, the evidence diminishes because of the first progression.

In I.2 the investigation is very crude. Earwicker is the subject of a rumor which eventually coalesces into a ballad. The persons responsible amplify the rumor from their own imaginations and it is greatly perverted in transit, being overheard at a racecourse, repeated incoherently by a drunk in his sleep, etc. In I.3 we may be in the next generation and a more scientific attempt is made: Earwicker's contemporaries (who sometimes resemble him) are interviewed. Their recollections of him are, of course, very diverse. In I.4 the mechanism of examination has become formalised, and after a trial the judges try to "bring the true truth to light" (96.27).

In the subsequent book I chapters there seem to be no surviving witnesses, but the document found by the hen in the midden can help. In I.5 this is scrutinised by paleographers, who successively consider the title, the envelope, the letter, its handwriting and finally its punctuation, which betray its author as Shem. After this the search necessitates systematic distinction of characters I.6 and an analysis of the character finally selected, Shem I.7. Shem makes the dumb speak and they give an account of Earwicker and Anna I.8, but the elm has still not told enough when nightfall petrifies the scenery. The proximity of I.2 ("in prefall paradise peace") is never regained, but then even this is partially conjecture and an arid memory of I.1.

It is important to appreciate the ambivalent attitude of humanity towards Earwicker. To some he is the target of research, "the cluekey to a worldroom beyond the roomwhorld" (100.29), and his true history is, as (52.22–23) says, what every son of a bitch would like to know. At the same time he might be dangerous to approach and must be fenced off and tabooed. An aspect of many taboos is the fear and avoidance of naming the thing tabooed, as Freud has shown.[3] This fear increasing as we proceed, there is a decrease in the frequency of names resembling "Earwicker." Counting the references from "earwakers" to "earwugs" in the Primary Index of Clive Hart's *Concordance to Finnegans Wake,* there are 13 in I.1–2, 8 in 1.3–5, 2 in I.6–8 and only 4 in the rest of *Finnegans Wake.* Similarly, the echoes of "Finnegan" diminish in book I. Considering all the words beginning "Finn" or "finn" in pages 1–50, 51–100, 101–150 and 151–200, the respective numbers are 10, 8, 2 and 1.

Obliteration of the giant's name constitutes defence by nonrecognition, but physical concealment is more important. This is the action, not only of the populace, but also of Earwicker himself, and it includes exile (pp. 51, 62, 98), entombment (pp. 66–81) and camouflage (p. 97). The distinction between these three processes is inexact. Shem, for instance, is "self exiled in upon his ego" (184.06), so at some levels exile can refer to a state of mind. The equation of Earwicker with Humpty Dumpty, the egg, suggests the same kind of thing—concealment within a psychological shell. Where physical exile is specified there are Mohammedan associations. At (51.29–31) Earwicker has gone to southeast England, presumably Sidlesham,[4] to escape persecution, but this is called the Lesser Pilgrimage, which is the Mohammedan journey to Mecca (but not Arafat, which is part of the Greater Pilgrimage). At (62.03) the word "hejirite" recalls Mohammed's hejira in 622 A.D. from Mecca to Medina, where his doctrine was more favorably received. At (98.04–08) Earwicker has "sidleshomed" and taken a new name on entering Islam (this is a normal practice for converts). In spite of these departures, however, he remains fundamentally in Ireland throughout *Finnegans Wake.*

The entombment of Earwicker facilitates a state of external inactivity in token of the foetal state, sleep, hibernation, coma and death. He lies in his cradle (80.17) or his bed (76.32). As a hibernating animal he feeds on stored fat (79.13) and as an over-wintering plant on starch which he has made from sugar (29.28). His grave apparently begins as the *down* (69.11) which is still there to see if you strike a lucifer, although the wall which did exist has vanished, as has the lost paradise (Valhalla, suggested by "wallhole"[5]) behind its "applegate." Matthew Hodgart[6] has identified *doun* as Armenian for "house," there being an Armenian cluster on this page, but it also echoes Gaelic *dun* ("fort"[7]), so the wall is partly that of the Magazine Fort in Phoenix Park. An attempt was made to blow up the Magazine to signal the beginning of the 1916 Easter Rising, but the sound was hardly noticed in the city. Nevertheless, it suggests Viconian thunder opening an era, the Ulyssean "ruin of all space" and the falls from masonry of Humpty Dumpty, the Master Builder, and Finnegan.

Earwicker's faithful citizens[8] (69.26) lock him in the *doun* to keep him inside probably and possibly also to protect him. It is for their own safety that they want to keep him inside. The respectful accents of the four old men at the end I.1 (24.16 et seq.) and the contemptuous ones of the *Ballad* singer are both masks of fear. The elaboration of much funeral custom has probably been motivated by fear of the dead.[9] The secondary desire to protect Earwicker is not devotion but apprehension of the nemesis which might follow insult to the corpse. The paragraph about the coffin (66.28–67.06) refers to fear of the dead. As I read it, it says that funeral requisites were needed because in their absence the dead would come back in the flesh, with malevolence ("thumbs down"), at midnight (like Cinderella's coach turning back into a pumpkin). Fear of retribution is manifested by the drunk who taunts Earwicker and throws stones at him, thereafter "reconnoitring through his semisubconscious the seriousness of what he might have done" (72.29–31). As the external imprint of Earwicker dwindles, his potency as a bogeyman grows. At (77.25–27) he is addressed by a formula which, though it is described as valediction, sounds more like exorcism. At (94.33–95.26) he is still further buried in the mind, and still more undesirable, being now physically repulsive and an object of sexual horror, "the badfather . . . and his old nickname, Dirty Daddy Pantaloons." But there is no consistent progression from good to evil, and Earwicker is as much connected with paradise as hell. I am reminded of the *Tibetan Book of the Dead,* where the soul is directed, on encountering the Wrathful Deities, to remember that they are only the Peaceful Deities under changed aspect.

The relation between the doun and the grave is unclear, but at the close of I.3 Earwicker is certainly in "earthsleep," with the cairns of his witnesses scattered around him. The "mighty horn" (74.04) suggests the one lying by the dead King Arthur, which had to be blown to restore him to life.

I.4 portrays a more complex burial in "a protem grave in Moyelta of the best Lough Neagh pattern" (76.21-22). *Moy* is the anglicised form of the Irish *magh* (Old Irish *mag*), plain. Mag Elta occurs in the *Lebor Gabála Érenn*, the Book of the Taking of Ireland, a compilation of manuscripts including the Books of Leinster, Fermoy, Lecan and Ballymote. A translation of R. A. S. Macalister is now available.[10] The first redaction tells of the clearing of four plains by the early invader Partholon (or Parthalón). On arriving in Ireland he found only one plain there before him, the Old Plain of Elta. It was called the Old Plain "for never did branch or twig of a wood grow through it." The second and third redactions add that it is called Mag nElta ("Plain of Flocks") "for the birds of Ireland used to be sunning themselves upon it." Macalister says that it is the isthmus of Sutton and the adjacent country North of Dublin. Partholon and all but one of his 9,000 followers died of plague "upon Mag Elta," and the *Annals of the Four Masters* record their burial at Tallaght, south of Dublin. Macalister regards the linkage of Tallaght with *Tamlachta* ("plague-grave") as an "etymological guess" by the Masters, which if correct, would extend Mag Elta south of the Liffey. Joyce uses the assertion in III.3 (see the entries in O Hehir's *Gaelic Lexicon* for 478.12 and 479.24) and it seems reasonable therefore to connect the "protem grave" with Yawn's "mound or barrow," and Earwicker with Partholon. The adultery of Partholon's wife Elgnat with his henchman Topa recalls the cuckolding of Arthur and Mark, and like Noah, Partholon had three sons. Their names were Laiglinne, Slanga and Rudraige. Partholon was also a guilty exile. According to the *Lebor Gabála* he killed his parents and fled to Ireland. The plague which destroyed his colony was sent in retribution for this. Macalister calls the Partholon story "the narrative of a fertility-ritual drama" and compares it with Set's murder of Osiris. The Old Plain of Moyelta also appears at (17.18), in connection with mass burial.

The connection of graves with lakes is another strand from the *Lebor Gabála*. According to the first redaction a lake burst forth at the digging of Rudraige's grave. According to the second and third this happened at the digging of Laiglinne's grave and Rudraige died ten years later, being drowned at the irruption of the lake named after him. The bursting-forth of lakes is of consequence in Irish mythology and forms the subject of a class of historic tales, the *Tomhadhma*.

Earwicker has a grave of the best Lough Neagh pattern. According to the *Parliamentary Gazetteer of Ireland* (Dublin, 1844-46) the waters of Lough Neagh were once universally believed to possess a petrifying power. Giraldus Cambrensis[11] recounts its creation when a wellspring was accidentally left uncovered. The water overflowed, and in forming Lough Neagh it annihilated a certain tribe deeply sunk in vice. Giraldus suggests a parallel with the destruction of the Cities of the Plain and the formation of the Dead Sea. It is possible that Lough Neagh is mentioned in I.4 because divine justice disposed similarly of the Parthalonians and the Lough Neagh tribe, but a more important connection derives from the account of its origin in the Metrical Dindshenchas.[12] The son of the king of Cashel, Eochu, with his wife and followers, were lent a horse by Oengus, with the injunction that they should turn its head and allow it to return when they had found a place to settle. They senselessly omitted to do this, and the horse strayed and made a well in the ground. Eochu fixed a lid on the well and built a house over it, but one day the well was left uncovered and the "cold depths of Lindmuine" rose up to drown him and all but one of his companions. The lough formed was Neagh after Eochu.

Eochu is not mentioned in *Finnegans Wake,* although his name includes the letters of H. C. E. The necessity for a connection is, however, seen when one examines T. F. O'Rahilly's *Early Irish History and Mythology,*[13] p. 291, n. 4:

> The Celtic Otherworld was often conceived as being situated beneath the sea or beneath a lake. In pagan times Eochu was believed to be lord of the Otherworld beneath Lough Neagh. In Christian times, after Eochu had been euhemerized into a mortal man, his connection with the lake was explained by inventing the legend that he was drowned when the lake burst forth and flooded the country. So the tradition recorded by Giraldus (Top. Hib. ii, ix) that fishermen on Lough Neagh could in calm weather see buildings (round towers) goes back ultimately to the pagan belief that Eochu had his residence beneath the lake.

These submerged buildings become visible at (601.04–07). The mention there of Atlanta ("atlanst!") implies the other variety of Celtic Otherworld, the fortunate isles to the West of Ireland.[14] The Otherworld is usually a joyous country where the dead are perpetually young and occupied in hunting and feasting. At (76.33), then, Earwicker is living beneath his lough in an "underground heaven, or mole's paradise." His grave is an inverted phallic lighthouse; as a vegetation god he can "foster wheat crops." This means to promote fertility, but it suggests also John Foster's Corn Law of 1784 "granting large bounties on the exportation of corn and imposing heavy duties on its importation," which did so much damage to the Irish. Having enlarged and waterproofed his grave, Earwicker retreats beneath its seven towers, which will presumably become the seven gables of (100.16). The populace cover the grave with a stone slab and as "time" passes they add funeral paraphernalia and grave goods. It must be understood that this is not entirely the continued elaboration of a single material grave but also a growth of elaboration accorded to the Earwicker graves of succeeding human generations. Thus in one sense the passage contains much more time than it does in another. Consideration of this confirms the fallacy of a naive temporal reading of *Finnegans Wake*. One should distrust statements such as the subsequent one (78.15–79.03) that after Earwicker had been three months in the grave, someone was seen there who looked like him, although the plain was involved in darkness. For one thing, "monads" suggests "minutes" as well as *"Monaten."* The feeling had circulated among his opposition that Earwicker was feeding and waiting to emerge, and when the person resembling him was falsely sighted he was attacked. The attack incorporates the Phoenix Park Murders of 1882 and the murder in *The House by the Churchyard*,[15] and the resulting corpse is laid to rest in Kate's filthdump by four hands of the four old men (80.16–18). Their song, *One More Drink for the Four of Us*,[16] is echoed in "And no more of it!" The new development in the Earwicker grave may appear to be its transfer to Phoenix Park, but at (80.07) it is partially St. Patrick's Purgatory, a dark tunnel of fear—supposedly a real entrance to purgatory—on an island in Lough Derg, so there is no spatial fixity. The real advance is the conceptual condensation of the coffin and the letter.

The "filthdump" is of course the kitchenmidden in which the hen of I.5 finds the letter written by Shem. Shem resembling Stephen Dedalus, the "loveletter, lostfully hers, that would be lust on Ma" suggests "foul long letters he had written in the joy of guilty confession and carried secretly for days and days only to throw them under cover of night among the grass in the corner of a field or beneath some hingeless door or in some niche in the hedges where a girl might come upon them as she walked by and read them secretly" (*Portrait,* III).

The letter in *Finnegans Wake* is a device uniting communications to the world from Shem, to Earwicker and Anna from their children, especially Shem, to Maggy from her loving sister and to "your majesty" from Anna. At one level it is *Finnegans Wake* itself.[17] On p. 80 its concealment is identified with the burial of Earwicker, but the equivalence of letter and coffin has already been anticipated in (66.23–31). The letter there lies dormant in a pillarbox, the half-brother of a herm. A herm is a monument, in this case Earwicker's tombstone. The coffin being a triumph of the illusionist's art accords with the letter being a triumph of Shem's art. At first sight it is naturally taken for a Shaun production. Parts of *Finnegans Wake* (e.g. 164.23–24 and much of III.1) concern the distinction of the arts for which the brothers are responsible, and these arts are linked here with the occupations fathered by Jubal and Tubal Cain.[18] The coffin made by Shem, then, had in I.3 been removed from Oetzmann's hardware premises.

A coffin encloses and protects the body. *Finnegans Wake* as a letter encloses, and by its mystery protects, the quiddity of Earwicker. I.7 does not say that Shem makes a coffin, but other connections between Shem and the grave do occur in book I. At (69.17–18) Earwicker enlarges his doun by renting the land to graze a sheep ("prime") and a goat ("cadet"). Primas and Caddy are the respective names of Shaun and Shem in (14.11–14), so Shem is a goat on top of the mound. This explains why, at (136.19), Earwicker "gates our goat" and why at (132.13) the print of his feet "is seen in the goat's grasscircle." It partially explains the question asked of Shaun by the judges at (89.19–21):

> The grazing rights (Mrs Magistra Martinetta) expired with the expiry of the goat's sire, if they were not mistaken? That he exactly could not tell the worshipfuls but his mother-in-waders had the recipis for the price of the coffin.

Esau and Jacob are mentioned a few lines above this. Shem losing his rights at Earwicker's death is like Esau losing his rights at Isaac's death. Jacob brought Isaac a meal of venison and stole Esau's blessing. Isaac's wife Rebekah, who prepared the venison, would know the recipe for it, and this recipe would be the price of Esau's rights. Shem-Esau, then, has to create the coffin-letter to recover the recognition he has lost to the usurper.

Earwicker's eclipse is hastened by a series of attacks upon him made by iconoclasts. At one level, there is only one attack on Earwicker, of which differing accounts are presented. At another level there are a multitude. It is however possible to distinguish seven main areas of direct attack in I.2-4:

1. pp. 30-31   King makes joke at Earwicker's expense
2. pp. 35-36   Cad asks Earwicker the time.
3. pp. 62-63   A man with a revolver and/or bottle threatens Earwicker.
4. pp. 70-73   An "unsolicited visitor" insults Earwicker and throws stones at him.
5. pp. 78-80   Earwicker, "the plaintiff," is struck.
6. pp. 81-84   Earwicker is beaten up by an "attackler."
7. pp. 96-97   Earwicker is hunted by Fitz Urse.

In making the first attack the king indulges "that none too genial humor" which originated with greataunt Sophy. Parnell had a greataunt, Mrs. Sophia Evens, who was a practical joker, so the king would appear to incorporate Parnell ("uncrowned king of Ireland") as well as several English kings. He applies the name Earwicker to Humphrey Chimpden, making him H. C. E. Now, the letter containing the misspelling "hesitency" which Pigott forged to implicate Parnell in the Phoenix Park Murders began "Dear E." The non-event described here appears then to be the transmission from Parnell to "Dear E" of a message—"Let there be an end of this hesitency." Earwicker of course hesitates continually throughout *Finnegans Wake*. The two persons accompanying the king form with him the usual triad of Earwicker's enemies.[19] As Leix and Offaly were devastated by Mountjoy and Drogheda was devastated by Cromwell, they may include those two figures, who are paired elsewhere in I.2 (at 39.08, Blount being the family name of Mountjoy, and in the first two stanzas of the *Ballad*).

The second attack may seem less offensive: Earwicker is merely asked the time. However, he interprets the question as an accusation and defends his position, whereas in the first case no response at all was indicated. In the third and fourth cases he is threatened with physical violence and in the fifth and sixth he is subjected to it. Complications arise here in connection with a fender and various sums of money, and these will require elucidation.

In the third attack Earwicker is carrying a fender. In the sixth a fender is left behind with him by his attacker. Like so many of the book I incidentals, the fender reappears in III.3. At (518.15-18) it is an "illegallooking range" and "an ersatz lottheringcan." Bonheim[20] reminds us that *Elsass-Lothringen* is German for Alsace-Lorraine. This region passed from French to German rule in 1871 and then back to the French after the Great War. One may presume that the attacks on Earwicker allegorize international conflicts and that the fender is a piece of disputed territory. This does not however explain its being a "confederate fender" at (84.09). At (84.34) it is a "claptrap fireguard" and at (524.08) "a piece of fire fittings." A fender surrounds and holds back something destructive, a fire, and similarly the territory lying between an offensive power and its objective may serve to hinder its advance. The *Finnegans Wake* manuscripts[21] go further and associate the fender with the coffin (which as stated encloses the dangerous body of Earwicker), but the connection has been excised from the final text.

In some attacks Earwicker pays his enemy. At (37.05) the Cad thanks him for guilders received. In the sixth one, the assailant owes Earwicker six pounds fifteen shillings, and offers to pay him if he can change a ten pound note. Earwicker doesn't have enough change but he gives the gunman four shillings and sevenpence (or seven shillings and fourpence) to spend on drink. He does not of course get the ten pounds. One may deduce from (86.30–31) that the 6.15.0 is Earwicker's rent. This page is very agricultural, so the rent may be that due for grazing animals on Earwicker's mound (see above). There is much allusion to pigs, and an attempt to dissect the subject has been made by Philip L. Graham.[22] I am unable to agree with all that Mr. Graham asserts, but it is clear that a pig is sold to pay the stated sum. It seems that at some time in Ireland one could refer to one's pig as "the gentleman who pays the rent,"[23] hence the term "gentleman ratepayer" (86.27).

The trial which follows this seems to be that of Earwicker's enemies since at (80.04) he is "the plaintiff." Shaun (87.11–18) accuses Shem of the attack. He adds that bad blood existed between Earwicker and Shem since before the Mise of Lewes (the agreement between Henry III and his barons) and compares them to the Mookse and the Gripes. Shem (91.24–33) denies ever having thrown a stick or stone at anyone, thereby referring to the fourth attack. The verdict (93.01) names both Shaun and Shem—Browne and Nolan—so both or neither must be guilty.

It is reasonable that as the fear and sublimation of Earwicker increase, successive attacks should manifest increasing violence. Perhaps the fifth attack is exceptional in having a more severe result than the sixth, but it is less vividly portrayed and it may in fact be more correct to regard them as a single unit. The seventh incident is the hunting of Earwicker by Fitz Urse. He escapes through camouflage or by hiding underground. A string of speculations on his fate or whereabouts then arrive by radio and telegraph. The last report (99.27–29) states that this time he has been really murdered, by the MacMahons. Now, Reginald Fitz Urse was the leader of the four knights who assassinated Thomas à Becket, and according to a legend[24] he fled subsequently to Ireland and founded the MacMahon family. So the final result of the last attack appears to be Earwicker's death by assassination. Colonel John Bawle O'Roarke, who wants to make sure that Earwicker is really "beastly dead," is John Boyle O'Reilly, who was in the Army as an agent of the Irish Republican Brotherhood. Many treacherous ballads proceeded from his unit. Because of this, it is conceivable that the *Ballad of Persse O'Reilly* takes its name from him. Although Earwicker now lies slain on the field of Verdun or on the seabed, a smoke-signal issues from his tower announcing (as at the election of a Pope) his continued embodiment, and lower on p. 100 his tangibility is confirmed by the persisting gravitational attraction he exerts.

I stated earlier that the obscuration of Earwicker extended to his name, person, memorials and to the stories about him. Having considered stories, name and person, I must now survey his memorials and the places sacred to him. Their accessibility lessens as one proceeds. Ye olde marine hotel, at which I.2 commences, is by (50.34–35) a destination from which none ever return. It may be the same as the house of Atreox, which has fallen in dust at (55.03). By (56.33) the location of its site is uncertain. Obviously at one level Earwicker is here already in the tumulus, but there is concurrently a projection of Finnegan at the end of I.1, lying on his bed while the four old men restrain him from rising. Their equivalence with Blake's Four Zoas has been suggested before,[25] but the passage seems to me to draw directly from plate 43 of "Jerusalem," which begins:

> They saw their Wheels rising up poisonous against Albion:
> Urizen cold & scientific, Luvah pitying & weeping,
> Tharmas indolent & sullen, Urthona doubting & dispairing,
> Victims to one another & dreadfully plotting against each other
> To prevent Albion walking about in the Four Complexions.

Albion, in the Sleep of Ulro, is of course Earwicker. The characters of the Zoas are implied. Armagh is cold and scientific ("a'm proud o'it"), Clonakilty pitying and weeping ("God help us!"), Deansgrange indolent and sullen ("say nothing") and Barna doubting and despairing ("whatabout it?"). There may be a reference to the Zoas' occupations in "plicyman, plansiman, plousiman, plab," which suggests the evolution of nomadic plaindwellers into farmers and then perhaps city plebians. It does not look like a Viconian cycle except in its rhythm. Tharmas is a shepherd, Urizen a ploughman and Urthona a blacksmith. Luvah would then be the "plicyman": in different parts of Blake he is a weaver and a vine-dresser but this hardly seems relevant. Also, this hypothesis sets the four in a different order to that in the verse. Blake influences the next page as well: in line 05 appear the King and Priest who "must be tied in a tether/Before two virgins can meet together." Weldon Thornton[26] discusses Joyce's use of this fragment in "Circe."

Effigies of Earwicker are, naturally, desecrated and abused. The Lewis Carroll waxwork is menaced by gamps and blackthorns (57.23). King Billy's equestrian statue appears at (75.15–16). It is also in *Ulysses,* and Thornton[27] points out that the historian D. A. Chart mentions a series of public assaults upon it. Attacks on effigies in *Finnegans Wake* come somewhere between attacks on the living body and demolition of its old habitation. Effigies are frequently destroyed in fertility rites and in festivals such as Sechseläuten and Guy Fawkes' Night. Guy Fawkes is remembered by Shaun at (87.04).[28] To anticipate I.8, Earwicker's enemies, who scrawl his sigla upside down on walls, also batter the Guy Fawkes effigy with cammocks (crooked staffs) at (205.28).

Violation of the dead remains of Earwicker is intermediate between that of his person and that of his effigy. The example given, which naturally occurs in the account of the grave, is that of Henry Luttrell (81.14), whose grandson became so unpopular during the Irish rising of 1798 that Luttrell's grave was broken open and the skull smashed with a pickaxe.[29]

I have emphasized the range of motivations leading to the effacement of Earwicker's shadow on the brain, but I must not ignore the erosion through uncaring natural forces which assist our forgetting. Sometimes they influence categories already considered: for example rain and low visibility at (51.03–08) do more than dissolve Earwicker's face: they make him hard to see from a distance. Consequently, in the heavy rain at (81.21), his assailant mistakes him for Oglethorpe.

The deterioration of the weather throughout I.2–4 can easily be followed. The first tableau is performed "one sultry sabbath afternoon" (30.14) but in the second (35.03) it has become gusty. At (39.02) Baldoyle is breezy. At (39.14) the weather is a pest and the rains are come, but as the echo is of "the winter is past, the rain is over and gone,"[30] the result is *Wakean* ambiguity. Gales are blowing at (43.27) and lower on that page Mr. Delaney anticipates a perfect downpour, but the water does not effectively arrive until the next chapter.

The whole of I.3 is embraced by the Irish climate. It begins in fog, cloud and humidity and closes with raindrops on Rathfarnham. I have called the weather "uncaring," but at some levels it is obviously personified. The clouds possess several meanings in *Finnegans Wake*. At the end of I.1 (29.11) Earwicker sins with the clouds alone for smile-down witnesses, but in I.3 his own plasticity of person makes him a cloud (50.36–51.02: "the shape of the average human cloudyphiz, whereas sallow has long daze faded, frequently altered its ego with the possing of the showers"). At (178.31) Shem prays to the cloud Incertitude. This might be Earwicker, but alternatively it could be Issy, who is a cloud at (82.20) and also in I.6 where she eventually falls as rain into the river (159.06–18). Then she is the river, and in passing out she will remember her fall as birth and the cloud as her mother (627.08–11).

Within I.3 we find it is the Lord's own day for damp (51.21) and that the rains have levelled the edifices built by kings (57.01). At (62.29) there is dense fog although the assailant mentions a blizzard. The descent of Issy ("the young reine") at (64.16) causes the river, as mad as she could be, to flood the plain. The topic of inundation, as I have shown, continues prominent at the beginning of I.4. Perhaps the large accumulation of Dutch words in pages 75–78[31] can be accounted for by the association of Holland with flooding and land reclamation. The Flood lasts until (80.20), when God commands its abatement and "the obluvial waters of our noarchic memory" withdraw. The introduction of Noah and his Flood provides a further instance of retribution by mass killing from above, the ones already quoted being the extinctions of the Parthalonians, the Lough Neagh dwellers and the Sodomites. As the Flood retracts we remember Earwicker and his tomb is before us, but Posidonius O'Fluctuary is told to desist from rolling away the stone at its mouth, and Shaun, who has brought his barrel, to take it back and not collect the letter.

As Earwicker is hibernating it now becomes cold (81.12–13) and the heavy rain (81.21) becomes cold rain (86.06). It is winter at (97.12), Earwicker being in winter coat, and the rain may have become snow as the streets are sledgy at (99.05), although (99.03) refers to "the ruining of the rain." The complete revelation of Earwicker by the water which had hidden and protected him was prevented on p. 80, as just stated, but at the close of the chapter its coming is foretold. Anna Livia has been "hiding the crumbends of his enormousness in the areyou lookingfor Pearlfar sea" (102.06–06), but now she will dispel the slanders which felled him, by writing her letter to the king. In an alternative mode, she will expose the truth involuntarily, like a hen scratching up a letter from a midden.

In the paragraph which closes I.4 we are the searchers for Earwicker, from whom we are separated by a distance as hopeless as that confronting the exiled Jews of Psalm 137. Earwicker is a lost race memory whose recovery we desire with a similar bitterness. We now realize that the oblivial water is in contact with him: it joins our home and our country of exile. We listen, as she bids us, to an illogical and allpervading babble. We never really understand what she is saying but the power in the words satisfies something and we continue resolute. Eventually it can make all other reading feel inadequate. And it never runs out.

Notes

1. Clive Hart, in *Structure and Motif*, pp. 69–75, suggests correspondences between points in *Finnegans Wake* and points on several temporal cycles.
2. *Letters*, I, p. 214.
3. See *Totem and Taboo*, section II.
4. See Clive Hart's *The Earwickers of Sidlesham* in *A Wake Digest*, ed. Clive Hart and Fritz Senn, (Sydney: Sydney University Press, 1968), pp. 21–22.
5. *Concordance:* Overtones.
6. Personal communication, 1969.
7. Brendan O Hehir: *A Gaelic Lexicon for Finnegans Wake*, (Berkeley: University of California Press, 1967).
8. Dutch *poorters*, citizens. In Leo Knuth: "Dutch in Finnegans Wake," AWN, VIII, 2, 27.
9. B. S. Puckle discusses this in *Funeral Customs* (London: T. Werner Lavrie, 1926), pp. 151–153. For example he considers the burial of suicides at crossroads an attempt to "maze" the spirit, so that it would be unable to find its way home.

10. Early Irish Texts Society, Dublin, 1938–56.
11. See section II, ix of *The Topography of Ireland* in *The Historical Works of Giraldus Cambrensis*, ed. T. Wright.
12. Ed. E. Gwynn, Royal Irish Academy, Dublin. See part IV (1924).
13. Dublin, 1946.
14. Joyce's pronouncement in his letter of 26 February, 1935 (*Letters*, III, p. 348) determines a linkage: "This melody is about Lough Neagh under which there is said to be buried a King of Atlantis. Others say Finn MacCool in anger took a sod of turf out of Ireland and flung it in the sea, thus making (1) Lough Neagh (2) Isle of Man."
15. See J. S. Atherton: *Books*, pp. 110–113.
16. See Matthew Hodgart and Mabel Worthington: *Song in the Works of James Joyce* (New York: Columbia University Press, 1959).
17. Brendan O'Hehir, *A Gaelic Lexicon of Finnegans Wake* (Berkeley: University of California Press, 1967), p. 53, points out that *leabhar* (80.14) is Irish for 'book.'
18. See the entry of Jubal and Tubal Cain in Adaline Glasheen's *Second Census*, p. 134.
19. I have discussed the nature of the triad in "A Structural Theory of Finnegans Wake," *AWN*, V. 6, 83–87.
20. *A Lexicon of the German in Finnegans Wake* (Berkeley: University of California Press, 1967), p. 148.
21. British Museum Add. MS 47471 B, p. 4b.
22. "The Middlewhite Fair," *AWN*, VI. 5, 67–69.
23. See for example the beginning of Act IV of Shaw's *John Bull's Other Ireland*.
24. See the article on Fitz Urse in the *Dictionary of National Biography*, vol. VII.
25. Atherton: *Books*, p. 236.
26. *Allusions in Ulysses* (Chapel Hill: University of North Carolina Press, 1968), p. 420.
27. *Ibid.*, p. 237.
28. *See Letters*, III, p. 339.
29. See the article on Luttrell in the *Dictionary of National Biography*, vol. XII.
30. Atherton: *Books*, p. 178.
31. Analysed by Leo Knuth in *AWN* V. 2, 19–28.

Concerning Lost Historeve

Book I
chapter v
Bernard Benstock

If it is correct to assume that the narrative line of *Finnegans Wake* concerns a series of Earwicker family imbroglios and the broadcasting of the rumors deriving from them, it is equally safe to contend that the basics of the plot have been covered in the first four chapters. Chapter five, therefore, marks a new beginning, in accordance with the new cycle within the Viconian scheme, although a distinctly separate approach to the material makes itself apparent. In parallel with the first chapter the tone here is once again of remote history, a sense of time past but barely perceivable and highly speculative, yet now there is a definite advantage: a single focus has replaced the diffuse examinations in chapter one. The piecing together of varying views in a series of disconnected digressions had succeeded in presenting alternate possibilities for introducing the materials of the confused past: now the all-important letter becomes the unique means of investigating the past events or event. As such chapter five is probably the most cohesive and least digressive chapter in *Finnegans Wake:* for a work that depends so much on its discursive accretions the *Wake* is rarely as economical in its presentation as in this chapter. Not brevity alone (this is hardly the shortest chapter) but concentration on an almost all-inclusive aspect gives it its frame. All material relevant to the letter undergoes examination, from who found it to who wrote it, from the words and accent marks intentionally committed to paper to the holes and stains and erasures that have been inadvertently introduced, from what it says to what it means, including the full range of textual and critical elucidation.

With the letter at the forefront chapter five contains (a) the longest single catalogue in the book—the names for the "untitled mamafesta," over 120 of them; (b) the fifth of the ten thunderwords; (c) one of the five variations in Joycean English of the Edgar Quinet sentence—"*Aujourd'hui comme aux temps de Pline et de Columelle . . .*"; and (d) the second longest sentence in the book, a four-page monstrosity set off by semicolons and colons.

Although this can safely be said to be *the* letter chapter, the actual text of that letter within chapter five does not give us either the first or the most complete version available in the *Wake*. Yet it may be the only instance in which the actual letter itself, the missive or manuscript as a document, can be viewed in *Finnegans Wake*. When introduced in the first chapter, materials from that letter are incorporated into the narrative once the pecking hen appears in the "battlefield" outside the museyroom. This "peacefugle, a parody's bird, a peri potmother, a pringlpik" (11.9–10) is both picking and pecking (and actually packing as well, sorting her finds in a "nabsack"—11.19). There is no attempt to differentiate between the words of the letter, designating the past, and the present scene and action, so that the first echoes of the key words of the letter are simultaneously a description of the night on which the hen is "picking here, pecking there" (11.12–13): "But it's the armitides toonigh, militopucos, and toomourn we wish for a muddy kissmans to the minutia workers and there's to be a gorgeups truce for happinest childher everwere" (11.13–16). There is no external indication here that a letter is as yet in question: only the Christmas greeting can be extracted through hindsight to be part of the letter that we eventually come to assume exists. Thereafter it is again the nocturnal scene of gathering and collecting, as a catalogue is elaborated of the junk that goes into the "nabsack." The list ends with some familiar items: "boaston nightgarters and masses of shoesets and nickelly nacks and foder allmichael and a lugly parson of cates and howitzer muchears and midgers and magget, ills and ells with loffs of toffs and pleures of bells" (11.22–25). There is no reason for the uninitiated reader to see the fragments of an epistolary document here either, but later echoes of many of these same phrases indicate that the Boston, Massachusetts, dateline has been incorporated, along with names and items that are central to the message of the letter. It is only with the closing series of kisses ("With Kiss. Kiss Criss. Cross Criss. Kiss Cross"—11.27) that it might become evident that this is from a letter.

The last version of the letter, by contrast, is the longest and most fully developed (and one can even suspect that it contains *more* than it actually should). It is unmistakably a letter, beginning with the traditional salutation "Dear" (615.12), and actually ending with a full signature ("Alma Luvia, Polabella"—619.16), although in identifying the authoress unquestionably as the heroine of the novel it is not as undisguised a signing as Joyce had earlier intended, "Dame Anna Livia Plurabelle Earwicker" (Add MS 47473). Much more than has ever been suspected to be within the pages of the letter is unfolded in this last declaration, but the basic scraps are nonetheless included: the letter-as-newspaper ("Fugger's Newsletter"—97.32) from Boston, Mass., is found in "Morning post as from Boston transcripped" (617.22–23); *foder allmichael* (Father Michael) returns as "pour forther moracles" (617.25); the *lugly parson of cates* is metamorphosed into "that lovelade parson, of case" (617.24–25); and *pleures of bells* easily blends into A. L. P.'s signature. As fully developed as the complete letter actually is in this final reading, it is essentially in a small pocket within several lines that the actual cluster of familiar elements appear.

There is good reason that neither in its initial nor in its fullest form does the letter motif have its primary sounding but in the version contained in the fifth chapter. Here again the basics are huddled together in a tight knot (on page 111) and in its entirety reads:

> originating by transhipt from Boston (Mass.) of the last of the first to Dear whom it proceded to mention Maggy well & allathome's health well only the hate turned the mild on *the van Houtens* and the general's elections with a *lovely* face of some born gentleman with a beautiful present of wedding cakes for dear thankyou Chriesty and with grand funferall of poor Father Michael don't forget unto life's & Muggy well how are you Maggy & hopes soon to hear well & must now close it with fondest to the twoinns with four crosskisses for holy paul holey corner holipoli whollyisland pee ess from (locust may eat all but this sign shall they never) affectionate largelooking tache of tch.
> (111.9–20)

It is difficult to resist the temptation to assume that the variation of the letter that appears here is *the* letter since it is in the chapter that deals exclusively with the letter. Some of the segments (that they have the weight of *motifs* is somewhat doubtful) are at their clearest in this chapter: Father Michael is very much himself; that parson of *cates* and *case* is simply the present of a wedding cake; Boston, Mass., is exactly as it appears on a map; and there is not much equivocation about the four crosses as kisses. Yet this sort of clarity may be misleading, especially since there is no evidence that James Joyce saw verbal literalness as his ideal in the writing of *Finnegans Wake*. If linguistic distortion informs *because* distortion has set in (as such warping accentuates significance in a dream), then the clear version here may be of lesser importance. Losing the twice-noted *parson* may be more of a loss than gaining something as ordinary as a wedding cake; failing to note Kate in the letter may be a serious omission; and there is many a gourmet who might prefer dainty viands (cates) to gooey cake.

A cross-listing of some of these segments as they appear at the major cluster areas is valuable in both an attempt to gain primary meaning and to note the way in which the portion in chapter five seems clearer and possibly most basic (see page 37).

Not only is the letter that begins on p. 111 (and presumably has its signature on p. 113: "Yours very truthful. Add dapple inn"— 113.17–18) the clearest conception, but the examinations of the letter that re-echo its phrases repeat its clarity. The four items singled out for scrutiny during the "Marxian" reading are "Father Michael," "Margaret" (in lieu of Maggy), "cakes," and "dear thank you." Their literalness is actually being mocked in this decoding: "Father Michael about this red time of the white terror equals the old regime and Margaret is the social revolution while cakes mean the party funds and dear thank you signifies national gratitude" (116.7–10). Codes are by their nature simple-minded: words, symbols, signs, letters, numbers are substitutes for real meaning, and once the key to the code is available the meaning of the message exists on a non-ambiguous level and is completely literal. *Finnegans Wake* is certainly not written in code-language and no single one-for-one ratio exists between the words Joyce includes and the equivalents that the "keyed" reader interprets. In this mock-Marxian decoding Joyce spoofs such simplistic readings in such verbs as *equals, means, signifies, is,* and in the comic disparity of the associations. (That the priest stands for the past and the young woman for the future almost makes Joycean sense—as it did in Ibsen—but *party funds* is trite and *national gratitude* intentionally silly.)

That the most commonplace of missives contains "lost histereve" (214.1) is easily understandable in Joycean terms: its very ordinariness attests to Joyce's reading of world history. But the more intriguing mystery might well lie in the salutation and the signature (the addressee and signer) and in the next examination of the fragments offers

a lugly paron of cates	a beautiful present of wedding cakes	cakes . . . beautiful present of waiting kates	A lovely pershan of cates		parting parcel of the same	lovelade parson, of case
boaston nightgarters and masses of shoesets	transhipt from Boston (Mass.)			bosthoon, late for Mass		Boston transcripped
	born gentleman	born gentleman	gentlemine born		ungeborn yenkelmen	bawl gentlemale
foder allmichael	poor Father Michael	father Michael F.M.			any much father	pour forther moracles
midgers and maggets	Maggy . . . Maggy . . . Maggy . . .	Margaret . . . Maggy's tea, or your majesty	maggy waggy		Madges Tighe	majesty
	dear thankyou	dear thank you			thanked you	Dear . . . thanks ever thanks, beloved
(10–11)	(111)	(116)	(280)	(301)	(369–70)	(615–19)

an intriguing possibility. It has generally been assumed that Maggy is a young girl (either the female in Boston writing to her Dublin relatives or the daughter about whom she writes or the Dublin girl being asked about in the letter: as the Maggies she approximates the dual existence of Issy, as in the Mime of Mick, Nick and the Maggies). The first cluster of letter material introduces midgers and maggets (in double plural), while the most literal version contains references to Maggy (and a variant in Muggy); the Marxian identification elevates her to a Margaret, and thereafter the new version contains the cast of characters: "there is many asleeps between someathome's ["allathome's health well"—111.11] first and moreinausland's last ["the last of the first"—111.10] and that the beautiful presence of waiting kates will until life's (!) be more than enough to make any milkmike in the language of sweet tarts punch hell's hate ["the hate turned the mild"—111.11–12] into his twin ["the twoinns"—111.17] nicky and that Maggy's tea, or your majesty, if heard as a boost from a born gentleman is (?)" (116.20–25). The commonplace here is the taking of tea (hence the milk, tarts, punch, cakes) and the family consists of Kate or Anna Livia (*life's*), children Mick, Nick and Maggy, and the master, a born gentleman. On the political level this tea party is in Boston as a rebellion against His Majesty the King of England. The transition from Maggy to majesty is particularly apparent in Madges Tighe in the late version of the letter in which the key words are the most disguised. In the final edition the salutation becomes multiple: "Dear. And we go on to Dirtdump. Reverend. May we add majest?" (615.12–13), implying beloved, husband, father, priest, God, king. This multiplicity is anticipated in the first instance as "Here, and it goes on to appear" (11.8), and repeated in various parts of the *Wake* where no letter material is particularly noticeable until it becomes somewhat intelligible as the opening of a letter in chapter 5: "Dear whom it proceded to mention." In itself the word "Dear" is a formal opening and meaningless without the designated person, but Joyce keeps the actually addressee secret until the last letter, although hindsight can find in a non-letter situation the suggestion of Maggy-Majesty: "Dear and lest I forget mergers and bow to you low, marchers!" (364.11–12). In Chapter 5, where the letter was obviously intended to be at its simplest, Joyce had at one point allowed the mystery to surface: the First-Draft Version begins, "Reverend/ Majesty well . . ." but this was deleted and the significance of the unfinished salutation preserved for the final copy of the letter.

The macrocosm of *Finnegans Wake* contains microcosms within microcosms, and the book itself begins with an address to the Reverend ("riverrun"—3.1) and although it ends with the word Joyce said was the weakest one in the language ("the"—628.16), that word is also the root for God (*the*, Welsh; *theo-*, Greek)—making the book cyclical in still another way. The letter chapter as an entity *contains* the document that reads from the vague opening, "Dear whom it proceded to mention," to the signature that suggests the letter to have been written by Anna Livia, "Yours very truthful." But the chapter itself ends with another signature, "Shem the Penman" (125.23), one that cannot easily be ignored. It is tempting then to see all of chapter five as a letter from beginning to end, just as the first chapter starting "riverrun" could be signed by Earwicker's initials at its conclusion, "he is ee and no counter he who will be untimendly respunchable for the hubbub caused in Edenborough" (29.34-36). And the fifth chapter does actually contain that same riverrun-reverend address in the opening invocation, the third word of which is the Farsi word for a letter, *name:* "In the name of Annah the Allmaziful, the Everliving, the Bringer of Plurabilities, haloed be her eve, her singtime sung, her rill be run, unhemmed as it is uneven!" (104.1-3). In *rill be run* the salute to the Reverend has its echo.

Just as the invocation proclaims the feminine figure of Anna Livia Plurabelle (*Annah/Everliving/Plurabilities*) so the document itself proclaims the revered, majestic father figure and is in the form of a wifely manifesto (the letter as document): "Her untitled mamafesta memorialising the Mosthighest has gone by many names at disjointed times": (104.4-5). Not only is it a manifesto as a proclamation but also in the religious sense that it makes manifest, it brings forth the Godhead. That it is the ineffable name of God that cannot be uttered is implied in its being "untitled," although several scores of titles are nonetheless advanced for it, substitutes that stand for the real name when the times (like now) are out of joint. Whereas the tetragrammaton was a shout in the street in *Ulysses*, "Hooray! Ay! *Whrrwhee!*" in *Finnegans Wake* it is contained within the titles of books, plays, songs, skits, stories, and music hall numbers. The exact number of titles remains in dispute since it is difficult on occasion to determine whether two segments separated by a comma are in actuality a single title or two different possibilities. That the collection of title possibilities is divided into three uneven groups separated by semi-colons may be accidental, and no particular pattern seems apparent within the three areas. The First-Draft Version began modestly enough with only *"Pro Honafrio, The Graons of a Briton, An Apology for a Husband, Can you excuse him."* These segments surface in the final draft, having undergone a sex-change: "The Groans of a Britoness" (104.14–15) is soon followed by a tentative title, *"An Apology for a Big* (some such nonoun as *Husband* or *husboat* or *hosebound* . . .)" (104.15–17). "Ought We To Visit Him?" (104.19) replaces "Can we excuse him," while the designation of Honafrio for Earwicker is dropped, to resurface in the lawcourts sketch of pp. 572–73 as Honofrius/Honufrius.

Whereas the original plan apparently called for a title and descriptive explanation that would concern the male figure exclusively with the female as authoress, the compendium of titles that form this catalogue points in many directions as well. The Earwicker husband is spotted in many of his aspects and guises. As sinner he is the object of his wife's efforts for his redemption, "for Old Seabeastius' Salvation" (104.6), yet there is reason to assume that he will undergo the cyclical fall-and-rise that befits the sacrificed god, "Knickle Down Duddy Gunne and Arishe Sir Cannon" (104.8–9). Culpability, as seen in the *O Felix Culpa* refrain (here presented as the temptress' backside, "Ophelia's culpreints"—105.18), echoes throughout the titles, "Gettle Nettie, Thrust him not . . . The Man That Made His Mother in the Marlborry Train . . . Nopper Tipped a Nappiwenk to his Notylytl Dantsigirls . . . Siegfield Follies and or a Gentlehomme's Faut Pas . . . Lumptytumtumpty had a Big Fall" (104.24; 105.8/10; 106.12–13/20), but the naughty little dancing girls have been culpable as well, even to the extent of sexually arousing his corpse: "How to Pull a Good Horuscoup even when Oldsire is Dead to the World" (105.28–29). The temptresses are his daughters ("Da's a Daisy so Guimea your Handsel too"—105.15) as well as the Stella-Vanessa pair when Earwicker is Jonathan Swift: "Which of your Hesterdays Mean Ye to Morra?" (104.23–24). The indiscretion in Phoenix Park provides its complement of titles: "Peter Peopler Picked a Plot to Pitch his Poppolin" (104.15); "What Barabas Done to a Barrel Organ Before the Rank, Tank and Bonnbtail" (105.15–16); "What Jumbo made to Jalice and what Anisette to Him" (105.17—with Alice as daughter and Anna as mother, this title implicates both; "Them Lads made a Trion of Battlewatschers and They Totties a Doeit of Deers" (105.33–34); "Abbrace of Umbrellas or a Tripple of Caines" (106.32–33). This last instance of the dramatis personae in the park contains the two girls and the three watchers, but Earwicker himself is absent from it.

Although essentially the subject of the titles in this catalogue, H. C. E. is not always present: some of the references are to other members of the household: "Anna Stessa's Rise to Notice" (104.8); "Amoury Trestam and Icy Siseule" (104.10); "Look to the Lady" (105.22); "Mum It is All Over" (105.35); "The Mimic of Meg Neg and the Mackeys" (106.10–11). But more important is the frequency of those designations that stress Anna Livia's view of the hero, where the emphasis is on the eye of the beholder. Where she is most involved, and speaks in the first person, are primarily those instances in which she discusses her sexual adventures. These cover the range from the seduction by the Viking invader to his domestication as her husband: "Hear Hubty Hublin, My Old Dansh" (105.18)—the coupling here is so obvious that they may well be a single, two-part title. The nostalgic glow of the past event colors some of the titling, and Anna Livia often presents herself as an old woman remembering, "E'en Tho' I Granny-a-be He would Fain Me Cuddle" (105.3), where her grandmother pose is belied by her position as Grania the young bride of the old Finn MacCool. The same double-value is present in "I am Older norethe Rogues among Whisht I Slips and He Calls Me his Dual of Ayessha" (105.18–20): the no in *northe* is balanced by the yes in *Ayessha* so that she moves from Molly's initial negative ("Mn") to her closing positive ("Yes"); Rider Haggard's She was two thousand years old while Mohammed's bride Aysha was nine; and duality implies the two maids in the park and the mother-daughter combination of temptresses. Like the Anna Livia of the closing soliloquy she implies at several occasions in these titles that she is passing him on from mother to daughter: "He Gave me a Thou so I serve Him with Thee" (105.36–106.1). Some of the titles are direct and unequivocal, like "I Ask You to Believe I was his Mistress" (which is followed by what may possibly be a subtitle, "He Can Explain"—105.13–14) and "In My Lord's Bed by One Whore Went Through It" (105.34–35), while others are simple enough from internal evidence: "He's my O'Jerusalem and I'm his Po" (105.6–7), where the masculine city identity is matched by the feminine river personification. Other items range from acceptance of the sexual conquest to the assertion that she as female was the sexual aggressor: "I Knew I'd Got it in Me so Thit settles That" (106.15); "He Perssed Me Here with the Ardour of a Tonnoburkes" (106.5–6); "The Flash that Flies from Vugg's Eyes has Set Me Hair On Fire" (106.26–27); "It Was Me Egged Him on to the Stork Exchange and Lent my Dutiful Face to His Customs" (106.17–19).

What at first glance appears to be an impersonal listing of topics, a comic catalogue dissociated from any direct involvement, is actually as personal a statement by Anna Livia about her husband as those contained in the last pages of the *Wake,* and just as diverse in her ambivalent attitudes toward him. What Joyce is offering here in objective form is a preview of that highly subjective monologue, with the variations in mood that we have learned to expect from the dying heroine. "It was for me goolden wending," she remembers nostalgically, "I am leafy, your goolden, so you called me, may me life, yea your goolden, silve me solve" (619.24/29–30), and in her earlier catalogue she included the title, "My Golden One and My Selver Wedding" (104.9) in much the same tone. When she is harking back to the early days of their young love, the same mood prevails and she asks to be loved now as then, "You will always call me Leafiest, won't you, dowling?" (624.22–23): "He Calls Me His Dual of Ayessha" (105.19–20). As often there is a note of resignation mixed with regret as she acknowledges that her life is ending, "I done me best when I was let" (627.13): "I Led The Life" (105.4–5); and her definitive "End here" (628.13) was anticipated by the title, "Mum It is All Over" (105.35). The caption which best suits the *Wake* itself also serves as one of the Mamafesta titles, "The Suspended Sentence" (106.13–14), only to be echoed by Anna Livia at the end as she acknowledges that the sequel of her own life can be read in "Tobecontinued's tale" (626.18).

During the course of Anna Livia's finale she rouses her sleeping husband and leads him out into the early morning, revisiting the scenes of their youthful love. With a burst of elan she notes, "It is very good for the health of a morning" (622.11–12), and it is that same sort of enthusiasm that can be found in the title, "Up from the Pit of my Stomach I swish you the White of the Mourning" (106.7–8). As they stroll through the familiar places. Anna Livia points out the house of the Old Lord whose door, like Earwicker's, she remarks, is always open. "His is the house of the laws," she comments (623.11), and it is apparent from her reverence that the Old Lord is not just a hereditary squire like Jarl van Hoother but also a God-figure, much like the revered being celebrated in the untitled mamafesta, where the simplicity of the designation of the "house of the laws" is paralleled by "His is the House that Malt Made" (106.27).

This tone of reverence applies to Earwicker at his best, as Anna Livia recreates him in her mind. She sees them, the Viking Corsair and the Irish maiden, as a romantic pair, "Proudpurse Alby with his pooraroon Eireen" (620.5–6), a kind of coupling that is present in the title-list in several instances, in "Thonderbalt Captain Smeth and La Belle Sauvage Pocahonteuse" (106.15–16), in "Allolosha Popfetts and Howke Cotchme Eye" (106.23–24), and even in "Armoury Treestam and Icy Siseule" (104.10). The proud Viking is admired in the revery and Anna Livia feeds his ego with such recollections as, "You were pleased as Punch, recitating war exploits and pearse orations to them jackeen gapers" (620.23–24), as among the titles one finds a similar ego-booster, "An Outstanding Back and an Excellent Halfcentre if Called on" (106.35–36). But most important in her recall of the young Earwicker are the sexual adventures they then enjoyed: these have been isolated from the catalogue, particularly such statements as "The Flash that Flies from Vuggy's Eyes has Set Me Hair on Fire" (106.26–27), which has its analogue in "I'm sure he squirted juice in his eyes to make them flash for flightening me" (626.15–16), while "He Perssed Me Here with the Ardour of a Tonnoburkes" (106.5–6) is approximated in her recalling, "And one time you'd rush upon me, darkly roaring, like a great black shadow with a sheeny stare to perce me rawly" (626.23–25). Such enthusiasms, however, are soon shortlived, and the mood of the finale is more often elegiac. "I thought you the great in allthings," she sighs with regret (627.23), as she had described him as "The Best in the West" (105.7), having come to realize that he is in decline. The cycle of his rise and fall is mirrored in the closing monologue in such phrases as "Humps, when you hised us and dumps, when you doused us" (624.13–14), as in the mamafesta it reads, "From the Rise of the Dudge Pupublick to the Fall of the Potstille" (105.22–23). Such disappointments notwithstanding, Anna Livia remains philosophic about the fallen hero, assuming that his was a human and common occurrence, that all men are guilty. Early in the soliloquy she acknowledges, "All men has done somthing" (621.32); in her mamafesta titles she includes, "Fine's Fault was no Felon" (106.25–26).

Whatever else these titles portend (and some still seem as random as anything in *Finnegans Wake*), they bound along toward a significant resolution, the run-on non-title that concludes the catalogue and serves as a description of the contents of the mamafesta, the argument of the text. Incorporated early in the composition of the section, and only slightly augmented for the final draft, it reflects Anna Livia's basic position. She is intent on exonerating Earwicker and squelching the rumors about him that she feels have been purposely and maliciously spread: "First and Last Only True Account all about the Honorary Mirsu Earwicker, L.S.D., and the Snake (Nuggets!) by a Woman of the World who only can Tell Naked Truths about a Dear Man and all his Conspirators how that all Tried to Fall him Putting it all around Lucalizod about Privates Earwicker and a Pair of Sloppy Sluts plainly Showing all the Unmentionability falsely Accusing about the Raincoats" (107.1–7). As definite as this defense apparently is, it should be remembered that this is Anna Livia's public statement on the subject, that her inner convictions on Earwicker's guilt or innocence are not necessarily disclosed here. The letter is a document for public consumption and the accusation against the "Snake" figure is more important to her here than any actual culpability by her husband. It is re-echoed at various stages of the final version of Alma Luvia's letter: "Sneakers in the grass, keep off!" (615.28–29); "Wriggling reptiles, take notice!" (616.16); "If all the MacCrawls would only handle virgils like Armsworth, Limited!" (618.1–2); "The cad with the pope's wife, Lily Kinsella, who became the wife of Mr Sneaker" (618.3–5). What Anna Livia is consciously composing is an apologia, but this is not her only function in the *Wake:* it is indisputable that she is also Biddy the hen digging about indiscriminately in the midden, and all she dredges up goes into the napsack, as she admits in her closing monologue: "Scratching it and patching at with a prompt from a primer. And what scrips of nutsnolleges I pecked up me meself. Every letter is a hard but yours is the hardest crux ever. Hack an axe, hook an oxe, hath an en, heth hith ences. But once done, dealt and delivered, tattat, you're on the ma;" (623.31–36). As letter writer she is her own censor; as a collector of "knowledges" she goes uncensored.

As in the rest of the *Wake* the tensions established in chapter five are between efforts to reveal and efforts to conceal. Fact-finding is as often fault-finding or the sort of whitewashing that finds no felon at fault. Biddy in particular seems to be malicious in her intentions and is herself implicated as a letter-writer; when she is innocently described as "a mere marcella, this midget madgetcy" (112.28) she is also involved within the contents of the letter, identified as a Maggy-figure (see the first version of the letter for *midgers and maggets*), and if the fragments on pages 112–13 are directly attributable to her, it looks as if she is catering to calumny rather than suppressing any unpleasantness: "All schwants (schrites) ischt tell the cok's trootabout him. Kapak kapuk. No minzies matter. He had to see life foully the plak and the smut" (113.11–14). The thunderword, the fifth in the book, that introduces this letter-fragment contains a *magger* that echoes her *madgetcy,* and if it in itself is a message, the hen may be a part of its meaning. As befits this "clearest" of chapters, the thunderword is the most comprehensive of all ten. It appears to be the least intrusive, being neither parenthetic nor a culminating comment or reaction nor a separate entity, but the most integrated into the context. Its clarity as such only means that it is composed of a majority of word-fragments rather than syllable-fragments and almost reads as a syntactically valid sentence: "Thingcrooklyexineverypasturesixdixlikencehimaroundherthemaggerbykinkinkankanwithdownmindlookingated" (113.9–11). Spaced out and mined for surface pun possibilities this thunderword can be read as "Things lie crookedly in (and out of) every pasture, six or ten, like (licentious) him around hers, the magger (his majesty), by kin or cancan, with down (low) mind through the locked gate or in the looking-glass." The pastoral scene, suggested by Biddy in the midden and the fall in the park, offers a shepherd's crook, milk cans, downy feathers, and a locked gate, but these may belie the cock's troot of smut. The guilty Earwicker locked in behind his gate and the lascivious daughter looking into her mirror are discernible in the last word, so that the thunderword itself may be a gossipy letter, despite the innocent echo of the kindly fowl offering a golden age in which "the manewanting human lioness with her dishorned discipular manram will lie down together publicly flank upon fleece" (112.21–13). An earlier pastoral scene, introducing the first instance of the Quinet sentence and investigating another document, "the tome of Liber Lividus" (14.29–30), presents in full innocence a parody of the drowned father, "Lean neath stone pine the pastor lies with his crook" (14.32).

Chapter 5 presents the second Joycean version of the Quinet sentence, and although the first is still fairly recognizable in its Irish setting, this new one is in much freer form. Stammered references to Quinet-Michelet and Vico-Bruno ("From quiqui quinet to michemiche chelet and a jambebatiste to a brulobrulo!"—117.11–12) help introduce the heavily disguised rendering of Quinet's assertion that nature survives man's civilization, that his cities and his battles give way to perennial flowers. Although much attention is given in this chapter to nature, the basic earth from which the hen scratches up history, the Quinet sentence here has lost most of its floral bloom:

> Since nozzy Nanette tripped palmyways with Higho Harry there's a spurtfire turf a'kind o'kindling when oft as the souffsouff blows her peaties up and a claypot wet for thee, my Sitys, and talkatalka tell Tibbs has eve: and whathough (revilous life proving aye the death of ronaldses when winpower wine has bucked the kick on poor won man) billiousness has been billiousness during milliums of millenions and our mixed racings have been giving two hoots or three jeers for the grape, vine and brew and Pieter's in Nieuw Amsteldam and Paoli's where the poules go and rum smelt his end for him and he dined off sooth american (it would give one the frier even were one a normal Kittle-licker) this oldworld epistola of their weatherings and their marryings and their buryings and their natural selections has combled tumbled down to us fersch and made-at-all hours like an ould cup on tay. (117.16–30)

Gone are Quinet's daisies and hyacinths and periwinkles, those eternal survivors of the battlefield, and in their place the turf cut out of the bog for the cottage fire and the clay for the teapot. What has been growing out of the earth has been transformed into intoxicants, and the residents of the home soil have emigrated to the New World and are dispersed. The cycle of life, birth-marriage-death in prosaic patterns, is what nature offers in lieu of the flowers, and only the *oldworld epistola* is there to be dug up. Its botanical significance is contained in *pistil*, but this is hidden in the more obvious *pistol*, the war relic dug up and enshrined in museyrooms, and in *epistle*, the letter that Biddy pecked up on Quinet's battlefield. Quinet's romantic idealism is eventually reduced to an *ould cup on tay*, the epistle bearing its familiar teastain. As Clive Hart has shown, the Quinet sentence and the letter motif are interinvolved in the *Wake,* and at four junctures major sounding of the two are close together. The battlefield willingly or unwillingly yields both persistent flowers and the hidden remains of man's historic past, the buried giant, the buried letter, and all the debris the hen salvages.

Although *what* the letter discloses is of vital interest here, at least as much attention is give to *how* the letter reveals its contents—the methods of examination. Of importance then is the identity of the narrative voice (or voices) within the chapter, and although it is a hopeful sign that Shem's signature concludes the chapter and might then be allowed to stand for the single narrator of its material, there are disquieting indications that the voice changes frequently, possibly from paragraph to paragraph. It is only by analyzing such changes that any pattern of narration emerges—and that remains a tenuous one. The opening invocation can be accepted as a Shemish celebration of the maternal figure and it cannot but be relevant that none of the many mamafesta titles in any way reflects discredit on Shem. (Considering that there is almost no room in this particular catalogue for elements of the brother battle, there is a slam included against Shaun: "Buy Birthplate for a Bite"—104.11).

The chapter proper begins immediately after the barrage of titles, and from the first it seems apparent that a somewhat pompously professorial voice is heard intent on explaining the significance of the writing of letters. From the initial statement, "The proteiform graph itself is a polyhedron of scripture" (107.8), the heavyfooted archeologist trips through his series of suppositions with touches of pedantic humor ("Amousin though not but"—107.23) and goodnatured condescension. But a blunt and demanding voice interrupts, insisting on a straight answer, "who in hallhagal wrote the durn thing anyhow" (107.36–108.1), and receives for his pain a lecture on the virtue of patience: "Now, patience; and remember patience is the great thing, and above all things else we must avoid being or becoming out of patience" (108.8–10). If it is a pedogogical Shem that began the explanations, it is then a hardheaded Shaun that demanded direct information without frills. The Shem who answers remains patronizing, but he does modulate his vocabulary to a degree and gets down to a more fundamental level of inquiry, identifying the father figure of the remote past, the surnameless Earwicker of the closing pages of the first and opening pages of the second chapter of the *Wake*. This reduction to a common level of comprehension is evident in the next passage, both in its matter-of-fact tone and its commonplace information:

> Naysayers we know. To conclude purely negatively from the positive absence of political odia and monetary requests that its page cannot ever have been a penproduct of man or woman of that period or those parts is only one more unlooked for conclusion leaped at, being tantamount to inferring from the nonpresence

of inverted commas (sometimes called quotation marks) on any page that its author was always constitutionally incapable of misappropriating the spoken words of others. (108.36)

That this is still Shemish can be seen from the tongue-in-cheek aspects: the speaker is no more concerned with delivering straight, unadorned facts than before, but anticipates the capacity of his heckler for jumping to conclusions. The false one that he therefore offers is that the absence of quotation marks means the absence of quoted material, since Joyce' readers are aware that he himself preferred the French *tirez* to the scorned "invented gommas" (374.10) and that the plagiarist may steal the words of others without the expetced documentation, deleting the quotation marks entirely.

The next portion begins in such colloquial fashion as again to suggest a change in narrators. The slangy statement that there is "another cant to the questy" (109.1) is further embellished with the insulting question, "Has any fellow, the dime a dozen type, it might with some profit some dull evening quietly be hinted—as any usual sort of onery iosser, flatchested, fortyish, faintly flatulent . . . every looked sufficiently longly at a quite everyday-looking stamped addressed envelope?" (109.1-8). Not just the slang that introduces the idea, but more importantly the subject matter of this paragraph makes it more than possible that Shaun the Post is once again intruding, this time to take over the examination for his own purposes. The concentration on the envelope, on the externals of the letter, certainly suggests the Shaunian preoccupations, and he soon turns the investigation into sexual byways. The envelope that covers the contents of the letter are like the clothes that cover the private parts of women. "Who in his heart," this narrator asks, "doubts either that the facts of feminine clothiering are there all the time or that the feminine fiction, stranger than the facts, is there also at the same time, only a little to the rere?" (109.30-33). Although lasciviousness as such is hardly the exclusive property of either Shaun or Shem, this kind of snickering suggestiveness and its envelope-externals emphasis seems to reveal Shaun the Post.

But this attempt to usurp the narrator's function and concentrate attention on the envelope instead of the letter proves shortlived. The narrator who takes back his role is less interested in Shaunian distinctions between fact and fiction and the Shaunian concentration on "the space of the time being" (109.22) than in the art-of-fact, artistic fiction ("Here let a few artifacts fend in their own favor"—110.1), and in time-consciousness, "sequentiality" (110.15). This artifact-finder now maintains his irreverent but knowledgeable tone and continues his investigation step-by-step. From general location, the isle of saints and sages ("Our isle is Saigne"—110.6), to the specific mound, the narrator sets his scene and the time of the find as midwinter. The hen that goes picking is like the child who found the Ardagh chalice, whom the narrator identifies with Shaun: "What child of strandlooper but keepy little Kevin in the despondful surrounding of such sneezing cold would ever have trouved up" (110.31-33)—in a later version of the letter, the born gentlemen are identified as the twins, "Jeremy Trouvas or Kepin O'Keepers" (370.8), which may be taken as a hint that Shem was the finder and Shaun the keeper. The found letter then reveals its battered contents: it has disintegrated in the hot midden, been stained with the orange peels buried there, as well as the original drop of tea while being written; the hen has pecked holes in it with her beak while retrieving it so that there are lacunae throughout. Moreover, these omissions might be further complicated by repetitions caused by the melting through of words from one side of the page to the other (the excesses of Maggy and well), so that the coherence of the message is marred. For all of its inadequacies, however, the letter is finally before us.

The Shem narrator retains his position during this historical account of the finding and viewing of the letter, and the analysis of its condition, except for an interjected "Why then how?" (111.25) part of the way through an impatient demand for specifics. That his listener is befuddled apparently amuses Shem and he taunts the slow-witted Shaun:

> You is feeling like you was lost in the bush, boy? You says: It is a puling sample jungle of woods. You most shouts out: Bethicket me for a stump of a beech if I have the poultriest notions what the farest he all means. Gee up, girly! The quad gospellers may own the targum but any of the Zingari shoolerim may pick a peck of kindlings yet from the sack of auld hensyne.
> (112.3-8)

But with this taunting Shem relinquishes the narration; Shaun's soberly ecclesiastical voice takes over, announcing his unquestioning faith in the hen in question: "Lead, kindly fowl!" (112.9). His straightforward message is a pollyannic belief in perfectibility, in the example set for man by the advanced bird. "For her socioscientific sense is sound as a bell, sir" (112.11–12), he pontificates, echoing his own envelope-theory: "to concentrate solely on the literal sense or even the psychological content of any document to the sore neglect of the enveloping facts themselves circumstantiating it is just as hurtful to sound sense" (109.12–15). From religious platitudes and courteous compliments regarding the "ladylike" behaviour of the hen, Shaun moves to augury ("Let us auspice it!"—112.18), predicting peace and prosperity for the future, insisting that they "are not justified, those gloompourers who grouse that letters have never been quite their old selves again since that weird weekday in bleak Janiveer . . . when to the shock of both, Biddy Doran looked at literature" (112.23–27). Rather than admit that he is confounded by the dark complications of the mysterious letter, Shaun slices through the darkness and maintains that he sees clearly and positively.

The letter that he interprets, after his sentimental celebration of the hen-authoress and insistence on her down-to-earth simplicity, is the one that tells the *cock's trootabout* Earwicker, with all its smut and foulness and without mincing matters. It reports the incident in the park, the father and his two fruitgirls/dancing girls, his foibles and the micturition, and signs it as coming from *Add dapple inn*. To Shaun this is an old story of feeble man's fall from grace: "Yet is it but an old story, the tale of a Treestone with one Ysold, of a Mons held by tentpegs and his pal whatholoosed on the run, what Cadman could but Badman wouldn't, and Genoaman against any Venis, and why Kate takes charge of the waxworks" (113.18–22). Shaun expects a simple answer and once again Shem returns to the complexities of his examination of the manuscript. As if Shaun had never interrupted or attempted to take charge of the proceedings, Shem continues with his search: "Another point," he begins (114.21), concentrating on the mysterious stain, postulating the theory of multiple authorship, and insisting that signatures are superfluous when everything in the letter is a signature of all things: "So why, pray, sign anything as long as every word, letter, penstroke, paperspace is a perfect signature of its own?" (115.6–8).

The major preoccupation that Shem now displays is presumably with a sexual reading of the letter, assuming that it involves the encounter of a prostitute and a curate (at first the clerical kind with a "perpetual soutane suit" and later as the bartender who "brings strong waters"—115.16–17/116.19). The scene is the pastoral one of *"prostituta in herba"* (115.15), or specifically in Phoenix Park ("Let a prostitute be whoso stands before a door and winks or parks herself in the fornix near a makeussin wall" (116.16–18), although the passage ends in various rural possibilities for sexual activity: "over country stiles, behind slated dwellinghouses, down blind lanes, or, when all fruit fails, under some sacking left on a coarse cart?" (116.33–35). In particular the Father Michael of the letter is identified as a lecherous clergyman fingering the young virgins who fall off their "bisexycle" before their entrances: "who picks her up as gingerly as any balmbearer would to feel whereupon the virgin was most hurt and nicely asking: whyre have you been so grace a mauling and where were you chaste me child?" (115.17–20). Shem luxuriates in the salaciousness of the psychoanalytic view of the situation described in the letter, and just as Shaun had assumed that it was a familiar old story, Shem concludes that " 'Tis as human a little story as paper could well carry" (115.36). Despite psychological and political readings the story remains a basic sex-love situation, and Shem varies from the sentimental to the earthy, acknowledging the universality of love as part of the cycle of life in repeatedly Viconian terms: "The lightning look, the birding cry, awe from the grave, everflowing on the times" (117.3–4); "a good clap, a fore marriage, a bad wake, tell hell's well" (117.5–6); "their weatherings and their marryings and their buryings and their natural selections" (117.27–28).

In full command now the Shem voice continues to make definite statements about the efficacy of the missive and directs them at his opponent, calling him "olmond bottlor" (118.5), "bafflelost bull" (118.7), and "Soferim Bebel" (118.18), since Shaun had previously addressed Shem as "baroun lousadoor" (107.36). In each of these two paragraphs Shem begins his argument from a position of strength, remaining assertive throughout, but perhaps losing confidence at the end of each. He maintains that every part of the letter is an indication of the whole and that the letter is a reliable document despite Shaun's attempts to discredit it: "we must vaunt no idle dubiosity as to its genuine authorship and holusbolus authoritativeness. And let us bringthecease to beakerings on that clink, olmond bottler!" (118.3–5). The mere fact that it is written evidence means that it must have been written at some *time* in some *place* by someone. Shem is defending the value of the written word, yet at his most assertive there are indications that he may be losing heart: someone, he reiterates, "wrote it, wrote it all, wrote it all down, and there you are, full stop. O, undoubtedly yes, and very potably so, but one who deeper thinks will always bear in the baccbuccus of his mind that this downright there you are and there it is only all in his eye. Why?" (118.13–17). In the final touch Shem may fall back on the argument that it is all in the eye of the beholder—or even more skeptical if *in the eye* has the power of complete dismissal, as in the expression, "My eye!" Yet he regains his confidence and answers his own question, *Why?*, with a strong, "Because, Soferim Bebel" (118.18).

The crux of Shem's confidence in the document is in its permanence through the ages, despite all the maulings it has undergone and (even more important) the changes that it has wrought upon itself. For Shem's "letter" contains within itself its bases for change: it is transitory and in a constant state of flux: it is flux itself. The human capacity to record the immediacy of experience (what Anna Livia declares when she says, "I wrote me hopes and buried the page"—624.4) is the essential, rather than any one specific message the piece of paper may contain. No document, however obscure or obliterated, is without meaning: "No, so hop me Petault, it is not a miseffectual whyacinthinous riot of blots and blurs and balls and hoops and wriggles and juxtaposed jottings linked by spurts of speed: it only looks as like it as damn it" (118.28–31). And he goes on to express his gratitude that any such document should exist, but with such fervor that the skepticism in Shem's basic makeup reacts against the excess of enthusiasm, even though he is "hoping against hope all the while that, by the light of philophosy, (and may she never folsage us!) things will begin to clear up a bit one way or another within the next quarrel of an hour and be hanged to them as ten to one they will too, please the pigs, as they ought to categorically, as strictly between ourselves, there is a limit to all things so this will never do" (119.4–9). The link between the letter and Quinet's sentence is that in both cases something permanent under the ground is expected to outlive the transitoriness of man's terrestial possession, but Shem seems to opt for man's own recording of his existence rather than a handful of hearty flowers.

At this juncture in the chapter a new narrative voice takes over, or perhaps it is only Shem putting on the mask of Sir Edward Sullivan. Just as the Ardagh chalice is an Irish artifact standing for the letter, so the Book of Kells represents *the* literary artifact, and Sullivan's transcription of it offers Joyce another opportunity for parody. The monster "sentence" spanning pages 119–123 is in Sullivanese and mostly dedicated to deciphering and commenting upon the orthography, describing the alphabet as it is sprinkled throughout the manuscript and the illuminated tidbits that frame the gospel. Our man Sullivan pays particular attention to the figures of Earwicker and Anna Livia, finding them in the capital E lying on its face (a "baffling chrismon trilithon"—119.17) and the delta, and marshals several *Wake* echoes not previously sounded in this chapter: *hesitancy*, 432 and 1132. Yet, although the obsession here is alphabetical and numerical, the contents of the familiar letter itself do not escape examination. Among the fragments isolated here for examination are *a born gentleman, Maggy, funeral;* the first is rendered into modern Greek (of sorts) as "to mpe mpron a gentlerman" (120.9); the "happy funeral" (280.11), which in its other transformations is a "grand fooneral" (617.26), a "grand funferall" (111.15), a "fun for all" (301.13), and "ephumeral" (369.33), is here an echo primarily of that "clear" letter, an italicized "funferal" (120.10); while the transition from Maggy to Majesty is at its clearest in the Sullivanian view of "variant *maggers* for the more generally accepted majesty which is but a trifle and yet may quietly amuse" (120.17–18). If it is true that this long "sentence" is Joyce's most specific reference to his own *Wake,* then several statements here are of particular interest: "the copyist seems at least to have grasped the beauty of restraint" (121.19–30); "always jims in the jam, sahib" (121.18–19); "the gipsy matting of a grand stylish gravedigging with secondbest buns" (121.31–32); and the oft-quoted "as if it were sentenced to be nuzzled over a full trillion times for ever and a night till his noddle sink or swim by that ideal reader suffering from an ideal insomnia" (120.11–14), *sentenced* here having the same connotation as Stephen's comment on his own *Hamlet* theorizing ("Are you condemned to do this?").

The Sullivan approach continues on up to the last paragraph of the chapter, first attempting to use the erudition of others (Duff-Muggli, Tung-Toyd, and a Punic admiralty report) to investigate the substance of the manuscript, and then concentrating on the peculiarities of the punctuation as he had on the numbers and letters. That the letter is being read by an Oliver Wendell Holmes sort of professor at his breakfast table sets up multiple possibilities concerning the necessary detective work involved and the mystery of the punctures attributed to the sharp-beaked hen. The professional type in question is "a grave Brofessor; ath e's Break—fast—table" (124.9–10), as "Yard inquiries pointed out" (124.8). That Holmes wrote *The Professor at the Breakfast Table* sets the morning scene at which the letter, having arrived in the morning mail, is being perused over breakfast.

(That the professor is grave is due to accentuation: the French *accent grave* in *a* changes the English indirect article into a French preposition.) While eating his ham and eggs and bread and butter ("smearbread and better and Him and newlaidills"—124.13–14) with his "fork" (124.9), this bread-eater ("Brotfressor"—124.15) seems to be myopically punching holes in the letter, "by punct! ingh oles (sic) in iSpace" (124.11–12). "These paper wounds" (124.3) then may have been made by the professor rather than the pecking hen, or his may have coincidentally been made directly upon hers: "that these two were the selfsame spots naturally selected for her perforations by Dame Partlet on her dungheap" (124.22–24). The *Yard* that made the inquiries is Scotland Yard, of course, so that Oliver Wendell Holmes equals detective Sherlock Holmes in this aspect of the investigation.

These last two paragraphs preceding the ultimate one are in themselves in the form of a letter. Toward the end of the second paragraph the writer is signing off: "With acknowledgment of our fervour of the first instant he remains years most fainfully. For postscrapt see spoils" (124.30–32). Yet, like the not-yets of the opening page of the *Wake,* the suggestion follows immediately that all this is to begin again, that nothing has as yet happened at the Inn of Father Adam in the middenheap of Eden: "Though not yet had the sailor sipped that sup nor the humphar foamed to the fill. And fox and geese still kept the peace around *"L'Auberge du Pere Adam"* (124.32–34). Without Earwicker's fall there is no "old story" to provide the contents for the letter, but only the Edenic world where lions-and-lambs and foxes-and-geese lie down together in the pastoral area surrounding Earwicker's pub (Fox and Geese is the name of an area south of Chapelizod). If this segment is indeed a letter, another microcosm within the macrocosm, then its salutation can be found in the opening words, "Duff-Muggli" (123.11)—Dear Maggy.

Since Shem is the subject of the final paragraph of the chapter, it is apparent that Shaun resumes narration of the finale. The Four Old Judges are attempting to track Shem down, "the writing chap of the salter" (125.7), and his name is given as "Diremood" (125.6), brother of "dearmate" (125.8). Like the Shem of the Penman chapter he is avoiding military service and has gone into hiding, perhaps having grown a moustache for disguise. Most significant is the fact that he is "formelly confounded with amother" (125.11–12), establishing the writer-amenuensis relationship between Anna Livia and Shem the

Penman; and since *fourmi* and *moth* are present, the entomological family relationships are hinted at. But Shem is also Shaun's twin, so he might well be confounded with another, his brother. Shaun's final insult condemns Shem as "that odious and still today insufficiently malestimated notesnatcher" (125.21–22), but Shem has his parenthetical comment before actually being named: "kak, pfooi, bosh and fiety, much earny, Gus, poteen? Sez you!" (125.22–23). This conclusion then leads directly into the questions-and-answers of the next chapter, a colloquy between Shaun the Post and Shem the Penman.

4

The Turning Point

Book I

chapter vi

E. L. Epstein

There are two ways to view the Questions chapter. One is to examine the chapter itself in detail for explication of some overlooked difficulties and patterns. The other is to open, or reopen, the larger questions of the form of the *Wake* and the Questions chapter's place in it. I will do both, since it turns out that treatment of the second question depends to some extent upon treatment of the first.

I,vi is a combination of a catechism and a list, the list elicited by questioning. This is by no means the first time a catechism form is employed in the works of Joyce. One could almost trace the catechism in this chapter back to self-questionings in *A Portrait,* especially in the diary entries at the end, and other passages in *Ulysses,* mainly to the questioning in Telemachus, Nestor, Proteus, Scylla and Charybdis and, of course, the Ithaca chapter, and to the lists in Cyclops and Circe. It is a useful device to elicit clear definition of psychological complexities. In *FW* itself there are many lists and many catechisms. The first page of *FW* contains what appears to be a list of the *dramatis personae* of the book. There are the many names of Persse O'Reily (44.10–14) and the listing of his attributes and actions in the "Ballad," and there are many others. Lists are, in fact, one of the main characteristics of the Joycean style. Catechisms are also commonly employed in the *Wake,* but it is only in the Questions chapter that a catechism *evokes* a list as its answer. Elsewhere in the *Wake,* a great deal of information is acquired through catechism, mainly with Shem doing the asking and Shaun on the answering end, but nowhere else does the answer outline the characters of the book so clearly as in I,vi.

There is unobtrusive ordering in and of the questions and answers themselves. For one thing, there is a definite short-long pattern in the first ten questions. Questions one, three, five, seven, and nine are very long questions, each with a very short answer, usually a short phrase, a name, or a sentence. Questions two, four, six, eight, and ten are short questions with long answers. This checkerboard pattern is broken at question eleven, where the question is rather long and the answer is enormous, and in question twelve, in which both the question and answer are two words each (unless all of the Shem the Penman chapter is intended to be the answer of the twelfth question).

The ordering of the questions themselves is apparently not significant (except for the position of the last question), but within the questions and answers themselves there is some hidden patterning. The four hundred parts of the enormous first question, in thirteen pages (I once fondly thought that these were three hundred and sixty-six parts, but a more careful count came to between three hundred and eighty and four hundred), are ordered by no principle amongst themselves, but the beginning and the end of the question provide, as is usual with Joycean polar opposites, a pattern: *Tree-Stone:*

> What secondtonone myther rector and maximost bridges-maker was the first to rise taller through his beanstale than the bluegum buaboababbaun or the giganteous Wellingtonia Sequoia, . . . and an he had the best bunbaked bricks in bould Babylon for his pitching plays he'd be lost for the want of his wan wubbling wall?   (126.10–12; 139.11–13)

The hero of the *Wake* remains the guilty builder throughout, whether he is Bygmester Solness or Nimrod constructing the tower of Babel—he is always Tim Finnegan or Humpty Dumpty wobbling on his own Dublin Wall. However, he is creator both in Time—the trees—and in Space—the bricks and stones; indeed, perhaps as Old King Coal, he is stone that once was tree, comatose fallen Man. This thematic opposition is usually associated with Shem and Shaun, but here we see both Shem and Shaun providing the alpha and omega for fallen man, and included in him.

These could be a few comments on a few of the other parts of the question not yet elucidated. "Is too funny for a fish and has too much outside for an insect" (127.1–2) probably refers to HCE as a lobster (*Hummer* in German). "If he outharrods against barkers, to the shoolbred he acts whiteley" (127.11–12) refers to HCE's commercial manners; employing the names of four famous London department stores (later there is also a reference to Selfridge's), the phrase has HCE out-Heroding Herod in his attitude toward the unruly proletariat ("barkers") while behaving with oily geniality to the wealthy and educated ("the shoolbred"). (The phrase acquires an ironic twist if the reader knows that William Whiteley was distinguished for his ironhanded attitude towards his employees.) The hero appears as Dublin in "a form like the easing moments of a graminivorous" (128.6–7)—Dublin *does* rather have the formless shape of a cowpat. "Blimp, blump" (129.7) conveys the notion of a deflated gasbag with great and comic economy. "Is the handiest of all andies and a most alleghant spot to dump your hump" (129.17–18), beside conveying the mountainous nature of the hero, in the Andes and Alleghenies (later we see that he disdains the Alps as *"nouvelles roches"* [129.35]), also contains an allusion to *Pilgrim's Progress*—Christian "dumps his hump" of sins at the top of the hill of Calvary. There seems to be a reference to the *Odyssey* at 130.19–20: "hanged hishelp from there hereafters"—in Book XXII, Telemachus hangs the unfaithful servant girls after the slaughter, though not quite from the rafters. There are obvious Dublin references in 130.27–31: the "twenty-four or so cousins germinating" in the U.S.A. are all the Dublins in America, while the "namesake with an initial difference" in Poland is Lublin; "his first's a young rose" (BUD) "and his second's French-Egyptian" (NIL) "and his whole means a slump at Christie's" (NUL–BID; Christie's, the famous London auction house.) Dublin is again referred to in the brilliant crossword puzzle clue at 130.34: "you and I are in him surrented by brwn bldns" (d*U*bl*I*n). In this clue "U" and "I" are literally in him, Dublin, surrounded by blind consonants; after all, he has an "eatupus complex" (128.36); Haveth Childers Everywhere, the citycreator, also tries to imprison his children in the city he has created ("we go into him sleepy children, we come out of him strucklers for life") (132.8–9). At 131.33–35 there is a high-spirited caricature of Ezra Pound at his bounciest, shaggiest, and Chinese-sagest: "has the most conical hodpiece of Confusianist heronim and that chuchuffuous chinchin of his is like a footsey kungaloo around Taishantyland." ". . . he was put to music by one shoebard" (133.26–27) might refer to Schubert's setting of passages from Ossian, or it might just be a reference to the UnFinnished Symphony. "Washes his fleet in annacrwatter" (135.6) refers to Eliot's Mrs. Porter and her daughter, who wash their feet (or something) in *The Waste Land*—at 135.7 occurs "missed a porter." To continue the Eliot overtones, there are a number of City churches at 135.9—St. Edmund, King and Martyr, a Wren church (1670-9) in Lombard Street; St. Dunstan-in-the-East, a Wren church (1670-9) in Great Tower Street; St. Peter-le-Poor, not a Wren church (constructed 1792, destroyed 1907) in Lower Thames Street; and a combination of St. Bartholomew-by-the-Exchange (Wren, demolished 1891) and St. Bartholomew-the-Great (pre-Great Fire), in Smithfield. Besides the references to the hero as a builder, we have here his commercial prowess combined with his piety; he is indeed "a gorgon of selfridgeousness" (137.33-34). However, "one lip on his lap and one cushlin his crease" (136.3-4) is the position of Judas in the center mouth of the triple-headed Satan in Dante's *Inferno*.

Flanked by tree and stone, the dozens of avatars of the male creative principle swarm toward the reader as if imitating the creator's resistless plenitude. Shaun picks the most gigantic of the forms of the hero for his answer—"Finn MacCool!"—and so deserves a full mark, but even so the answer is dwarfed by the question devised by Shem.

Shaun creates a poem of love as answer to the second question, rudely phrased by Shem as a variant on "Does your mother know you're out?" This phrase was once very common as an expression of scorn and an implication of immaturity. "Mike" responds, in the meter of "The Bells of Shandon," by forecasting the rôle of Anna Livia as reconciler of her quarreling sons; as Time, the ever-rolling stream, she bears all her sons away, and as the Prankquean she forces them to reverse their personalities. In the Lessons chapter Shem and Shaun change sides (of the margins) after being "bathed" in the text (287.18-292.36). In the answer, Shem and Shaun, as Church ("cowld Clesiastes") and State ("hot Hammurabi"), espying her "pranklings," renounce their quarrels for ever, or at least for "a night."

The third question is the one that Shaun apparently answers incorrectly—"he misunderstruck and aim for am ollo of number three of them . . ." (126.7-8). It is not easy to determine his error. His answer to the third question, a rather silly version of the motto of Dublin, seems to suggest that, in his authoritarian way, he assumes obedience to be the only duty of the citizen, or the material prosperity ("obesity") is the only measure of the felicity of a civilization. (He apparently believes that Man lives by bread alone; he certainly is obsessed by food all through the book.)

The next three questions deal with the Four Old Men, Sackerson the servant, and Kate the Slop, three entities that have lost their mature powers and remain as superannuated and subservient beings. The answer to the question of the Four Old Men is brilliantly composed, consisting of, among other things, the four regional accents of Ireland, four metals (gold, silver, copper, iron), the characteristic products of the four provinces, and, most striking of all, the complete inability of the regions of Ireland to unite—when they try to "harmonise" their responses, by ringing a chime of bells, the upper partials of each bell interfere with those of its neighbors, leading to a dreadful jangle through which can be clearly discerned a ferocious quarrel about money. The four provinces do not "harmonise" any more than do the Four Gospels. This is neither the first nor the last time when Joyce comments sardonically on the political shortcomings of Ireland. Two more points: Shaun, whose voice is behind that of the old men, will not recognize death, the end of man. Although he carefully contrives it that each city-name answer will be of six letters, distorting "Delfas" and "Dorhqk" in the process, he will not allow any of his cities to have a "nuinous end," even if he must reverse the first and last letters of "Nublid" to effect this. In addition, I would hazard a guess that the four italicized words in the answers—"we'll," "leave," "more," "your"—may represent the sounds of, respectively, a golden bell, a silver bell, a copper bell, and an iron bell, and the four italicized words in the attempted chime of bells at the end—"neople, Shandeepen, feepence, Aequallllllll"—are distorted in the direction of the "gold" and "silver" sounds of "we'll" and "leave," appropriately enough, when the money is not divided "aequalllllllly."

The Four Old Men, concupiscent and ridiculous as always, are directing their love-song at Issy, an anticipation of their love-poem in II,iv (398.31–399.28), and as in that poem, they are offering her a life of economic and sexual servitude.[1] Little more can be expected from the "paúpulation" of Ireland; *paulus* "small" (Lat.) combines with *Paúpus* "grandfather" (Gypsy-Romany), to suggest the little old men of the provinces of Ireland making late, loveless marriages.

Questions 5 and 6 are about the servants of HCE. Joyce seems to be suggesting that they both share the socially deprived situation of negroes: Sackerson is called "Pore ole Joe," the name of the song in Britain that is Stephen Foster's *Old Black Joe,* while "Summon in the Housesweep Dinah" is based on "Someone's in the house with Dinah" from "I've Been Working on the Railroad," a song associated with blackface comedians in Britain since the song was introduced by the Christie Minstrels in the nineteenth century (see 175.35-6; see *Ulysses*

436 for a minstrel rendition of "There's someone in the house with Dina"). One of Sackerson's rôles is bouncer and general Dogberry in HCE's pub; in II,iii, "the Sockerson boy" announces closing time ("Polizeinstunde") on 370.30, and attempts to put the fear of the Lord into the drunken customers ("to pump the fire of the lewd into those soulths of bauchees, havsousedovers") while all the time rinsing up their dirty bottles. Sackerson's thunderous threats to the customers, backed up by the fear (or the fire) of the Lord, is foreshadowed on 141.16–17: "lewd man of the method of godliness": in Romany "mitoovelesko-godli" means "thunder," or literally "my God's noise," and may be concealed in "method of godliness."

Questions 7 and 8 present no difficulties of interpretation, except perhaps that the answer to Question 8 provides an interesting numerological pattern. There are fourteen clauses patterned on "they war loving, they love laughing" and so on, and fifteen rhyming/alliterating words in the phrases that follow—"as *born* for *lorn*" and so on; *fourteen* plus *fifteen* equals *twenty-nine,* the number of the maggies. Also "born—lorn—lore—love—live—wive—wile—rile—ruler—ruse—rose—hose—home," thirteen of the fifteen rhyming/alliterative words, make up a chain of a type invented by Lewis Carroll, one of the aspects of Shaun.

The main difficulty with Question 9 is its syntax, which is more complex than that of any other sentence in the *Wake* (with the possible exception of 193.32–195.04, the gigantic sentence that announces the arrival of Anna Livia and the true commencement of the "story" in the *Wake*). Reduced to its bare bones, it appears to ask the following question: If a human being were now accorded a sight of "old hopeinhaven" (the old Adam, or Adam Kadmon, the universal man, the universe in the shape of man, combined with old Copenhagen, Wellington's "big wide harse"), then *what* would that far-gazing forgetter (*Vergesser,* Ger.) seem to be dreaming of? The answer, "A collideorescape," combines a theoretical view of the atomic structuring of the universe, as a product of random processes, and a justification of ultimate patterning (by repetition of random events), as in a kaleidoscope. However, the syntactic complexity of the question itself imitates the universal "collideorescape," with a great surface complexity combined with an underlying simplicity.

Joyce had a predecessor in this sort of imitative syntax. Milton, in Book 8 of *Paradise Lost,* provides a sentence of great complexity, also on the subject of universal order:

> When I behold this goodly frame, this World
> Of Heaven and Earth consisting, and compute
> Their magnitudes, this Earth a spot, a grain,
> An atom, with the firmament compared
> And all her numbered stars, that seem to roll
> Spaces incomprehensible (for such
> Their distance argues and their swift return
> Diurnal) merely to officiate light
> Round this opacous Earth, this punctual spot,
> One day and night in all their vast survey
> Useless besides; reasoning I oft admire
> How Nature wise and frugal could commit
> Such disproportions, with superfluous hand
> So many nobler bodies to create,
> Greater so manifold, to this one use,
> For aught appears, and on their orbs impose
> Such restless revolutions day by day
> Repeated, while the sedentary earth,
> That better might with far less compass move,
> Served by more noble than herself, attains
> Her end without least motion, and receives
> As tribute, such a sunless journey brought
> Of incorporeal speed, her warmth and light;
> Speed, to describe whose swiftness number fails.
> (*Paradise Lost,* VII, 15-38)

The basic syntactic structures of both sentences are similar:

Joyce: If X, then what Y?
Milton: When X [then] I . . . wonder Y.

In addition, the speech in *Paradise Lost* is contrived by Adam, the old hopeinhaven of Joyce's question. The *Hamlet* references in the Joyce sentence ("Camelot prince of dinmurk"), and the repeated "seems," which evoke Hamlet's comment to his mother, "Seems, madam! Nay, it is; I know not 'seems' " in *Hamlet* I.ii.76, are also to be found in the Milton. "When I behold this goodly frame, this World" echoes Hamlet's "this goodly frame, the Earth," in *Hamlet* III.ii.309.

Both in *Ulysses* and in *FW* Joyce reiterates his belief that the universe is based upon the void, upon incertitude, or "unlikelihud," to

Book I, chapter vi . . . Epstein / 63

quote the Prankquean. Random events, random resemblances in language, these are the raw materials for his art, its content and its form. Yet he believes that, even if the universe of events and actions is based upon "hophazards" (615.7–8), pattern will emerge as a result of repetitions, given enough time; in fact, the whole question foreshadows 614.21–615.10, the passage ending the male section of the *Wake*. Ultimately the random universe orders itself in time, even if a great deal of time is required for the operation of this "collideorescape."

Question 10 is framed as a smoky, fiery query, to which Issy replies in her most irritating and coquettish vein. Though "bitter" and "sour" appear among the cinders of her lovers' hearts, she only finds herself "sweet" (143.29, 33). With false innocence she explores Tristan's body in imagination and exclaims, upon reaching a "tickley" area, "Funny spot to have a fingey!" (144.35). The bat that symbolizes sexual passion in "Nausicaa" begins to fly on 146.32, with Issy's exclamation "Sh!" As her hushings increase—"Shsh!" (148.04), "Shshsh!" (148.16), and "Shshshsh!" (148.32)—the bat, "longears," continues to flit, and her passion increases—"Amory, amor andmore!" (148.32). The object of her passion, Amory (Tristran), is in some danger, however, The mention of Norma's aria "Casta diva" on 147.24, and mistletoe on the line above, forecast her role as the castrating virgin priestess of the moon, in Book II,iii (360.23–361.17). Her lovers pay for their pleasure.

Question 11 is asked by Shem about Shaun himself, by no means the last time this occurs in the *Wake;* indeed, Shaun is occupied with justifying himself most of the time. In this case, he enters pompously into a complex lecture, complete with examples, of his justification of his attitude towards his brother. Despite its length, there is little which needs to be said about the answer to this question (except perhaps to note that Burrus and Caseous, as Brutus and Cassius, are to be found in Dante's *Inferno* in the other two mouths of the three-mouthed Satan, as rebels against order in the person of the head of the Roman state). Shaun's jealousy is so apparent, and his lack of balanced judgment so obvious, that his answer is almost transparent. However, even he cannot conceal the truth—the Mookse suffers the same fate as the Gripes, and both Burrus and Caseous are bypassed for Antonius, the Tristan-figure. Burrus and Caseous, like the Mookse and the Gripes, are mixed figures. Caseous, mainly the Shem-figure, is referred to as "brutherscutch" or *Butter*scotch, and also as "tyron" which, while the Greek for "cheese," also suggests the name of Wyndham Lewis' journal *The Tyro* (163.8–9); while the Gripes is also mostly Shem, his name, Niklaus Alopysius (155.31) contains the Greek for 'fox,' -alopēs; he is both grapes and fox. In fables, timeless paradigms of experience, the changeover from Shem to Shaun is expressed as a unity in one figure of both brothers. The answer ends, however, with a clear expression of Shaun's fear and hatred of his brother, "I'd fear I'd hate to say" (168.12).

The twelfth question-and-answer pair is the most enigmatic. First of all, whose voice is it we hear saying "We are Shem"? In the introduction to the chapter it is declared that Shaun "left his free natural ripostes to four of [the questions] in their own fine artful disorder" (126.8-9); that is, he allowed four of the answers to be in the voices of the characters the questions concern. These four are question 4 (the Four Old Men), question 6 (Kate the Slop), question 10 (Issy), and question 11 (Shaun himself). By this analysis, it could not be Shem himself who answers question 12. Second, why is there a grammatical error in the Latin of the question, "Sacer esto?"? "Esto" is the second or third person imperative or optative singular form, not the question form which the phrase requires.

Both of these questions can, I believe, be answered by locating the source of the question. It is almost certainly to be found in Horace's second book of satires (*Sermones*), the third satire. Joyce prepared the second book of satires (with the exception of the seventh satire) for honors in Latin at the university in 1900.[2]

In the satire, lines 168 to 186 tell the story of a wealthy man, Servus Oppidius, who lectures his two sons on his deathbed on the proper way to preserve his property. Like Shem and Shaun, his two sons, Aulus and Tiberius, are polar opposites in personality, the former being prodigal and spendthrift, the latter being intensely avaricious. The father cautions them not to reduce or increase the value of the property. (The latter adjuration is necessary, since the avaricious son might be led to acquire a bad reputation by his practices; he is warned by his father that he resembles in his avarice a famous moneylender nicknamed "Hemlock" (*Cicuta*), famous at the time for his cunning and insatiable greed.) Moreover, the father specifically cautions them against seeking public office as aediles or praetors, since the largesse they will be expected to dispense to the people would use up their inheritance:

> uter aedilis fueritve
> vestrum praetor, is intestabilis et sacer esto.   (11. 180-1)

"Is intestabilis et sacer esto" seems to bear the meaning "May you (he) be outlawed and taboo (or accursed)." "Intestabilis" refers to civic disability—that is, the legal inability to testify or make a will because of infamy. "Sacer" bears the meaning of "taboo," because it means ultimately "reserved for the specific handling of the gods," whether because holy or greatly sinful. This double meaning of "sacer" doubtless pleased Joyce, as would the double disgrace, outlawry by the State and Church, so to speak, expressed in the phrase in 1.181 above.

The meaning of "esto" is difficult to establish, in Horace as it is in Joyce, but for a subtler reason; the scholiast on Horace suggests "sit" for "esto" because the phrase refers to the action of *either* one or the other of the brothers, which would require the use of the third person singular subjunctive (or optative) form of *esse*, "sit," rather than the second person imperative singular, "esto." However, it is possible, that "esto" is a *third* person imperative singular, a usage reserved for antiquated or poetic texts.[4]

Since Joyce certainly knew enough Latin to realize that "esto" is not an interrogative form, I consider that he left the Horatian phrase as it is in the satire to evoke this particular context. With this interpretation in mind, the phrase could now be paraphrased "Is it you who are referred to, as one or both of the brothers in the Horace satire, as set apart, for good or evil?"

Why is the answer in the plural, "Semus sumus!"? Mrs. von Phul suggests that it is either indicative of a royal "we," or that Shem is as "myriad-minded" as Shakespeare, "and in him are all the characters of the dream."[5] While both of these interpretations are possible, I would suggest a third possibility, based upon the uncertainty, described above, about the actual speaker of the phrase, and of the place of I,vi in the *Wake*.

Book I was, except for chapters i and vi, composed as a whole in 1923–24; the first and second drafts of these six chapters were completed in less than six months.[6] Then Joyce began to work on Book III, and did not return to Book I until 1926, when he began the first draft of I,i, and began to work on I,vi. I,vi, as Hayman says, was "a section designed to balance and integrate other aspects of the book."[7] Joyce drafted answers to the first ten questions, but was unable to complete the chapter, or at any rate to draft an answer to the eleventh question (and presumably the twelfth also), until the summer or fall of 1927, by which time he had worked out schemes for Books II and IV.[8] I,vi is, therefore, a chapter which was added when much of the plan of the book had been worked out in Joyce's head, and the eleventh and twelfth questions were completed when the *whole* plan of the book was clear to him. To determine the place of I,vi in the plan of the *Wake* and to answer the puzzling questions about "Semus sumus," we should consider what part the chapter *does* play in the *Wake*.

It seems to me that the primary function of the first ten questions is to provide an immense broadening and deepening of our knowledge of the characters in the "drame" at a time when we are preparing to understand a story laid out in time in which they are all involved, in Books II and III. Book I was, according to Joyce, an "immense shadow,"[9] by which I think he meant that the actual "action" of the book does not begin until Book II, when the children begin to grow up and learn about themselves and their parents. II,i and ii provide the learning; II,iii overthrows the father, and II,iv brings together the new young bride and groom as Tristan and Isolde. In Book III we see the guilty father—castrator Shaun gradually assuming the mantle of fatherhood, which weighs him down from Shaun to Jaun to Haun to Yawn to the role of somnolent father, Mr. Porter. The "action" of the *Wake*, therefore, takes place in time only in Books II and III—that is, in the space of one night, between lighting-up time (in II,i) and incipient dawn (in III,iv). The rest of the "action" is non-temporally presented in Books I and IV, thus dividing the *Wake*, appropriately enough, between Space and Time, the deathbone and the lifewand. In this scheme, the first ten questions and their answers in I,vi provide an enormous widening of information about the characters in the *Wake* just before they are about to go on stage for their nighttime drama, which is thereby expanded to universal dimensions. In addition, we come to hear the voices of some of the characters, only a few of whom (like Kate) we have heard before. We hear the Four Old Men, Kate, Issy, and Shaun himself, as well as a bit of the voice of the young ALP (beginning to flow) at the end of the Mookse and the Gripes.

To grasp the significance of the twelfth question and answer, however, we must also look at the *Wake* as a whole.

The *Wake* still bears signs of its composition. Since I,vi was composed after I,v and I,vii were drafted (in considerable detail), the end of I,v and the beginning of I,vii still dovetail very neatly.

To all's much relief one's half hypothesis of that jabberjaw ape amok the showering jestnuts of Bruisanose was hotly dropped and his room taken up by the odious and still today insufficiently malestimated notesnatcher (kak, pfooi, bosh and fiety, much earny, Gus, poteen? Sez you!) Shem the Penman.

Shem is short for Shemus as Jem is joky for Jacob.

The portrait of Shem in I,vii was originally introduced by the last section of I,v. As the book now stands, I,vii seems to be a continuation of the twelfth answer in I,vi, even if this means leaving what seems to be a loose end at the end of I,v. This is, however, not true; between the drafting of I,v, vii, and the creation of I,vi, Joyce had apparently reached the conclusion that the brothers were to combine into a Buckley/Tristan figure preparatory to becoming the new/old father. The brothers in I,vi are not separate characters but really one personality, and therefore the twelfth question *and* the twelfth answer are spoken by them *both*, now one and the same person, in unison. They are acknowledging the acceptance of the Shem-principle of temporal process as an essential element in the book.

This interpretation does four things: 1) it explains the plural form of "sumus" and the presence of two brothers in the Horace allusion; 2) it ties up the loose end of I,v; 3) it helps to suggest the continuity between the fifth, sixth, seventh, and eighth chapters of Book I, and the relationship of Book I to Book II; and 4) it suggests who the "speaker" of the chapter is.

> I,vi begins,
> So?
> Who do you no tonigh, lazy and gentlemen?
> The echo is where in the back of the wodes; call him forth!
> (126.1–3)

I would suggest that this is the voice of Shem calling forth his Shaun-half from the back of the "wodes"; Shem asks the questions, and "Who do you no tonigh, lazy and gentleman?" is a question, as is "So?" If the *Wake* is a letter from ALP, nevertheless the voice throughout is the voice of Shem, who, as the Penman, creates the words for the voices of nature. In the physical object which is the individual copy of the book *Finnegans Wake*, "Shaun" is the material of the page and binding and the ink on the page, and "Shem" is the "subvocalic" representation of the marks on the page which is the "reading" of the text by the reader. Shaun is an object in space, a book, and Shem is a process in time, a reading. Within the *Wake* itself Space and Time divide the telling of the story, which means that at two points in the book the mode of narration changes. One of the points occurs at the end of Book I. It is my contention that the final form of Book I was conditioned by this formal requirement. The spatial ordering of Book I must merge into the temporal ordering of Books II and III, and the last sections of Book I provide this transition.

To take things in reverse, I,viii shows time operating already; ALP is flowing and the "sound-movie" of *Finnegans Wake* is about to begin. However, at this point the movie projector is running too softly and slowly for a "persistence of vision" or of sound to operate, so all we hear is an almost undifferentiated murmur, and all we see is a twilight effect on the screen. (The image clears and the sound comes up as Book II begins.) The chapter preceding this pre-visual, pre-auditory phase of the story is I,vii, which on the surface is a violent attack on Shem by Shaun; but the ending of the chapter begins the sound-movie projector, when Shem points the deathbone and the quick are still (the visual continuum of life is atomized into thousands of "still" photographs), and Shem raises the lifewand, and the dumb speak (the sound-track, a continuous track on the film, begins to produce noise over the sound-system). The sound produced, ". . . Quoiquoiquoi-quoiquoiquoiquoiq!" is the sound of a sound-movie's sound-track when the film is unreeling too slowly to be either heard or seen clearly. When the projector finally picks up speed, we hear the sound "O," the first sound of the next chapter, I,viii. Therefore the whole of the Shem the Penman chapter is leading to the creation of a sound-sight film-projection system, a deathbone-lifewand system. The division between sight and sound occurs at p. 187 with the commencement of the Justius-Mercius section, when Shem is commanded to "stand forth" from the text by his visual brother (187.28), and when Mercius "speaks" for himself. (The previous unity of the brothers is indicated by the fact that Justius is speaking "to himother" and Mercius "of hisself" (187.24; 193.31). Time actually "begins" in the book within the enormous sentence on 193.32–195.4. The syntactic backbone of the sentence is "now . . . it is to you, . . . to me, . . . you alone, . . . to me [note the changes of person] . . . that our turfbrown mummy is acoming . . ." (194.4, 12, 12–13, 14, 17, 22). The speaker exclaims "thank

Movies" for the return of ALP, since it is a sound-movie that is beginning.

This pattern of I,vii, a violent attack upon Shem followed by a structurally significant point in the creation of the "story" of the *Wake*, also occurs at the end of I,vi. Shaun, in answering the eleventh question, attacks Shem violently; the twelfth question and answer, spoken by both brothers, admits the necessity of "Semus," the voice, and the movement in time, of the story. I,vi and vii therefore cause the story to begin, first by suggesting the possibility of a Time-element (Semus) added to the Space-element which has dominated the book up to this point, and then by showing how the Time element brings in the story of the development of the children, the overthrow of the father, and the accession to fatherhood of the combined son-figure, Tristan.

The introduction of time into the spatial realm is one of the most important structural tasks of Book I, and the process begins with the words ending the last line of I,v, "Shem the Penman." This is the first and only time in the whole of the *Wake* when the complete and unaltered title of Shem is used. In fact, except for a passing mention at 94.11, it is the *first time in the Wake* that the name of Shem appears. I believe that this unique appearance signals the entrance of Shem, the principle of sound and temporal process, into the *Wake* as a character. (He is always present as the text actualizing itself in the reader's mind whenever the book is read, of course.) His intrusion, marked by Shaun's question to him in Russian, "How are you today, my dark sir?", precipitates the violent invective of I,vi and I,vii, since he is an alien temporal principle intruding into a hitherto unchallenged spatial realm and questioning its total validity. After the initial quarreling is over, however, sound and sight are both carried away by their turfbrown mummy, as in the Mookse and the Gripes, the sound movie begins, and the "story" is told.

> Time like an ever-rolling stream
> Bears all its sons away . . .
> (Isaac Watts, Psalm XC, Stanza 5 [1719])

Notes

1. See Ruth von Phul, "Five Explications," *A Wake Newslitter*, New Series III, 4 (August 1966), 85.
2. Kevin Sullivan, *Joyce among the Jesuits* (New York: Columbia University Press, 1958), p. 159.
3. *Schol. in Hor.*, ed. H. J. Botschuyver (Amsterdam, 1935), p. 326.

4. Von Phul, 85.
5. Von Phul, 85.
6. Richard Ellmann, *James Joyce* (New York, 1959), pp. 801–03; David Hayman, *A First-Draft Version of Finnegans Wake* (Austin, Texas, 1963), p. 22.
7. Hayman, p. 27.
8. Hayman, pp. 27, 296–97; Ellmann, p. 802.
9. Breon Mitchell, "Marginalia from Conversations with Joyce," *A Wake Digest,* ed. C. Hart and F. Senn (Sydney, Australia, 1968), p. 81.

5

The Artist as Balzacian Wilde Ass

Book I
chapters vii–viii
Robert Boyle, S.J.

The two pages of chapter seven which set forth Joyce's clearest and most profound statement of the literary artist's aim and operation, pages 185–186, emerge from Joyce's lifelong development of a vision of the literary artist, with contributions from Aristotle and Plato, Dante and Shakespeare, Christ and Ignatius, and, not last among many, Balzac and Oscar Wilde. Wilde's contribution is most obvious on 186:8, where Shem the artist, persecuted and exiled, like the author of *De Profundis,* that "farced epistol to the hibruws" (*FW,* 228:33–34), wanes "doriangrayer" in his spending of himself, out of the bowels of his misery, in the service of art.

Joyce's development of his notion of the artist is partially portrayed in Stephen Dedalus,[1] but it achieves its full flowering only in Shem. Joyce illustrates some of the stages of his great insight in his literary products from his early poems, *Dubliners,* and Stephen Hero through *Portrait* and *Ulysses* into the pages of *Finnegans Wake,* which best set forth his image of the artist joyfully creating out of his suffering self the cosmos of words in which we can merge with him, if we will. In *Dubliners* it was a matter of seeing with the artist. Together, the work assumes, we could observe the object as it is in itself, in all its scrupulous meanness, as we saw the language adapt itself to the external object. Through *Portrait* and *Ulysses* there is a motion inward, from the external object to the acting subject, until, in *Finnegans Wake,* no external object remains. There is only the cosmos of language in which we find ourselves tangled, and we can see and feel nothing but that. There is no clear and definable "scrupulous meanness" any more, but a flux of complicated and intermingling human activity, purely verbal, which may make clearer to us how deceived we were if we really once thought that, as the young Joyce claimed for *Dubliners,* we were peering with the spiritually deprived Irish at a mirror held before us to reflect our own paralysis. This, at any rate, seems to me the main thing Joyce learned perhaps in part from Balzac but most certainly from Oscar Wilde, and, while Joyce does not, it may be, probe more deeply into the philosophical depths of the esthetic notion than did Wilde (who went deeper than most of us can), he does manage, as a far greater aritst, to express the notion more powerfully than could Balzac and Wilde, the two artists he calls upon in this climactic image.

Perhaps the clearest, if over-simplified, way to see Joyce's development of his image is to compare it to the development of thought from Matthew Arnold's aim for the artist, "to see the object as it is in itself," through Pater's stress on the impression the object makes on the observer—thus moving inward and giving a basis for "art for art's sake"—to Wilde's dismissal of the external object in favor of the inner experience itself, which, according to his insight, was the only thing obtainable all along, and the most valuable to human beings. Thus Wilde can lay down the principle of his "new aesthetics" (a principle analogous to, but more profound and far-reaching than, Hopkins' principle of sprung rhythm as a base for structure), that "Art never expresses anything but itself."[2] Now Wilde can proceed from Arnold's speciously objective "to see the object as in itself it really is" to the essentially subjective "to see the object as in itself it really is not."[3] It is to this extraordinary insight that Joyce comes in *FW,* 185–6, and, with all the gleaming wealth of Wilde's examples and rhetoric in those Platonic dialogs Mr. Best so much admired (and from which Stephen's best gems are mined), Joyce carries further the expression of Wilde's doctrine, most effectively in the eucharistic image brought to a climax in "transaccidentated" (*FW,* 186:3–4).

I have tried elsewhere to chart the course of Joyce's use of Catholic eucharistic imagery for his artistic ends.[4] In *Portrait* he used it as Matthew Arnold might have, seeing the bread transmuted into an object available for feeding the culture-starved masses, a food external to giver and to eater. In *Ulysses* the shift begins on the opening pages with Buck's ridicule of the naive realism inherent in much post-Tridentine Catholic discussion of the Eucharist, in which the peculiar situation of the accidents of the bread and wine threatened to overshadow the divine substantial operation of Christ. It was this perception of the difficulties in the Thomistic stance which led Scotus to coin "transaccidentation" (which may be traced in the N.E.D.) and Luther and other reformers to repeat the term. The Thomistic explanation, at least as it developed, tended to stress too much, like Matthew Arnold, the object as it is in itself. Thus Buck's ridicule becomes pointed, though Buck himself, as his own anti-Wildean stance suggests, does not realize the implications of his lampoon. Joyce does, though, most fully, as I shall attempt to show in the treatment of the mirror imagery, from Buck's anti-Wildean cracked mirror to Bella Cohen's Wildean magic mirror in "Circe," where the artist Joyce, like the Shem of 186:3, reflects from his own individual person the dividual chaos of human language, which, according to Wilde (in a statement which would not likely have emerged from Matthew Arnold, and might not cause surprise if it were attributed to some contemporary structural linguist), "is the parent, not the child, of thought."[5]

Language is the human mirror in which alone we can see ourselves fully, and the language is not an external object embodied in ink, any more than the eucharistic Christ is embodied in bread. Language is the dynamic operation of an existing mind, and if we can become immediately involved in the language, re-created in us, of an intense and perceptive individual, we will have tapped the source of human mystery, and the united stars of the true Miltonic-Uranian cosmos can shine in the darkness of the squid-self's ink.

As, in Catholic belief, Christ in himself summed up and completed human experience, and in the eucharist makes his complete living self available to his lovers, so in Joyce's analogy the artist gives himself in his ink to his hearers and seers, and makes all the intensity of what is "common to allflesh, human only" available to them. It is the human experience which Matthew Arnold as well as Wilde ultimately wanted, and Joyce, never out to reject anything human, manages like Christ to encompass all of human experience (or at least not to exclude any facet of it). He does not, like Christ, do it to carry men to something beyond the human, but, like Balzac, to provide a human, not a divine, comedy.[6] Limiting himself to human experience, which, he was like Wordsworth profoundly aware, rocks from time to time from the shock of mysterious hidden forces, Joyce the artist manages to create a verbal cosmos most satisfactory and, in the sense explained, complete. This is one of the reasons he succeeded better than did Wilde, who never, as I can now understand the matter, fully extricated himself from the moral dilemma in which Arnold and Pater, like the whole esthetic tradition we have known through Sidney and Shelley, were bogged down.

Joyce did not reject that tradition, as I can dimly perceive the matter, but he blithely ignores its moral dilemmas (or transcends them) in *Finnegans Wake,* as Stephen Dedalus with his concern for the conscience of his race probably did not. Joyce does not say that the Aristotelean aim of acheiving the virtuous man (meaning the man who does right) is false. He merely, in his magic mirror, reflects what he experiences, and leaves mystery intact. Those who suppose that Joyce the artist attacks or defends religion (or anything else) have, I judge, limited and cheapened in themselves a vision which in Joyce does not attack or defend anything human, but embraces and uses all that happens inside and outside the crystalline universe, and refuses only to make human reason the norm and limit for its operation and scope. Thus Catholic faith becomes a most useful analog for Joyce, since it stresses, in its insistence on the existence of strict mystery, both the limits of reason and the possibility of somehow knowing something, at least in its effects on what we can experience, about what is beyond reason. Buck, like the blond cop of 186:17, attempts to operate within reason exclusively, and thus, as the cop judges the artwork to be ink, Buck judges the eucharist to be bread. They are both right in the main (reasonable, and hence at sea in ultimate matters), but out of the wading depth in which alone they are safe. The consecrated bread, in Catholic doctrine, conceals (to reason) and reveals (to faith) the divinely and humanly operating Christ, and the ink, in Joyce's image, conceals (to the Philistine) and reveals (to the true Hellenist) the humanly operating artist. So Joyce, who refused to receive communion, no doubt on grounds like Stephen's, based not alone on reason but on fear of operations beyond the grasp of reason, fully used Catholic doctrine to Wildean ends, and managed thus (as in other ways too) to reach a depth of expression Wilde could not attain.

A glance at two of the mirror images in *Ulysses* (pp. 8/6 and 553/567) will, I judge, give background to the deepened reflection of self we find in Shem. Buck, who confidently tells Haines that he and Stephen have gone beyond Wilde and paradoxes, holds before Stephen a cracked looking-glass of a servant, recalling Wilde's statement that art treated as a mirror reduced "genius to the position of a cracked looking-glass."[7] Stephen, looking in Buck's mirror, sees himself, poor dogsbody. This is the mirror of Matthew Arnold, not of Wilde, for according to Wilde, the mirror of art does not reflect reality but rather determines it. This is the mirror of the rationalist, the moral mirror of Hamlet, which, according to Wilde, Shakespeare used only to indicate Hamlet's madness.[8]

But in "Circe," the magic mirror of Bella does not reflect what is in front of it, but "realizes in fact what has been dreamed in fiction,"[9] so that Stephen and Bloom see not themselves but first a dummy Shakespeare who metamorphoses into a somewhat more lively Cunningham, both of them cuckolded and usurped, both models of the ventriloquist behind them, the invisible Joyce, of the young and mature characters in front of them, and even of us, invisible spectators behind the fictional observers. We, like the artist, are thus in a position to see that the mirror is subjective on both sides, and that we have gone somewhat beyond Wilde's own position, which would (I suppose) have shown us the operating ventriloquist as well as his dummies providing the determining models for the receptive characters and for us. Or rather, Wilde, as I can now guess, would not have thought of the dummies within the mirror, but would have had the artist operating directly on the observing characters, or perhaps directly on us. Joyce provides levels which help to convey some of the indirections by which language operates.

In *Finnegans Wake,* we have entered the mirror, so that there is nothing being determined outside of it. The language now has no reference to what is happening outside our immediate experience of it. Matthew Arnold would now be at a loss, as I see the matter, since the object he wanted to use as a norm and touchstone has totally disappeared. Oscar Wilde would feel a sense of complete satisfaction, I judge, since he would find fulfilled what he took to be the essence of art and of criticism, "the record of one's own soul."[10] If indeed the soul is to find divinity, it will find it not in objects outside itself, but in itself, through contact with mysteries revealed not by other objects but by its own mysterious self. The artist, Wilde says, "Will look out upon the world and know its secret. By contact with divine things, he will become divine."[11] This accords with the Catholic belief Joyce early learned in regard to the eucharist, and provides a good base for Joyce's combining of the mirror and the eucharistic images.

The Picture of Dorian Gray is an attempt by Wilde to deal with his own doctrine in a creative work, where the three principal males are projections of aspects of himself, as he points out: "I am so glad that you like that strange coloured book of mine: it contains much of me in it. Basil Hallward is what I think I am: Lord Henry what the world thinks of me: Dorian what I would like to be—in other ages, perhaps."[12]

In Wilde's novel, both Sybil Vane and the picture of Dorian show the difficulties in subordinating art to nature. Sybil can attract Dorian only with the perfection of art, when she is determined by Shakespeare, and merely disgusts him when she offers him her loving natural self. The picture can by magic accept the effects of Dorian's evil and selfish choices, but in the end it effects his destruction—art subordinated to morality is dangerous, or rather, fatal, seems to be the moral. As Wilde said, this concern with morality is an artistic error when it appears as a lesson or an example.[13] Wilde wanted to escape that moral trap, but did not quite succeed. Joyce did escape it, by accepting, like Whitman, evil along with good, devils along with angels, without suggesting, in the cyclic flow of his verbal cosmos, any desirable subordination of one to the other, simply accepting what he humanly and intensely experienced, and expressing that as directly and perfectly as he could. Matthew Arnold operated in a world which offered or seemed to offer objective norms by which an object could be judged as good or bad. Joyce operates in a world where the sole and constantly shifting norm is the intense experience of the self. Touchstones and analogs thus become at best revelations of the self to the self, at worst mere self-deceptions, and no certainty other than the intense experience is possible. It is the voice of Matthew Arnold, in part, which speaks through Justius when he accuses Mercius of total subjectivity and lack of certainty: ". . . you have reared your disunited kingdom on the vacuum of your own most intensely doubtful soul" (*FW*, 188:16–17). And it is the voice of Oscar Wilde, in part, who admits with Mercius that he is "haunted by a convulsionary sense of not having been or being all that I might have been" (*FW*, 193:35–6), the constantly shifting artist finding the fullness of his being in the more comprehensive being of the dynamically operating woman, imaged in the living waters from which he takes the power to make the dumb speak.

Dorian Gray has been often tied to Balzac's *Peau de Chagrin*, and in Joyce's imagination here the two works offered types useful to him—young men who found the effects of their choices taken on by magical artifacts which eventually brought the men to destruction. Balzac's "peau" furnishes the background, if I am not mistaken, for Joyce's Shem writing with indelible ink on his skin.[14] Balzac's Raphael sees the mysterious oriental seal of Solomon and then the Sanskrit words etched into the ass's skin, so deeply that they seemed to have grown there:

> ... et lui fit apercevoir des caractères incrustés dans le tissu cellulaire de cette Peau merveilleuse, comme s'ils eussent été produits par l'animal auquel elle avait jadis appartenu.
> —J'avour, s' écria l'inconnu, que je ne devine guère le procédé dont on se sera servi pour graver si profondement ces lettres sur la peau d'un onagre.[15]

The magic skin, in its language from the lost past, promised him that he could have whatever he willed, but with each choice the skin would shrink, and when it disappeared, the young man, progressing likewise toward dudhood, would die.

For Wilde, Balzac was the creator who brought forth the 19th century.[16] Wilde modeled himself on Balzac's characters while he was in Paris, thus illustrating his doctrine that art determines nature, and when he returned to the continent as an exile after his release from prison, he called himself Sebastian Melmoth. The immediate source for his name was the character in his grand-uncle's book, *Melmoth the Wanderer*, about a man who, having sold his soul to the devil, wanders restlessly about Europe. The same book, by the Rev. Charles R. Maturin, uncle of Wilde's mother, had intrigued Balzac, who wrote a book allied to the magic of *Peau de chagrin*, *Melmoth réconcilié*, dealing also with the Faust theme of Maturin's book. Balzac's Melmoth, to save his soul, had to repent and pass his demoniac passion to another person. This, as is evident, is even closer to Wilde's theme in *Dorian* than is *Peau de chagrin*, and the novel would no doubt, owing to the family relationship, have attracted Wilde even more strongly. All of this alchemical mumbo-jumbo is grist for Joyce's treatment of his alchemist too, and comes into play in his tieing together *Peau de chagrin* and *Dorian* as it does later in his picture of Shem like the imprisoned Wilde writing his Hebrew journal in his cosmic jail, his "obscene coalhole," and sending this "gheol ghiornal," the "epistola," as Wilde intended to entitle the letter Ross called *De Profundis*, in imitation of papal epistles to the world, off to the high-brows who condemned him:

> ... and fire off, gheol ghiornal, foull subustioned mullmud, his farced epistol to the hibruws. (228: 32–34)

Sebastian, pierced with arrows, becomes subustioned, because (no doubt) Wilde was busted even below the point of having nothing left, and perhaps because he was still deeply interested in the area below the bust. And Melmoth, the honey moth, becomes mullmud, since Wilde, a troglodyte now more than a star-gazer, dwells so much on the darkness and destructiveness of his fleshly lusts, based on his common clay.

This context of Wilde as model for Shem as Balzac was model for Wilde has, like everything in *Finnegans Wake,* its direct and its ironic aspects. Joyce asserts (though with laughters low) more even than Wilde, or than Shelley, that the artist creates his age, and he includes this notion in his image or Shakespeare in Bella's mirror as well as in his more cosmic image of Shem's cuttlefish ink, which both screens him and spreads the darkness of the creative void around the neat crystalline universe. And, in irony, he shows Shakespeare as a strangling dummy hideously warped by our modern whore-house age, and he shows Shem's little fearful exudation of ink, which is his life-blood, judged to be merely ink by the blond cop. Not for this Philistine cop is it, Caliban that he is, to pierce the surface and to read the perilous symbol.

Green, gray, and black were deeply personal colors to Joyce the artist as he spent his eyesight in the service of his art. In September, 1928, he wrote to Miss Weaver of his warding off blindness "by dressing in the three colours of cecity as the Germans divide them,"[17] that is, green, gray, and black. With the gold involved in "Dorian" included, the colors of the Irish flag echo the "pious Eneas" epic hero who ironically leads off this poet's descent to dudhood. Then throughout the paragraph other avatars prepare for the ultimate darkness, in which, however, in a miracle like that of Shakespeare's Sonnet 65, the keyman of the wild will shine bright too: he has been betrayed like Esau, a small rebel like the Mensheviks (also a son of man, a menschavik), an alchemist seeking a miraculous change, an artistic historian seeking to unfold a "continuous present" (Joyce adopted Wyndham Lewis's contemptuous phrase describing *FW*—cf. *Letters* III, 188n.), a quasi-divine though hiding saviour, and a squid. The squid image derives from an early review of *Ulysses,*[18] and Joyce here uses it in a context which throws some light on AE's comment to Lizzie Twig (if indeed it was Lizzie) in *Ulysses,* pp. 163/165. There he refers to "the two-headed octopus" and quotes Pater on the Mona Lisa, "the head upon which the ends of the world have forgotten to come." Wilde speaks also of Pater's passage[19] in stating how Pater the critic, through the music of his prose, reveals to us a secret of which Leonardo's picture (the "object") knows nothing. Pater leads us, Wilde says, to create in ourselves the beautiful verbal cosmos which goes beyond any intention of the artist, precisely Joyce's aim in *Finnegans Wake*. And AE, as he speaks to Lizzie of Lisa, echoes Wilde, I should think, more than Pater. (If Milly is watered-down Molly, then Lizzie could be considered vinegared-down Lisa.) The Scotch accent, I suppose, belongs to Carlyle, who as End of the World whirls cosmically through the murk of "Circe" (*U*, 596/507), preparing the way for Elijah—as, presumably, Carlyle and Pater, who might here, in AE's mind, represent philosophy and art, prepared the way for AE the spokesman for farmers and leader of a group of faithful hermetists, twoheaded indeed! Shem as squid squirts ink into the cosmos, screening himself as hidden creator from the crystalline world, but at the same time revealing his presence in the ink which conceals him. I take it that the crystal cosmos, no doubt the rational seeing crystal eyeballs which perceive the ink, is also Milton's crystal world, limited and complete, which can apodictically express rational certitudes like the ones which follow, "This exists, that is it," and bring us to a seeming, satisfying certitude. And then, I take it, we may think that we can, like Finn waking up, expel the devil, who can be told to take, not the hindmost, but himself. And now the pen-king, in spite of lags and gags and a trinity of Jesuit "geegees" (*FW*, 120:21), sets about assembling "Eblania's conglomerate hords" (as on 614:25), accomplishing like Bloom the miracle of circling the square (as this book structured in fours and eights does also); having killed priest and king (church and state, Ignatius and Parnell), the artist-clown, brandishing his bell-laden champion pen, unlocks the whirling cosmos, "the wilds of change" in the chaosmos of Alle so beautifully celebrated on pages 118–19:

> . . . every person, place and thing in the chaosmos of Alle anyway connected with the gobblydumped turkery was moving and changing every part of the time: the travelling inkhorn (possibly pot), the hare and turtle pen and paper, the continually more and less misunderstanding minds of the anticollaborators, the as time went on as it will variously inflected, differently pronounced, otherwise spelled, changeably meaning vocable scriptsigns.

This much and a great deal more is suggested to me as I attempt to recreate Joyce's cosmos in myself, temerariously and confusedly trying to fulfill more than Wilde could have dreamed possible his ideal of creative criticism. If some of it is mine and not Joyce's, so much the better, in Wilde's view, so long as it is interesting and beautiful and perceptive. According to Wilde's doctrine, I can and should do to Joyce (if only I could!) what Pater did to Leonardo. I am not, however, trying to do anything of the kind, not only because I am no Pater, but because I have been brought up in a Matthew Arnold approach to literature and criticism from which I have only partially freed myself. Even so, I am not sure that I have avoided projecting views and feeling of my own into Joyce's text (or perhaps better, taking into account Joyce's eucharistic image, into the living and hidden Joyce). But then I'm not sure that Joyce's book, like Christ's eucharist, does not require so personal a response that such mingling of subjectivities is inevitable—and desirable. It does seem to me, however, that sane criticism at least demands that one try to distinguish between what he may be providing from his own experience and what he finds in the experience of the original creator. I'm trying to do that, and whatever I offer here, I judge to be, at least probably, the product of Joyce's imagination.

In any case, I have set forth, as well as I now can, what I perceive (or think I perceive) of Joyce's magnificent image of the artist in operation. In the clash of Mercius and Justius which follows, the charges brought against Shem the true artist include many of the charges leveled at Wilde too. Justius introduces the charge of sodomy on 188: 23-24: "And here, pay the piety, must I too nerve myself to pray for the loss of selfrespect to equip me for the horrible necessity of scandalisang (my dear sisters, are you ready?) by sloughing off my hope and tremors while we all swin together in the pool of Sodom?" He then launches into the remarkable paragraph which Bernard Benstock considers the highlight of the chapter[20] a passage which powerfully puts forth Wilde's doctrine that the artist draws his material out of himself: ". . . you with your dislocated reason, have cutely foretold, a jophet in your own absence, by blind poring upon your many scalds and burns and blisters, impetiginous sore and pustules. . ." (189: 30-33). It is easy to see why, in Benstock's valuable perception of the chapter, this paragraph becomes *the* highlight. *The* highlight for me, as I suppose is evident, is on pages 185-6. Every orchestral conductor determines the highlights according to his own insights and circumstances, and hopes that Stravinsky would concur. In any case, the passage just quoted develops into a charge like that leveled at Wilde during his trial.[21] Shem is accused, on 190: 33-36, of literary homosexuality, of being a prosodite instead of a sodomite, mating masculine monosyllables of the same numerical mus. "Antinos" indicates that Justius is identifying Mercius with Antinous, the youth beloved by Hadrian, and the rather dense passage indicates that Justius's charge is that which the prosecutor thrust on Wilde, that he is using his style (or prosody) to conceal his scatology. "Mus" is a Latin masculine ending, "sum" backwards, and "mouse" (which, according to Partridge, can signify both mouth and penis). And instead of a blackfriar, he is a "quackfriar" (191:1), the wild goose whose life-giving priestly quacking ends this chapter.

In his final words, Shem as Mercius indicates his unity-in-fault with his brother and with all humans, the doomed and the dominating. He is the pick of the "wastepaperbaskel," which ends significantly with the name of God. Shem shares his being, as I take it the floating pronouns and the varying rhythms indicate, with his brother and, most of all, with his mother, as she takes over until his climatic artistic gesture and formula at the end. He tends to blush at the obscenity of the dead universe, until through the activity of a woman he finds a resurrection and new life. This, I take it, is the symbolism suggested throughout Joyce's work and stressed in these feminine chapters of Book I, chapters five through eight. These make up the feminine circle of the two gyrating circles that comprise the infinity symbol formed by the eight chapters of this first book, an eight that turns like the circling eights of the final chapter of *Ulysses*, which, as I see it, laid the ground for the structure of *Finnegans Wake*. And the artist finds his fulfillment in the woman who speaks through him in the next chapter and, most fully, in the final waking pages of this greatest of human epics.

Notes

1. I have attempted to trace some aspects of this development in "Astroglodynamonologos" in *New Light on Joyce,* ed. by Fritz Senn, Indiana University Press, 1972, pp. 131–140, and in "The Priesthoods of Stephen and Buck" in *Approaches to Ulysses,* ed. by Staley and Benstock, University of Pittsburgh Press, 1970, pp. 29–60.

2. "Intentions," *The Artist as Critic: Critical Writings of Oscar Wilde,* ed. by Richard Ellmann, Vintage Books, 1970, p. 313. Hereafter referred to as *C.W.*

3. *C.W.,* pp. 366 and 369. A lucid and valuable survey of the shift of attitude involved appears in "Arnold, Pater, Wilde, and the Object as in Themselves They See It" by Wendell V. Harris, *Studies in English Literature,* XI, 1971, pp. 733–47.

4. "Miracle in Black Ink: A Glance at Joyce's Use of His Eucharistic Image" in *James Joyce Quarterly*, X, Fall, 1972, 47–60.
 5. *C.W.*, p. 359.
 6. In the first draft, Joyce had "common to all flesh, mortal only," *A First-Draft Version of Finnegans Wake*, ed. by David Hayman, University of Texas Press, 1963, p. 119. I suspect that the final "human only, mortal" accompanied the entrance of Balzac into the passage.
 7. *C.W.*, p. 307.
 8. *C.W.*, p. 306.
 9. *C.W.*, p. 311.
 10. *C.W.*, p. 365.
 11. *C.W.*, p. 407.
 12. Letter to Ralph Payne, Feb. 12, 1894, *The Letters of Oscar Wilde*, ed. by Rupert Hart-Davis, Harcourt, Brace & World, Inc., New York, 1962, p. 352.
 13. *C.W.*, pp. 240–1.
 14. For a translation and discussion of the Latin passage on p. 185, in which Shem concocts from his bodily wastes, deposited and prepared in a Grecian Urn, his caustic ink, see my *"Finnegans Wake,* Page 185: An Explication," *James Joyce Quarterly*, IV, Fall, 1966, pp. 3–16.
 15. *La Comédie Humaine*, Vol. 27, ed. Jacques Lambert, Paris, 1954, p. 35.
 16. *C.W.*, p. 309.
 17. *Letters of James Joyce*, III, ed. by Richard Ellmann, Viking, New York, 1966, p. 269.
 18. I discuss this briefly in the article cited in note 4 above, pp. 57–8. The review, by N. P. Dawson, is titled "The Cuttlefish School of Writers," *Forum*, 69 (1923), p. 1182.
 19. *C.W.*, p. 367.
 20. *Joyce-again's Wake*, University of Washington Press, 1965, p. 225. Benstock stresses on p. 119 that the squid's ink paints the story of humankind in many hues, and perceptively notes the division in Wilde's character suggested by the golden "Dorian" and the faded, distorted "Gray." He sees all three principal male participants in *FW* masquerading as Oscar Wilde, pp. 21–2, and he sees Wilde in "the wild man from Borneo," p. 203; this is, I believe, the figure who shakes his "bell-bearing stylo," which I take to be the style Wilde put above any rational meaning as well as the artist's pen, on 186: 15.
 21. See *C.W.*, pp. 435–38. Joyce, in his essay on Wilde, defends him against charges that he was outside the normal or desirable areas of humanity, *The Critical Writing*s, ed. by Mason and Ellmann, Viking, 1964, 203–5. Joyce stresses Wilde's own discussion, in *De Profundis*, of the importance of sin for the artist, that act of self-assertion against the other, which, Joyce says that Wilde knew, is a central Catholic insight, the "felix culpa," that, in the human world we experience, only through separation does atonement become possible. In a letter to Stanislaus (*Letters* II, 150), Joyce imagines the charges which the prosecutor, by reading between the lines, would base on part of *Dorian*, and admires Wilde's aim of putting himself before the world. He thinks, though, that Wilde lacked the courage to "develop the allusions in the book." Joyce may have come to realize that it was not so much courage as effective technique that Wilde lacked; had he been as powerful and innovative an artist as Joyce, he might have more closely foreshadowed *Finnegans Wake*. He had the right intention, anyway. He knew, "it is simply concentrated race-experience" (*C.W.*, p. 384).

Music and the Mime of Mick, Nick, and the Maggies

Book II
chapter i

M. J. C. Hodgart

> The scheme of the piece I sent you is the game we used to call Angels and Devils or colours. The Angels, girls, are grouped behind the Angel, Shawn, and the Devil has to come over three times and ask for a colour. If the colour he asks for has been chosen by any girl she has to run and he tries to catch her. As far as I have written he has come twice and been twice baffled. The piece is full of rhythms taken from English singing games. When first baffled vindictively he thinks of publishing blackmail stuff about his father, mother etc etc etc. The second time he wanders off into sentimental poetry of what [sic] I actually wrote at the age of nine: "my cot alas that dear old shady home where oft in youthful sport I played, upon thy verdant grassy fields all day or lingered for a moment in thy bosom shade etc etc etc etc." This is interrupted by a violent pang of toothache after which he throws a fit. When he is baffled a second time the girl angels sing a hymn of liberation around Shawn. . . Note specially the treatment of the double rainbow in which the iritic colours are first normal and then reversed.
>
> (Joyce, letter to Harriet Shaw Weaver, 22. 11. 1930)

In *Finnegans Wake* it is always difficult to see the wood for the trees. For this chapter Joyce has fortunately given us a fair amount of information about the wood or macrostructure; it is not too difficult to complete the outline from p. 236 to the end of the chapter with the help of *A First Draft Version*. The praise of Shaun-Chuff by the girls turns into an apocalyptic vision of feminism. The Devil, Shem-Glugg, apparently dies (239), but makes a comeback (240) and writes, as he has threatened, rude stories about his parents (241). There is a beautiful interlude as night falls on the animals of the Phoenix Park Zoo (244–245). The Devil makes a third set of three guesses about the color of the girls' drawers, but fails as tiercely as before (252). Again he is mocked by the girls, but now the parents appear to stop the games and send all the childen to bed (255)—the question remains unanswered. The Age of Play is over, too soon will come the tasks of school (256). The father's rectal thunder ends the cycle (257), the curtain falls on the play-within-the-play; after prayers soon all is mum (259).

Joyce also gave some information about the trees or microstructure when he mentioned in another letter to Miss Weaver (4. 3. 1931) some of "the books I am using for the present fragment which include Marie Corelli, Swedenborg, St. Thomas, the Sudanese War, Indian outcasts, Flammaion's The End of the World, scores of children's singing games from Germany, France, England and Italy and so on." I can't claim to have identified all this material but the children's games are not too hard to find. For example, "Withasly glints in. Andecoy glants out. They romp it a little, a lessle, a lissle. Then rompride round in rout" (226.28) is based on "Lubin Loo": "Put your right foot in, put your right foot out; shake it a little, a little; and turn right round about." If you have a memory of an infant singing that, as I have, you will readier appreciate the eerie charm of the chapter. Children's games are a primitive kind of musical drama, and so opera, as we shall see, is a major constituent of the chapter; there is also a kind of ballet, employing the language of gesture, bringing in the theories of Sir Richard Paget and the Abbé Jousse. Swedenborg was presumably drawn on for angelology, Marie Corelli's *The Sorrows of Satan* for demonology. Since the latter, with its attendant topics of witchcraft and black magic, is so prevalent in the Mime, I propose to deal with it in a little detail.

The Devil is traditionally worshipped by a coven of twelve witches. A major poetic source for this worship is Robert Burns' "Tam O' Shanter": (229.21) "tomashunders," (255.04) "Tamor," (241.25) "tammy," (240.30) "shantungs." The Scots names for the Devil, quoted by Burns, are "Clootie" (239.18), "Hangie" and "Hornie" (several references to the last two, especially "horneypipe" 231.31). The worship consists largely in kissing the Devil's arse, hence (251.11) "Blackarss," also "black arts" with witches, devils, and sorcerors in the context. The witches in Shakespeare's *Macbeth* appear several times. For a list of the traditional demons one need look no further than Milton's "Nativity Ode" and "Paradise Lost" I and II. All or nearly all of them appear in the Mime or in Book I, chapter vii which deals with Shem as devil: Beelzebub, Moloch, Chemos (177.05) "shemozzle," Baalim, Ashtaroth, Thammauz, Dagon, Belial, Mammon, Azazel (258.07) "Azrael." More elaborate lists can be found in *Lemegeton* and other grimoires, conveniently summarized by R. Cavendish in *The Black Arts,* including Astaroth, Astarte (232.12) "astarted," Nergal (234.31) "nargleygarley," Behemoth (244.36), Lilith, and so on. The *Grand Grimoire* (243.09) "grimes" tells how one may make a pact not with the Devil but with one of his subordinates, Lucifuge Rofocale: Joyce mentioned the latter to Jolas for a note in *transition,* glossing (250.27) "Rosocale," cf. (354.32) "lucifug lancifer."

Black magic and sorcery play an important part in this chapter, as they did in the intellectual life of nineteenth-century Europe, and, I am sorry to say, again do so in the mid-twentieth century. (At this point I have to state that I do not believe in magic, white or black, or astrology or the occult or ESP, and I do not want to go into the question of whether Joyce did so or not.) The most important author and practitioner of the nineteenth century was Eliphas Levi (244.35) "Eliphas" (230.34) "levirs," and of the twentieth, Alastair Crowley, who believed that he was a reincarnation of Levi and called himself the "Great Beast" of the Apocalypse: hence (232.28) "crowy" (229.12) "Crowhore" (231.05) *"alas that dear."* He is named more clearly outside the chapter as "Crowalley" (105.27), but he is very clearly called the Great Beast and associated with Levi in the Phoenix Park Zoo episode: *"Great is Eliphas Magistrodontos"* (244.35). Crowley was associated with McGregor Mathers, the founder of the occultist Order of the Golden Dawn, of which W. B. Yeats was an active member. I cannot find Mathers in this chapter, though he is named several times elsewhere in the *Wake,* but the Order appears at (22.18): "Radium Wedding of Neid and Moorning and the Dawn of Peace." "Perdunamento" (220.21) is based on *Perdurabo,* the magic motto-name that Crowley assumed on joining the Order. W. B. Yeats assumed the more interesting motto-name of *Daemon est Deus inversus* which, if not quoted, is beautifully Joycean.

Less spectacular than the calling up of evil spirits are the various species of fortune telling; the most notorious, again in vogue today, is the Tarot pack. Space forbids a full treatment of this subject, but

86 / A Conceptual Guide to *Finnegans Wake*

if the reader will inspect a standard Marseilles pack/deck while consulting Hart's *Concordance* he will be able to judge whether the following is correct or not. The four suits are *Epeé,* swords, spades (222.22, 250.35), *Coupe,* cups, hearts (242.04), *Denier,* coins or pentacles, diamonds (256.29), *Baton* or *Baston,* wands, staffs, clubs (254.14). The following are the twenty-two Major Trumps: I think I have found nearly all of them but shall give reference only to the more interesting.

    0. *Le Mat,* Fool. "matt" (245.29), "fools" (238.24), "Fools" (222.23).
    1. *Le Bateleur,* Juggler.
    2. *Papesse,* Female Pope.
    3. *L'Emperatrice,* Empress.
    4. *L'Empereur,* Emperor.
    5. *Pape,* Pope. "pop" (223.10), "papavere's" (227.16).
    6. *L'Amoureux,* Lover. "amourmeant" (231.08).
    7. *Chariote,* Chariot. "jarrety" (222.31).
    8. *Justice,* Justice.
    9. *Hermite,* Hermit.
   10. *La Roue de Fortune,* Wheel of Fortune. (221.12, 227.10, 235.21).
   11. Justice.
   12. *Le Pendu,* Hanged Man. (243.26, 248.15).
   13. (No French name), Death.
   14. (No French name), Temperance.
   15. *Diable,* Devil. (passim).
   16. *Le Maison Dieu,* Falling Tower. "maize" (244.21), "towerable" (224.12).
   17. *L'Etoile,* Stars.
   18. *Lune,* Moon.
   19. *Soleil,* Sun.
   20. *Le Jugement,* the Day of Judgement. (257–258).
   21. *Le Monde,* the World.

The Tarot itself appears in various "tar's," of which at least six can be found in the *Concordance.* Other methods of divination are mentioned: "telling fortunes" (221.13), "card, palm, tea" (221.14), and doubtless much more could be gleaned from the Mime.

I turn to a more congenial topic, namely, operas that have to do with the Devil or devils. The very first is "robot" (219.23), which points to Meyerbeer's *Robert le diable*. The most striking is Weber's *Der Freischutz* (1821). Act I: Max (tenor, 248.34), in love with Agathe (soprano, 250.27, "Aghatharept"), is eager to win a shooting competition to decide who is to be the next head ranger, but loses in a trial. Kaspar (bass, 256.35, "Caspi") who has sold his soul to the evil spirit Zamiel (spoken part, 242.20, "Samhar"), advises Max to get magic bullets from Zamiel. Act II: Agathe is nervous, though calmed by her friend Aennchen (one of ALP's names) when Max tells her he must fetch a stag he has shot in the haunted Wolf's Glen (223.03 "Woolf," 221.08 "Glen"); the music of the Wolf's Glen scene that follows is some of the most famous in Romantic music. I shall not describe the rest of the plot, which has a happy ending with a chorus of bridesmaids (220.03 "Bride's" 237.06 "bridawl," 234.36 "chor"). This bridal chorus is associated in the Mime with the chorus of flower-maidens in *Parsifal,* of which one of the chief characters is the wicked magician Klingsor, creator of the magic garden. There are many references to Parsifal and the flower-maidens, but, as we shall see, in the context of the angelic rather than the demonic. On the latter theme, one of the best known operas is Gounod's *Faust:* Mephistopheles appears as "muffinstuffinaches" (225.11); Marguerite and her Jewel Song *"Faites-lui mes aveux"* as "uniomargrits . . . avowals" (249.12). Mozart's *Magic Flute* also deals with the conflict of good and evil magic: "magical helmet" (220.26), also referring to the magical helmet of the *Ring*; "Rasche . . . Mitscht" (222.10–11), the Queen of Night's aria *"Der Holle Rache"*; "Neid and Moorning" (222.18), night and morning, the Moor; "Arrest thee, scaldbrother . . . ill s'arrested" (223.19–21), the magician Sarastro, plus *"Arretez, mes freres"* from Saint-Saens' *Samson et Dalila*; "the benighted queendom" (241.22); "Sara's drawhead" (254.12), Sarastro.

The plot of the Mime centers on the asking and answering or failing to answer three questions or riddles, and this is also given extended treatment in operatic terms. Question-master in television feature: "In what two well known operas do Questions and Answers figure prominently?" Experts on panel: *Turandot* by Puccini and *Siegfried* the third part of Richard Wagner's *Ring*." "Full marks." At the risk of spelling out the obvious, here is the plot of *Turandot*: In a fairy-tale China it is decreed that Princess Turandot will only marry a suitor if he can solve three riddles that she sets; failure means instant death.

("*Gli enigme sono tre—la morte e una!*") In Pekin arrive an Unknown Prince (whose real name is Calaf), his father Timur, a deposed king of Tartary, and attendant slavegirl Liu. Calaf falls in love with Turandot and decides to attempt the riddles, although he is advised against this by Ping, Pang, and Pong, the three ministers, and by Timur and Liu. Calaf remains resolute ("*Non piangere, Liu*").

In Act II Turandot explains why she has made such a cruel decree: a thousand thousand years ago a princess was abducted and raped by a barbarian, and she is the reincarnation and avenger of this princess; ("*In questa reggia*"). The Prince answers the first two riddles correctly with "*la speranza*" (hope) and "*il sangue*" (blood). When the third is set, "What is the ice that gives you fire?" he hesitates, but gets it right as Turandot herself. He has now won the Princess, but to save her from humiliation he generously allows her to answer a question: if she can find out what his name is, she will be free and he will die. In Act III heralds proclaim that no one in the city must sleep until the Prince's name is discovered ("*Nessun dorma*"); Liu is arrested and tortured but does not reveal Calaf's name. She reproaches Turandot, predicts that she will capitulate to the Prince, and then commits suicide. In the very last part (completed by Alfano after Puccinni's death), the Princess does melt, and Calaf tells her his name, which she announces to the people is "love."

Turandot's and Calaf's names are half hidden and half revealed throughout the Mime: "turquashed" (235.08); "tourments of tosend years" which also introduces the thousand thousand years of "*In questa reggia*" (230.13); "t . . . t . . . t . . . t . . . t . . . tourtoun" (227.35); "dot" (232.27 and 238.01). Cf. "taeorns," also bringing in the theme of past aeons and epochs (236.20), and she is hidden in the thunderword (257.27) and elsewhere. As for Calaf: "Only the caul knows his thousandfirst name" (254.19); "calaboosh" (240.24); "calico" (240.25); "Calavera" (255.14); "prince" (254.35); "the hero, Capellisato" (255.01). His father Timur appears: "Timor" (231.10) and "Tamor" (255.14), which also means that his true name is "Amore." After a three question sequence we have the three ministers: "Ping an ping nwan ping pwan pong" (233.28). Little Liu is hidden away in: "Anne-liuia" (236.17). Later Shaun sings "*Non piangere, Liu*" in pidgin Chinese: "no belong sollow mole . . . Fu Li's" (426.16). Fragments of the questions and answers appear in both English and Italian.

In *Siegfried* the young hero has been brought up by the evil Nibelungen dwarf Mime. A wanderer enters who is Wotan in disguise; he asks Mime to set him three questions, offering his own head as forfeit. He answers all three correctly, naming the Nibelungs, the giants, and the gods, and then sets three questions to Mime, on the same conditions. In fear Mime agrees, correctly answers the first and second (the Walsungs, and Nothung the famous sword), but when the wanderer asks as the third question: "Who will reforge the sword?" he cannot answer. The wanderer tells him the correct answer, which is that the sword can be reforged only by one who has never known fear—and that turns out to be Siegfried. The wanderer does not take Mime's life, but says that the fearless one will take it, as duly comes about.

The Mime of Joyce's title (219.18) refers to Wagner's dwarf and head god here and elsewhere: "if you guess mimic miening" (313.23); "Mimmy" (226.15); "mimosa" (247.36); "wenderer" (245.24); "wondering" (229.14); "forget . . . gnawthing," forge Nothung (231.20–22). "Ring" is a common word in the Mime, describing also the girls' dance-game; the last words of the cycle, spoken not sung by Hagen: "*Zuruck vom Ring!*" ("Get back from the ring"), are quoted at (249.20): "Oh backed von dem zug!" Siegfried and Sigmund are named in "signur's" (243.16), *Die Walkure* in "valkyrienne" (220.05), Brunnhilde in "healing and Brune" (246.32), and Freia in "freytherem" (231.13). Siegfried's horn, as he journeys down the Rhine, is heard in "Rhinohorn" (245.01). At the end of the Mime there is an extended Apocalypse, mentioning *Gotterdammerung* (Twilight of the Gods): "gttdmmrng" (258.02), followed by: "Hlls vlls," which means Valhalla, Wallhall, the palace of the gods destroyed at the end of the cycle. To go from last to first, as one often does in *Finnegans Wake*, we hear Wotan's first words in the *Ring* (*Rheingold*) which are addressed to Walhall, "*Du wonnige selige Saal*": "ing . . . joyous guard . . . palashe . . . wonner" (246.13–15).

"Rhinohorn" (245.01) "toran" (245.10) introduces not only Siegfried's horn, but also *"Der reine Thor,"* the pure fool, Hauptmotiv of *Parsifal*. Parsifal is an analogue of Chuff, and the Blumenmadchen, flowermaidens of Klingsor's enchanted garden, of the girls who worship Chuff like so many teenyboppers. Flowers are of course a basic part of the Mime, the most important being the heliotrope, the answer to one of the riddles. There are many echoes of his name in "Percy" and "Persse" throughout the *Wake*; the girls dance round him in a "ring," singing "come," and these are commonly repeated words in the chapter. Parsifal is sexually pure and resists temptation (cf. "innocent," pp. 235, 240), and in this and other respects he is like the heroes of *Patience* by Gilbert and Sullivan, who are especial favorites of Joyce.

In the latter work, Reginald Bunthorne (a Fleshly Poet) and Archibald Grosvenor (an Idyllic Poet) are pursued by a chorus of "Rapturous Maidens": "Why, what a most particularly pure young man this pure young man must be!" Cf. "Bunnicombe . . . the herblord the gillyflowerets so fain fan to flatter about" (254.35–36). The Ladies Angela, Saphir, Ella, and Jane all put in an appearance as well. Among the many other Gilbert and Sullivan references is a pleasant one to *The Mikado*: "Where is our highly honourworthy salutable spousefoundress. The foolish one of the family is within. Haha! Huzoor, where's he? At house, to's pitty. With Nancy Hands" (244.18 ff). A parody of Japanese polite constructions is followed by Pitty-Sing and Nanki-Pooh, and the Lord High Executioner Koko appears in: "Cococream . . . sticksword" (236.4–5). The most elaborate allusion is: "Luiz-Marios Josephs" (243.36). It is well known that this is one of the many references to Napoleon's Josephine and Marie-Louise, and also to three tenors, Ludwig, Mario, and Joseph Maas, who appear elsewhere. It is not so obvious that it contains also the three "kings" of *The Gondoliers,* Luiz, Marco, and Giuseppe, as well as a minor opera by Montemezzi, *L'Amore de Tre Re* (cf. "mezzo" in the previous line). On the previous page, *Trial By Jury* is used, as Mable Worthington has pointed out, to bring in the theme of an old man in love with a young girl.

It is impossible to do justice to the dense clusters of operatic references in the Mime except by producing long and cumbersome lists. I can only suggest that the reader use his own "do-it-yourself" kit; let him look for operatic allusions to maidens, flowers, and fairytale-like plots (like Rossini's *Cenerentola,* "Cinderella"), and he should be able to improve on my own far from meagre findings. I confess that I have not yet found much about ballet in the *Wake,* and perhaps Joyce was not so interested in this art form. But the traditional British pantomime, which like *Parsifal* usually contains a transformation scene, is almost as important in the Mime as in the last section of the *Wake*. One would expect to find names of heroines from many operas in so female a chapter (Carmen, Santa, Lola, Mimi, Lucia, and so on), but Joyce also decorates his text, to a degree that will not be believed except by opera buffs and collectors of historical discs, with the names of singers: in "Shaun" (III,i) of tenors, in the Mime mainly of sopranos and contraltos. The repetitions of "tur" and "turn" conceal not only

Turandot, but also the most famous singer of this role Eva Turner. "The flowers of the ancelles' garden" (227.17) refers not only to the Blumenmadchen, but also to the soprano Mary Garden, who also comes in at (252.33). Many others can be discovered by looking through the entries in *The Oxford Dictionary of Opera*. The importance of this topic is announced by the bold opposition of the tenors McCormack and Sullivan at the beginning of the chapter (222).

In this discussion I seem to have moved from the wood to the trees, from plot and structure to a web of allusions, but I begin to doubt whether there is really much distinction drawn between the two in *Finnegans Wake*. To put it in Wagnerian terms, one cannot say that the essence of *Tristan und Isolde* is in the plot concerning the love-lotion (as Bernard Miles calls it), rather than in the sequence of chromatic harmonies that spell out "*Liebestod.*" The essence of the Mime is the evocation of childhood, innocent and gay, but with sinister undertones of black magic and death. The shadow of death falls over a beautiful passage near the end, which concerns legitimate drama rather than opera:

> Home all go. Halome. Blare no more ramsblares, oddmund barkes! And cease your fumings, kindalled bushies! And sherrigoldies yeassymgnays; your wildeshaweshowe moves swiftly sterneward! For here the holy language. Soons to come. To pausse.
> (256.11–15).

The basic quotation is the dirge from *Cymbeline:* "Fear no more the heat o' the sun, . . . Golden lads and girls all must,/ As chimney-sweepers, come to dust." "Cease your funning," from *The Beggar's Opera,* implies that the children's play is over; Moses's bush is a burned-out case. The Anglo-Irish dramatists Sheridan, Goldsmith, Yeats, Synge, Wilde (*Salome*), and Shaw take their final bows before: "The curtain drops by deep request" (257.31–32), from the hymn "The day thou gavest, Lord, here endeth,/ The darkness falls at thy behest." The chapter moves to its end in religious and specifically Old Testament terms: the awe inspiring effects of the Viconian thunderclap are worked out in terms of the *Shema* ("Hear, O Israel," *Deuteronomy* 6), and a dense combination of quotations from "Sisera's Song" (*Judges*, 5), *Genesis,* and the *Psalms* (258). At the very end, there is a shift to the *Anglican Prayer Book,* with its grave and soothing cadences. Joyce wrote the chapter in a year of great affliction, partly caused by his daughter's and his own health. He must have seen himself as Job, on whom the Lord heaped miseries, and yet, as he wrote to Miss Weaver: "I think the piece I sent you is the gayest and lightest thing I have done in spite of the circumstances." Stoicism and humor finally prevailed. Lord have mercy on us, indeed, but "incline our hearts to keep thy law": the mummers' show must go on.

>Loud, heap miseries upon us yet entwine our arts
>with laughters low!
>Ha he hi ho hu.
>Mummum. (259.7–10).

7

Night Lessons on Language

Book II

chapter ii

Ronald E. Buckalew

What is *Finnegans Wake* about? This, says Atherton in *Books at the Wake*, is the fundamental question of *Wake* criticism.[1] Among other things, *Finnegans Wake* is about language. Both explicitly and implicitly, Joyce discusses the role of language in the family, society, history, and art. Yet language is not only the chief means by which these institutions are codified, shaped, and perpetuated, but an institution itself. The nature of this institution as seen in its limitations and potentialities, Joyce also thoroughly explores. The exploration of language is especially prominent in the "Night Lessons" chapter (II,ii), but it is an important element in the *Wake* as a whole.

Tindall calls the three chapters of which "Night Lessons" is the center "the densest part of the *Wake*,"[2] but the reader does not get far into the first page of the book before its style and language become its most conspicuous features. The style compels us to look at the language at the same time that we strive to break through its opacity to get at its meaning and at the narrative behind it. This foregrounding of the language calls attention to its function as mediator between man and man and as the means by which man narrates and interprets his past and present experiences, whether real or imagined. In "Night Lessons," the different tones and styles of the central text, the two sets of marginal comments, and the footnotes, serve to differentiate the speakers. Here Issy's racy, colloquial wordplay in the footnotes ("Making it up as we goes along." [268. n.2]; "Skip one, flop fore, jennies in the cabbage store." [271. n.2]), contrasts most markedly with Shaun's solemn, Latinate paragraph headings in the right margins (to p. 293, when they move to the left), such as his "CONCOMITANCE OF COURAGE, COUNSEL AND CONSTANCY. ORDINATION OF OMEN, ONUS

AND OBIT. DISTRIBUTION OF DANGER, DUTY AND DESTINY. POLAR PRINCIPLES" (270-71.R1). But as these "doldorboys and doll" (266.18) do their homework "in the studiorium upsturts" (266.13), language provides the means by which Shem (with the help of geometry) irreverently exposes his mother to his brother, while it also makes possible the accompanying innuendo. This means of communication, therefore, is central to the basic human conflict in the family between brother and brother, son and father, and daughter and mother. It serves to differentiate individuals and to define roles through the normal kinship labels while binding together each speaker and hearer. It is in the nature of fiction, moreover, that this bond exists simultaneously on two levels, on one between the characters of the fiction and on another between author and audience. With the language foregrounded through distortion and wordplay as it is in *Finnegans Wake*, it becomes at once both subject and object, both means and end.

The role of language as both uniter and divider of members of a family may be extended outward to society as a whole and backward into human history. Within the cyclic pattern of history to which Joyce subscribes, language is the means by which history, in the sense of an account and interpretation of events, is made and preserved. In Book III of his *House of Fame,* Chaucer describes a high rock of ice on which famous names are inscribed. Those in the shade remain clear, but those in the sun are obscured, their particular location being arbitrary. Just as Chaucer uses this and other images to portray the accidental quality of both the completeness and the accuracy of historical records, so Joyce uses the hen's letter in the dung heap, the twelve gossiping customers in the pub, the two washer-women in "Anna Livia Plurabelle," as well as the blendings and distortions of names of historical personages, such as "Dook Weltington" (371.36, Duke of Wellington and Dick Whittington), "Stonewall Willingdone" (10.2, Wellington and Stonewall Jackson), and "Wallisey wanderlook" (312.29-30, Wellington and Alice in Wonderland). At this last example and also much else in the book suggest, the line between history and fiction is dim indeed.

Since Joyce in his fiction was portraying "the ideal eternal history" within the Viconian framework,[2] he was in a sense an historian, much as his fellow Celt, Geoffrey of Monmouth, was in his *Historia Regum Britanniæ,* itself a blend of history and fiction designed to recall the glorious past of the British people. Perhaps Joyce saw himself as an ironic successor to Geoffrey. As a writer, however, Joyce was chiefly a creator of a fictional world as well as an interpreter of the history of the race.

Joyce's chosen medium, language, preserves the literary art of the past, but it does so with limitations. English works like *Sir Gawain and the Green Knight* or *Piers Plowman,* works which Joyce may have been echoing in such alliterative passages as "I heard he dug good tin with his doll, delvan first and duvlin after . . . by dredgerous lands and devious delts . . ." (197.20–22), are now at least as opaque in language as the denser sections of *Finnegans Wake.* This medium also challenges the powers of the artist as he attempts to wield its established elements of sounds, grammar, and vocabulary to fit his purposes, or to shape those elements into slightly novel molds when the established forms do not seem adequate. Joyce told his friend Eugene Jolas, "I have discovered that I can do anything with language I want."[4] He is speaking here as the God-like creator of his fictional universe. In this respect he sounds like one of his fallen hero's literary relations, Humpty Dumpty in Lewis Carroll's *Through the Looking Glass:*

>"The question is," said Alice, "whether you *can* make words mean so many different things."
>"The question is," said Humpty Dumpty, "which is to be master—that's all."[5]

Joyce was certainly the master, but not in the purely arbitrary way that Humpty attempted to be. Although Joyce, like Carroll before him, showed that the limits of conventional language can be stretched, he also demonstrated that these limits exist. It is worth noting that Joyce said, "I can do anything *with* language . . ." not "*to* language." The artist may fully exploit the linguistic resources available to him, but he cannot create them, beyond those creative possibilities which are themselves part of the available resources. Joyce is the creator as shaper or molder, but not the creator *ex nihilo.*

In *Finnegans Wake* Joyce shapes his language more freely than had probably ever been done before. Had he not had models and sources of inspiration among his predecessors, however, in addition to the fertile milieu in which he worked, it is unlikely that he would ever have created *Finnegans Wake.* Among his predecessors were Jonathan Swift in his *Journal to Stella,* and Lewis Carroll (Charles Lutwidge Dodgson) and Edward Lear in their nonsense works in poetry and prose.

Joyce's debt to Swift's work in general is very great, and the wordplay of the *Journal* is often cited as an important stylistic influence. It may, however, be overrated. Most of the *Journal* is not in "little language" at all and the brief portions that are were often revised by the early editors. Since Harold Williams' scholarly edition of 1948 was not available to Joyce, he probably used J. K. Moorhead's Everyman's Library edition of 1924. A very small fraction of this is in the "little language," and this language itself consists basically of three simple devices: whimsical abbreviations, such as *MD* and *Ppt* for Stella; a baby talk style achieved by a few regular letter replacements, such as *z* for *th*, *r* for *l* and *l* for *r*, *d* for *g* and *g* for *d* (or *l*), and by some word reductions, such as *ee* for *your* and *oo* for *you*; and very rarely a mildly disguised phrase in which random letters are inserted between the letters of the phrase, so that every other letter must be disregarded to get the message. Instances of this last device are to be found in Letter XLI (Feb. 21, 1711–12), "His business was, that I would hoenlbp ihainm itaoi dsroanws ubpl tohne sroeqporaensiepnotlastoiqobn," which unmasked is "help him to draw up the representation";[6] and in Letter XVII (Mar. 7, 1710–11), "He gave me al bsadnuk lboinlpl dfaonr ufainfbtoy dpionufnad," which is "a bank bill for fifty pound."[7] These seem intended primarily as part of a clever game, although they would also prevent a casual or hurried reader from immediately understanding them should the letter have been opened in transit. If, however, Swift really expected that his letters might fall into the wrong hands, he would probably have eschewed his baby-talk style. Examples of this style are "Bed ee paadom Marom, I'm drad oo rike ee Aplon" (Beg your pardon Madam, I'm glad you like your Apron) in Letter XLIII (Mar. 21, 1711–12);[8] and "So here comes ppt [Stella] aden [again] with her little watry postscript; o Rold [Lord], dlunken [drunken] Srut [Slut] drink pdfrs [Swift's] health ten times in a molning [morning]; you are a whetter, fair I sup Mds [Stella's] 15 times evly [every] molning in milk porridge. Lele's [there's] fol [for] oo [you] now, and lele's fol ee [your] Rettle [letter], & evly kind of sing [thing];" in Letter L (July 19, 1712).[9] This style, which Swift refers to in Letter XLIII (Mar. 11, 1711–12) as "ourrichar Gangridge" (our little language), is usually found at the closings of letters or occasionally elsewhere when Swift is being personal and wishes to suggest intimacy and affection. Although such a style may have given Joyce a hint or two, it hardly seems sufficient to account for the distortions and wordplay of *Finnegans Wake,* which are much more extensive, more visual than aural, and quite different in purpose. Jolas tells us that "A British clipping came saying that Joyce was trying to revive Swift's *little language* to Stella. 'Not at all, said Joyce to me. I am using a *Big Language*'."¹⁰ Most striking in this respect is the fact that Clive Hart's *Concordance* cites no occurrences in the *Wake* of such common "little language" words as *deelest, lele, logues, richar, rettle, sollahs,* and *zis*. The nearest Joyce comes to directly following Swift is in the phrases "Vely lovely entilely!" (299.25) and "She velly fond of chee" (166.31). Swift, however, would have used *rovery* for *lovely,* and, furthermore, the contexts of these two passages suggest that Joyce intended a Chinese effect. *Chee* here refers to *tea,* the next line mentioning "this eastasian import." In terms of style, therefore, Joyce owes nothing particular to Swift, even though some general influence may exist.

In contrast to Swift, the influence of Carroll and Lear was particular as well as general. Here Joyce had models for the use of portmanteau words, doubtlets or "word ladders," coinages, and other wordplay within a dream world context, one where the imagination of the artist is given full rein to connect and blend people, places, and events as if they themselves were words. In Carroll's work we find also the combination of explicit and implicit concern for language which is prominent in such parts of *Finnegans Wake* as "Night Lessons." Atherton argues that Joyce "was not at first aware of all the parallels with Carroll's work," citing Joyce's 1927 letter to Miss Weaver in which he claims not to have read any of Carroll until a few weeks before he wrote the letter, "though, of course," he said, "I heard bits and scraps."¹² If, however, the "bits and scraps" included such pieces as Carroll's "Jabberwocky," and if Joyce also knew such works as Lear's "The Pobble Who Has No Toes," the basic influence on his style could have existed prior to the more extensive reading or sampling that led to the numerous references in the text to Carroll, to Alice and her world, and to other works of Dodgson, as well as to those of Lear. In Lear's "Pobble" we have the phrase "tinkledy-binkledy-winkled a bell," as well as his coinage *runcible* in "He has gone to fish for his Aunt Jobiska's/Runcible Cat with crimson whiskers!"¹³ *Pobble* occurs twice in *Finnegans Wake,* as in "the whole pub's pobble" (334.24), and near this first instance we have the word *tinkledinkledelled* (345.26).

Even if Joyce did not see Carroll's *Alice's Adventures in Wonderland* and *Through the Looking-Glass* or Lear's *A Book of Nonsense* until after he had gotten well into his work, he could still have encountered important samples of their work and that of other nonsense writers in the two collections edited by Carolyn Wells: *A Nonsense Anthology* (1916) and *A Whimsey Anthology* (1906). The first contains "Jabberwocky" and "The Pobble." In both are works not only by Carroll and Lear but also by Gelett Burgess, W. S. Gilbert, and many others, some famous, such as Jonson, Pope, and Thackeray, and others anonymous. From such "bits and scraps" as these from *A Whimsey Anthology*, Joyce could have derived hints for his sustained tour de force:

> Sol fa—Tanta-ra-ra! Shriekery, squeakery, strum, strum,
> Louis d'or—couldn't get more—packery, backery, glum, glum!
> (p. 119)
>
> Dull humdrum murmurs lull, but hubbub stuns.
> Lucullus snuffs up musk, mundungus shuns.
> Puss purs [sic], buds burst, bucks butt, luck turns up trumps;
> But full cups, hurtful, spur up unjust thumps. (p. 54)

These volumes are full of such wordplay, much of it uninspired, but nonetheless linked with *Finnegans Wake* in the experimentation with words, spellings, and sounds. This interest in punning, wordplay, dialect humor, and parody was characteristic of much comic journalism and burlesque theater in the late nineteenth century, a tradition from which Carroll and Lear drew and to which they contributed. Joyce could also have drawn from this tradition, quite apart from any direct influence of Carroll and Lear on his work.

The influence of his own times, of the milieu in which he lived and worked, was certainly the chief reason for Joyce's interest in language and for the peculiar style which he created as both expression of and comment on that interest. Important forces which encouraged his style and helped provide its elements were Joyce's language background and training, the rise of the discipline of linguistics accompanied by strong movements for spelling reform and an international auxiliary language, and the linguistic and imagistic experimentation of contemporary writers. These developments in linguistics and literature were manifestations of social changes and philosophical currents, particularly the move toward structuralism with its concern for the system of elements and their relationships in both structural linguistics and new criticism. That feature of Joyce's thesis which Ellmann describes as "the typical character of every particular, whether person or incident" is analogous to the structural linguistic concepts of phoneme and morpheme. In these every particular sound or minimal meaningful form in a language manifests one or another sound-type or form-type. These concepts were being developed by Edward Sapir, Leonard Bloomfield, and others, during the 20's and 30's, while *Finnegans Wake* was being written. They and the *Wake* may both be manifestations of a general philosophical disposition of the time.

Joyce's increasing exploitation of the medium of his works is not surprising when we consider the role language played in his life. Growing up in Ireland at a time when Irish nationalism was increasing as fast as the use of Gaelic was declining, would naturally turn an intelligent boy's attention to language. When this context was enriched by his studying in Jesuit schools where Latin played a major role, it is no wonder that Joyce majored in foreign languages at the university. This Jesuit schooling crops out in the *Wake* in modified forms of the heading with which the pupils began their written lessons: *Ad Majorem Dei Gloriam*. It appears both as "at maturing daily gloryaims" (282.6) and *"Ad Majorem l.s.d.! Divi gloriam."* (41814). In addition to Joyce's study of Latin in school, his undergraduate interest in Ibsen stimulated his study of Dano-Norwegian. His basic range of languages is indicated by the five translations he made of James Stephens' English poem, "Stephen's Green," one each in German, Dano-Norwegian, French, Italian, and Latin. Among the letters edited by Ellmann are over a hundred written originally in one or another of these languages, except for Latin. Reading experimental novelists in these languages, such as Mallarmé and Hauptmann, further increased Joyce's conscious awareness of the medium of the writer and sensitized him to its possibilities. His language teaching, chiefly in Paris and Trieste, which required fluency in at least two languages and the ability to manipulate equivalent elements in both, also helped sharpen his appetite for words and his skill in handling them. This work certainly sensitized him to the forms, the nuances of meaning, and the peculiar features of English words. In an early letter written in Trieste to his brother Stanislaus, Joyce summed up the results of his first nine months abroad. In it he claims that he has "learned German and Danish fairly well" and says, "I write much better now than when I was in Dublin."[15] Part of this improvement was no doubt the fruit of extensive exercise of his talents during this time, but part of it can be attributed to the linguistic stimulation which resulted from his foreign residence and his work. Such benefits continued to accumulate over the years and culminated in *Finnegans Wake*.

An invaluable foundation for this later development was his own Irish dialect. Because Joyce grew up in Dublin where he could hear varieties of Irish English and also British Received Pronunciation, his ear for speech differences was well trained. His awareness of these differences would naturally increase over the years as he heard more and more RP through English friends and through visits to England and as he recalled the voices of his family and of his friends and acquaintances of his early years in Ireland, as well as having these memories renewed by his visits to Ireland. Joyce's having heard contrasting dialects from an early age would itself have increased his language awareness in general, but the Irish dialect in particular was well suited to encourage a fondness for puns and wordplay. One feature of Irish English that would have this effect is the pronunciation in Joyce's day of *ea*-words with an *ay*-sound rather than an *ee*-one. Thus, *heal* would be homophonous with *hale* rather than *heel*. An educated speaker, however, who knew that in RP and many other English dialects the *ea*-words were homophonous with *ee*-ones, and who was writing chiefly for such an audience, would feel an ambivalence of association in these *ea*-words that would encourage playing with them. Two related features of Irish English which are more pregnant in this respect are the tendency for voiced stops, especially final ones, to be devoiced, so that both *back* and *bag*, and both *cap* and *cab* may be pronounced the same, and for there to be one pair of sounds, usually dental affricates (/tθ/ and /dˣ/), where Standard British and American English have two pairs, namely voiceless /t/ and /θ/ and voiced /d/ and /ð/, the first of each pair an alveolar stop and the second a dental fricative. The result is that the words written *tin* and *thin* are homophones. When this second feature is compounded with the first, we have potentially homophonous sets of words, such as *wreath, wreathe,* and *read; breath* and *bread; oath, oat, owed,* and *ode; both, boat, bowed,* and *bode; troth, throat,* and *throwed*. The possibilities for punning and other wordplay in such a dialect are mindboggling, and Joyce's work, especially *Finnegans Wake*, suggests that they did indeed rattle in his mind.

Although these dialect features are important preconditioners of Joyce's style, they also help to account for particular words in the *Wake*. Joyce puns on *wake* and *weak* (both pronounced /wek/ in turn-of-the-century Irish English) in "at Tam Fanagan's weak"

(276.21–22). The pun on the name *Persse o'Reilly*, and perhaps *Pears* soap also, in the lines,

> Yes, pearse.
> Well, all be dumbed!
> O really? (262.8–10)

is more apparent if the *ea*'s are pronounced /e/ as in *say* rather than /i/ as in *see*. The same sound correspondence lies behind the altered spelling of *tea* in "thounce otay" (262. left margin) where we may also have alliteration, considering the colloquial tone and the consonant features mentioned above. This consonant relationship must also have suggested to Joyce the amusing alteration of *Catholic* to *Catalick* (158.4), whereas the reverse spelling alteration provides the pun on tongue and *thing* in "anythongue athall" (117.15–16) and on *through* and *truth* in "twofold throughts" (288.3) in a passage with *t*-alliteration. The relationship of the series "Niggs, niggs and niggs" (183.5–6), to "Ichts nichts on nichts!" (343.20), "Nixnixundnix" (415.29), and "Nichtsnichtsundnichts!" (416.17) is closer when one realizes that in the Irish dialect *niggs* may be homophonous with *nix*.

The dialect homophony of the word *each* and the name of the letter *H* is important to the understanding of a Joycean joke at the expense of G. B. Shaw. G. B. S., as an avid advocate of spelling reform, attempted to demonstrate what he considered absurdities of English spelling by respelling *fish* as *ghoti*, using the *gh* of words like *laugh*, the *o* of *women*, and the *ti* of *nation*, where they represent /f/, /ɪ/, and /š/, respectively. Among the night lessons on language is the footnote, "Gee each owe tea eye smells fish. That's U." (299.n. 3). Here Joyce replaces Shaw's letters *g, h, o, t,* and *i* with words (*each* standing for *h*), and then a word with a letter (*U* for *you*). Thus, while giving Issy a typically irreverent comment, Joyce also implies that he thinks Shaw's reforming "smells fish[y]." After all, look at the fun one can have with the present system!

The proposal of Shaw which Joyce was mocking here was one manifestation of a movement, especially strong in the late nineteenth and early twentieth centuries, which helped call attention to the superficial forms of words and the multiple ways English has of rendering its sounds. A related movement was that for an international auxiliary language. This movement was burgeoning during Joyce's lifetime and could not go unnoticed by a person with Joyce's interest in popular culture, his international perspective, and his involvement in the use and study of numerous languages. In a survey of this movement, *One Language for the World* (New York: Devin-Adair, 1958), Mario Pei writes,

> The two decades that close the nineteenth century witness the great flowering of constructed languages, including both Volapük and Esperanto, along with at least forty other serious projects of varying merit.
> The period between 1900 and 1920 is dominated by Esperanto and its brood, but many other valuable suggestions appear, at the very least forty in number. It remains for the years since 1920 to multiply both popular interest and types of proposal. (p. 94)

Among these later proposals is Basic English, first promulgated in 1930 by Charles Ogden. This consisted of a simplified English based on a vocabulary of 850 words, 600 of them nouns, which by means of paraphrase, such as "take part" for *participate,* could express any idea. Joyce refers to this scheme and Volapük while apparently mocking artificial languages in general:

> For if the lingo gasped between kicksheets, however basically English, were to be preached from the mouths of wickerchurchwardens and metaphysicians . . . , where would their practice be or where the human race itself where the Pythagorean sesquipedalia of the panepistemion, however apically Volapucky, grunted and gromwelled, ichabod, habakuk, opanoff, uggamyg, hapaxle, gomenon, ppppfff, . . . (116.15–33)

Finnegans Wake in general may be seen as an ironic comment on international language proposals, Basic English in particular. Whereas most inventors of international auxiliary languages aimed for simplified grammar or vocabulary, Joyce's procedure was to enrich his expression by complication. A person with Joyce's sophistication, knowledge of languages, and sense of humor surely found much to laugh at in the spectacle of international congresses held by hordes of zealous speakers of Volapük or Esperanto. Eugene Jolas tells us, in fact, that Joyce "often talked with a derisive smile of the auxiliary languages."[16] While mocking their means, Joyce may nevertheless have sympathized with their aims, and he certainly had in common with them the attempt to create a new means of expression. Since their attempt came first and was known by Joyce, it may well have provided him with another source of inspiration for his own.

M. J. C. Hodgart suggests that Joyce may have gotten much if not all of his knowledge of Volapük, Esperanto, and Novial from Otto Jespersen's *An International Language* (Copenhagen, 1928). He also cites some passages in the *Wake* based on Volapük (34.13) and Esperanto (52.14, 160.29, and 565.25).[17] Another possible source is Jespersen's earlier work, *Two Papers on International Language in English and Ido* (Copenhagen, 1921), in which a number of those languages which appear in *Finnegans Wake* are mentioned, such as Universal and Idiom Neutral as well as Volapük ("what with moltapuke on voltapuke" [40.4–5]), Novial ("tuned in to hear the topmast noviality" [351.15]), and Ido ("tell her in your semiological agglutinative yez, how Idos be asking after her" [465.12–13]). There may also be a pun turning on Danish *maal* ("language") and the artificial *Mezzofanti-Sprache* in Joyce's itinerary which opens the "Night Lessons" chapter and includes "Mezzofanti Mall" (260.21–22). Some of these languages (Universal, Idiom Neutral) appear in a sentence in which Joyce seems to be poking fun at some of the names, suggesting that they are as distinctive as the labels *concubine, prostitute,* and *street arab*. There is, to my knowledge, no Sordomutics or Florilingua, for example, but *-lingua* is common in names like *Mundelingua* and *Pasilingua*. "The olold stoliolum," says Joyce,

> ... is told in sounds in utter that, in signs so adds to, in universal, in polygluttural, in each auxiliary neutral idiom, sordomutics, florilingua, sheltafocal, flayflutter, a con's cubane, a pro's tutute, strassarab, ereperse and anythongue athall. (117.12–16)

A kind of interlanguage which has developed in various parts of the world at different times out of a need for a compromise between two or more natural languages is the pidgin. Such a language is spoken by people doing business with each other or between a master and his servants or slaves. Pidgin has interested those studying the problem of an international auxiliary language and also anthropologists and others concerned with intersecting cultures. Joyce seems to have been among them if we may judge from his use of brief passages that appear to represent a variety of pidgin English, as well as his use of the name in "Tipatonguing him on in her pigeony linguish" (584.3–4). In a passage in "Night Lessons" treating the events in Phoenix Park in cycling and Arthurian terms, we suddenly encounter, "all boy more missis blong him race quickfeller all same hogglepiggle longer house blong him" (285.6–8). As Shaun responds enthusistically to Shem's geometry lesson with "So analytical plausible! . . . it will be a lozenge to me all my lauffe" (299.26–29), he followes it with "More better twofeller we been speak copperads" (299.30). When the two are later at odds, we again meet the same style, "he fight him all time twofeller longa kill dead finish bloody face blong you" (303.30–32). The same kind of unsophisticated earthiness that Joyce seems to suggest in these passages appears also in the fable of the Ondt and the Gracehoper when the Gracehoper prays: "Nefersenless, when he had safely looked up his ovipository, he loftet hails and prayed: May he me no voida water! Seekit Hatup! May no he me tile pig shed on! Suckit Hotup!" (415.33–35). A longer passage in the same vein (485.29–34) has enough Chinese elements in the context ("shanghaied," "Tsing tsing!" Confucium") to indicate that Chinese Pidgin English is intended there. The others may be Melanesian rather than Chinese. All of these, however, produce a sudden change in style that calls the reader's attention back to the language just as he perhaps felt he was getting used to it. This is only one such device among many, because Joyce does not allow us to forget that we are reading a surrealistic-type prose that may change in style or even language at any moment, regardless of subject or speaker. Although pidgins develop to bridge a linguistic gap, Joyce uses them within his language to create one, at least momentarily.

In contrast to those artificial and semi-natural languages which are intended to facilitate communication by bridging different natural languages, are the cants or argots designed by thieves and others outside the law to keep the ordinary person from understanding what is being said in his presence. An important Irish cant was Shelta, referred to in a quotation above as "Sheltafocal" (11.14) as well as in "Shaun replied under the sheltar of his broguish" (421.21–22). This cant, a reduced form of which is still used by the Irish Travelers in the American South,[18] was based on Gaelic. It is discussed along with other cants in R. A. Stewart Macalister's *The Secret Languages of Ireland* (Cambridge: Cambridge University Press, 1937), a book which Joyce made use of as soon as it appeared. Adaline Glasheen lists in the *Wake Digest* (pp. 48–51) some of the cant words Joyce incorporated. Macalister's book obviously came out too late for it to have contributed a strand to Joyce's original creation of the *Finnegans Wake* style, but the *Wake* and the secret languages have features in common, "for," as Dounia Christiani noted while discussing the large Danish element in the work, "surely the *Wake* is arcane by intention."[19] And as Macalister notes, "talking in riddles has been at all times a favourite amusement among the Celtic peoples."[20]

One of Joyce's favorite riddling devices in *Finnegans Wake* is the introduction of various languages other than English. Explicit references to specific languages just in the footnotes of "Night Lessons" are "None of your compohlstery English here!" (271. n. 3), "Traduced into jinglish janglage . . ." (275. n. 6), "my old nourse" (279. n. 20), "Translout that gaswind into turfish . . . " (281. n. 2), "Parsee ffrench for the upholdsterer . . . " (296. n. 1), and "Basqueesh, Finnican, Hungulash and Old Teantaggle, the only sure way to work a curse" (287. n. 4). In the last one Joyce is punning on the names *Basque* (with *bak-sheesh*), *Finnish* (with *Finnegan*), *Hungarian* (with *Hungarian goulash*), and perhaps *Old English* or names with *Old* in general (with something like *tea* and *crackers*). Although Joyce's frequent use of language names suggests his pervasive consciousness of languages, his use in his text of the languages themselves is even more striking. Shem's marginal comments are some of the briefer ones and illustrate the variety of languages used. There are at least seven different languages represented besides English, of which the following are samples: Latin—"Non quod sed quiat" (263.L3); Italian—"Undante umoroso" (269.L1); French—"Pas d'action, pen de sauce" (274.L2); Spanish—"Vive Paco Hunter!" (286.L1); Greek— "οὐκ ἔλαβον πόλιν" (269.L2); German—"Dondderwedder Kyboshicksal" (283.L2); and Danish—"Forening Unge Kristlike Kvinne" (267.L3). As these examples show, Joyce's foreign language is often distorted and mixed to produce puns and jokes. Thus the last of those just cited is a rearrangement, as well as a respelling, of the name of the Danish YWCA (Kristelig Forening for Unge Kvinder), so as to change the initials KFUK to a more English-like FUKK. Among the blends of two languages are the Spanish instance above, the German-Latin "Verschwindibus" (270.L3), and the Danish-French "Pige pas" (272.L1). The reader of *Finnegans Wake* who soon becomes accustomed to a text peppered with foreign phrases and bilingual puns, must also deal with extensive passages in such languages as Latin (287.20–28) and French (281.4–13).

Most of this foreign matter is in the better known languages of Western Europe, but Joyce is believed to have used about forty different languages, including artificial ones, from the evidence of a holograph list (B.M. Add. ms 47488, f. 180) and of the text. In the mathematical section of "Night Lessons," one of the lesser known languages crops up to bedevil the reader, although Joyce at least gives him a clue as to what dictionary to consult, when he follows the passage with "allahthallacamellated, caravan series to the *finish* of helve's fractures" (285.21–22, italics added). The preceding four lines run, "kaksitoista volts yksitoista volts kymmenen volts yhdeksan volts kahdeksan volts seitseman volts kuusi volts viisi volts nelja volts kolme volts kaksi volts yksi!" (285.17–21). Although *volts* is not a Finnish word, the others are the Finnish numerals meaning "twelve" to "one." All together they suggest an electric charge (thunder and lightning) associated with the creation in *Finnegans Wake* through the merger of zero and one. This interpretation is implied by passages nearby, such as "helve's [heaven's] fractures" (285.22), "*A stodge Angleshman has been worked by eccentricity*" (284.L1), "A Tullagrove pole . . . may be involted into the zeroic couplet" (284.5–10), "find . . . how minney combinaisies and permutandies can be played on the international surd! pthwndxrclzp!" (284.11–14, where the last "word" contains twelve consonant letters, and if the first *p* is ignored, and the *w, x,* and *z* replaced with the vowels *u, e,* and *a,* respectively, we have *thunderclap*), and "Imagine the twelve deaferended dumbbawls of the whowl abovebeugled to be the contonuation through regeneration of the urutteration of the word in pregross" (284.18–22). This last might be glossed in part as "In the beginning was the word, and that word was a thunderclap, and its echoing and elaboration are epitomized by *Finnegans Wake*."

The use of numerous languages in addition to English in his work enabled Joyce to enrich the texture and broaden the range of reference. Not only do we have both distorted and undistorted English, but the sounds, shapes, and referential world of many other languages and cultures. This contrapuntal framework on an English ground bass not only reminds us of man's many voices but also unites them into the single voice of HCE in his role of Here Comes Everybody. Yet it is part of Joyce's game with the reader, too, like an Old English Riddle that ends with *Frige nama*, "figure out my name." Whether the reader is amused or awed or both, he is bound to be exercised by the experience, and in accord with Joyce's fascination with the magic of words, probably exorcised as well.

An example of this broader range of references and Joyce's playing with his reader is his double use of a couplet of Ibsen's, which in the original runs,

> I sørger for vandflom til verdensmarken.
> Jeg lægger and lyst torpedo under Arken.

This has been rendered by Christiani, who discovered it in the *Wake*, as "You provide the flood for the world-field. I shall gladly put a torpedo under the Ark."[21] The couplet appears in disguised form in the course of a dialogue in the "Yawn" chapter, but it is marked off by being both a single speech and italicized:

> —*Day shirker four vanfloats he verdants market.*
> *High liquor made lust torpid dough hunt her orchid.*

The other and earlier appearance, though slightly closer to the original, is not marked off from its context in any way. It goes, "They seeker for vannflaum all worldins merkins. I'll eager make lyst turpidump undher arkens." (364.28–29). Here Norwegian and English blend, as do Ibsen and Joyce, and Ibsen and Earwicker, the master builder. The style of *Finnegans Wake* is such that we would scarcely recognize this blending, however, were it not that the reading of the *Wake* is a corporate enterprise. How much more of the work is similarly waiting to have such facets revealed?

Although the poetry of Ibsen's original only dimly comes through Joyce's versions, Joyce gives it a poetic quality of his own. He follows the second version with a piece in a rather different style: "With her shoes upon his shoulders, 'twas most trying to beholders when he upped their frullatullepleats with our warning." (530.26–27). It is a marked characteristic of *Finnegans Wake* that its style varies drastically, but to a considerable extent this style is poetic in its rhythm, frequent rhyme, pervasive alliteration, and imagery. This poetic quality of *Finnegans Wake* is a reflection of both contemporary literary trends and the particular technique and language which Joyce developed.

The early twentieth century was a period when the media of art and communication had become for many the center of attention. In the study of language and in the creation of art and literature, as well as music, many directed their attention to the linguistic code and its properties, in the case of linguistics and literature, and to the physical qualities of paints and colors and other artistic substances. This was a time of experimentation in many fields, but in the world of art there were movements such as futurism, cubism, vorticism, and imagism, movements in which artists often modified and distorted the usual representations of objects or delighted in the object or form for its own sake. In part, *Finnegans Wake* is in this vein. Although Joyce goes beyond his language by enriching the content rather than ignoring or subordinating it, he nevertheless takes pleasure in the sounds and forms of words and sentences, creating a complex kind of musical score with his language. In this respect, it is not surprising that some of *Finnegans Wake* reads like nonsensical nursery rhymes. The primary function of a passage like the following seems to be the enjoyment of the rhythm, rhymes, and alliteration:

> Braham Baruch he married his cook
> to Massach McKraw her uncle-in-law
> who wedded his widow to Hjalmar Kjaer
> who adapted his daughter to Braham the Bear.
> (284. n. 4; the lineation is added here and in the following passages.)

One suspects that the words were chosen more for their sound than their meaning, although they allude to Irish historical figures, and they also remind one of the nonsense verse of Carroll, Lear, and others in the paradox of a man marrying off his own widow! Similar are the following:

> Wait till spring has sprung in spickness
> and prigs begin to pry
> they'll be plentyprime of housepets
> to pimp and pamper my.
> Impending marriage.   (279. n. 17–18)

> . . . so from Nebob see you never stray
> who'll nimm you nice and nehm the day.   (270.27–28)

> Ten men, ton men, pen men, pun men, wont to rise a ladder.
> and den men, dun men, fen men, fun men, hen men, hun men
> wend to raze a leader.   (278.18–21)

One could multiply such examples many times over, but they suffice to illustrate that Joyce's wordplay is far more than a matter of puns.

He is also more than just a fun man, however, as the last passage clearly refers to Tim Finnegan's climbing his ladder and to Shem the Penman and all his ilk who wish to rise in the literary world. It also refers to the still larger number of dunners, writers of messages such as the hen's letter, among others, who wish to bring down (raze) anyone who succeeds. Yet it probably refers as well to those who, like the Fenians, want to raise a leader, and perhaps raze some too.

None of the passages just quoted were originally arranged as poetry as they are here; they were printed in the *Wake* as prose. One of the major features of early twentieth-century literature was the blurring of the artificial boundary between poetry and prose. Free verse is one manifestation of this trend; *Finnegans Wake* is another. Just as this work challenges conventional concepts of genre, it also modulates frequently from prosaic rhythms to poetic ones and back again. The poetic quality is achieved in part through Joyce's extensive use of familiar phrases and common sayings and in part through parallel structures with lots of alliteration and rhyme. Common expressions tend to have a regular rhythm which carries over even when they are parodied or otherwise played upon, as in "On the name of the tizzer and off the tongs and off the mythametical tripods" (286.22–24) or "the dimpler he weighed the fonder fell he" (282.19–19) or "This is the glider that gladdened the girl that list to the wind that lifted the leaves that folded the fruit that hung on the tree that grew in the garden Gough gave" (271. 25–29). Although the next passage is not based on a familiar expression, a similar rhythmical effect derives from the parallelism and the alliteration of *n* and *k*:

> Can you nei do her numb? asks Dolph, suspecting
> the answer know. Oikkont, ken you, ninny? asks Kev,
> expecting the answer guess.   (286. 25–28)

Oftentimes the two devices of familiar expressions and poetic sound patterns are either used together or juxtaposed, as in

> For hugh and guy and goy and jew.
> To dimpled and pimpled and simpled and wimpled.
> A peak in a poke and a pig in a pew.   (273. 13–16)

On one level here is our enjoyment of the balanced rhythms, the rhyming of *hugh, jew,* and *pew,* as well as the *-impled*'s, and the alliteration of sounds represented by the *g*'s and the *p*'s. On another is our pleasure in recognizing patterns of meaning—the names *Hugh* and *Guy,* the opposed labels *goy* and *jew,* the elaborately pleated wimple in contrast to the concept 'simple.' On a third level is our recognition of the double play on "a pig in a poke," ending in a rhyming sound (/uw/) that ties the whole passage together.

In spite of the reader's enjoyment of such passages, however, he may not understand them at first on more than a superficial level. The reason is that in exploiting the resources of the language, Joyce often produces morphological or syntactic forms which may obscure the surface meaning, although ultimately they enrich it. It has recently been fashionable in linguistics to stress the creative aspect of language, the extent to which the individual user creates what for him, at least, are novel structures and sentences even though they are based on established patterns. Yet nowhere else, perhaps, do we witness so fully "THE INFLUENCE OF COLLECTIVE TRADITION UPON THE INDIVIDUAL" (268.R1) as in language. Joyce demonstrates both tradition and originality as he plays the role of writer as creator. He uses the sound patterns, words, sentence structures, meaning relations, and familiar expressions that are part of the shared experience of himself and his speech community, but he modifies and distorts them, and combines them in unorthodox ways. Sometimes the distortions are slight, sometimes great, but before we get to the denser sections like "Night Lessons," we have had a chance to practice on the more transparent ones. Here we are challenged the way a child is who is first learning his language. Like him we need a certain degree of exposure, coupled with a willingness to learn and supported by the assumption that it all means something once the system is learned. So Joyce may change spellings, make up new words, combine words that we do not expect to find together, or insert some foreign material, but he does not at first do all of these at once, and he usually keeps his basic sentence structure intact.[22]

One of the major causes of the density of the language of *Finnegans Wake* is the abnormal or unexpected collocation of concepts. Because we assume that the meanings of the words we hear or read cohere in ways we can comprehend, we are quick to correct or reinterpret a use of a word that is not conventional in the light of our own experience with the language. When a student writes, as one of mine recently did, that Shakespeare's use of *do* was "obligatory," explaining that he could use a simple verb construction with or without a form of *do,* we immediately assume that the writer inadvertently used the wrong word and not that he is writing in a dialect where obligatory means "optional" or in a mode where contradictions are intentional. With Joyce, however, our expectations are constantly flouted in a way that Lewis Carroll would have enjoyed. For example, in "Dear and I trust in all frivolity I may be pardoned for trespassing but I think I may add hell" (270. n. 3), we have several words that do not seem to add up. Particularly, what does "add hell" mean? If we try to associate it with other important words in the passage, such as *frivolity* and *trespassing,* we may be tempted to think of it as equivalent to "raise hell." The tentative quality of the rest of the clause ("I think I may"), as well as the extreme politeness elsewhere in the sentence, calls that supposition into question, however. Since the sentence is not really part of a larger context of sequential discourse which could be brought to bear on it, we cannot confidently judge the tone. Yet if we replace a few words in Joyce's sentence with ones similar in form but more appropriate to each other and to the rest of the sentence in meaning, we get a perfectly clear sentence: Dear *Stannie* I trust in all *sincerity* I may be pardoned for *presuming* but I think I may *ask help.* There are two kinds of word replacement in this new sentence. In the first, all but one of the substituted words are of the same grammatical class as the words they replace: *ask* is a verb like *add; help* is a noun like *hell.* In these instances the original sentence is grammatical in the sense that Noam Chomsky's famous "Colorless green ideas sleep furiously" is grammatical, that is, the word classes occur in the order that English grammar requires and thus that English speakers expect. Just as many other meaningful sentences can be made on the same pattern as this one, such as "Colorful young gypsies dance vigorously" or "Deadly new germs spread virulently," so, too, many of Joyce's sentences in *Finnegans Wake* can be "translated" similarly.

The one word that was not replaced with another of the same grammatical class was Joyce's *and,* here changed to *Stannie.* In this case Joyce had linked an adjective and a pronoun by *and* ("Dear and I"), violating the normal grammatical restriction that conjoined items belong to the same class. Here we can either change the *and,* as was done, to collocate *dear* with a noun, or replace the *dear* with a noun or other pronoun and keep the *and,* as in "Dad and I." This kind of problem is particularly difficult when the classes of words joined are incompatible, as here, and not just rearranged. Such rearrangement is present in the note following: "He is my all menkind of every desception" (270. n. 4). When *all* and *my* are used together before a noun, we expect the *all* first, as in "all my friends." Otherwise we expect *whole* before a mass noun as in "my whole family." The order "all my men-," therefore, is what we would expect. Because *my* does not normally occur with *mankind,* we need to adjust this also. Joyce here appears to be blending several possible constructions, such as "all my men," "my old man," and "all mankind." Within the context of the whole sentence (the particularlizing pronoun *He* and the blend of *description* and *deception* into *desception*) as well as of the whole book, we can read this phrase as a reference to HCE in his dual roles as Issy's father (a particular man) and "Here Comes Everbyody" (human beings in general), with also a suggestion of HCE as her potential lover and also all lovers ("He is my all men- . . . "). By successfully conflating several mutually incompatible syntactic constructions, Joyce calls attention to the several different meanings that he brings together at one time. Although it is at first hard for the reader to see all this going on, the sentence achieves a marked poetic force and conceptual power once it is dissected, deciphered, and reintegrated.

The means by which the portmanteau word *desception* is created reflects another very important characteristic of the language of *Finnegans Wake:* its visual orientation. One has to see the word written this way for there to be a second word implied. According to Gross, "the basic language of the *Wake* is English, and spoken English at that."[23] Although the rhythms and tone of the work, both within dialogue and outside it, are those of speech, much of the richness and difficulty of it derive from the written forms, supplemented as they are by such visual devices as the geometric diagram of ALP (293), the diminishing and increasing letter sizes in "greater THaN or less THaN" (298.13), the Doodles family (299. n. 4), the nose-thumbing marginal sketch (308.L3), and the whole parody of scholarly annotation in the margins and footnotes of "Night Lessons." That Joyce joked about G. B. Shaw's zeal for spelling reform, as noted above, is hardly surprising when we consider the importance of orthography in the *Wake*. Joyce's consciousness of this importance is underscored by the numerous references throughout to alphabets, futharks, runes, cuneiform, and letters in general. An important instance is "Every letter is a godsend, ardent Ares, brusque Boreas and glib Ganymede like zealous Zeus, the O'Meghisthest of all." (269.17–19). Although many of Joyce's spelling distortions are designed to alter pronunciation, many others are not. The foregrounding of *faked, filmed* (?), and *folk* in "A phantom city, phaked of philim pholk" (264.19–20) is purely visual, as is the play on *Europe's* in *"Youreups"* (300. n. 2). Similar is "If I gnows me gneesgnobs the both of him is gnatives of Genuas" (274. n. 2). The twelve-consonant sequence "Pthwndxrclzp!" (284.14), and other tricks like it are also made possible by what amounts to Joyce's Book of Kells. One such trick is the mirror (looking-glass) image associated with Issy-Alice. It is very unlikely that anyone would attempt in speech (or comprehend it if it were attempted) the reversal of form in several of the words in the following sentence: "O Evol [love], kool [look] in the salg [glas] and ees [see] how Dozi [Izod] pits what a drows [sword] er." (262. n. 2)

The most important and pervasive orthographic device is the use of the initials of Humphrey Chimpden Earwicker and Anna Livia Pluribelle, as well as the various representations of the 00 symbol associated with them. The initials HCE, which are woven into the text throughout the book, would hardly be significant in speech. They are often reinforced in the text by capitalization, as in "the Harbourer-cum-Enheritance" (9264.8–9), "Even Canaan the Hateful" (264.9–10), and "Eat early earthapples. Coax Cobra to chatters. Hail, Heva, we hear" (271.24–25). Besides the fact that one cannot capitalize in speech, there is the additional problem of the different sound values of the letters used for his name Although *Chimpden* begins with a /č/ (*ch*) sound, the letter used for it is normally just *c*. Most often this letter represents a /k/ sound in the words containing the initials, as in "Honour *commercio's* energy" (264.1, italics added) and "Hoo *cavedin* earthwight" (261.11). Sometimes it represents an /s/ sound, as in "Ecclesiastical and *Cellestial* Hierarchies" (298.L2) and "this habby *cyclic* erdor" (285.1–2). Only occasionally does the word whose initial *c* is used begin with a /č/, such as *chatters* above and "Haroun *Childeric* Eggebert" (4.32). Even a *ch* spelling does not always represent a /č/, as seen in the difference between the first and second ones in "Eche bennyache" (302.28). Joyce even plays with this deviaton by using the letters *s* and *k* on occasion instead of *c,* as in "Shaun, son of Hek" (420.17) and "he*s* hecitency Hec" (119.18, italics added). Similar variations arise with the different sound values of *H* (/h/ and nothing), *E* (/i/ and /ɛ/), *A* (/æ/, /a/ /e/, and /ɔ/), and *P* (/p/, and /f/ with *h*).

Joyce goes beyond the plain use of the initials in "O hce! O hce!" (291. n. 1). This footnote follows the statement, "short wonder so many of the tomthick and tarry members in all there subsequious ages of our timocracy tipped to console with her at her *mirro*rable gracewindow'd hut" (291.7-9, italics added), and if one takes the hint and reads the footnote backwards as a mirror-image, it becomes "echo echo," a kind of visual onomatapoeia. Akin to this is the cry, "Echo, choree chorecho" (584.33-34), following a rooster's crowing in the lines above it.

The sexual significance and the two *O*'s of the "O hce!" passage suggest that it belongs with the numerous occurrences of the important double-O symbol associated with Alp and Creation. It appears not only in the geometry diagram as the two intersecting circles, but also as the infinity sign in a passage permeated with implications of sex and Creation. Besides the visual images suggested by the referents of the words "dumbbawls" (284.19)—dumbbells and balls—and "bissyclitties" (284.23)—bicycles and female genitals, we have related expressions, "zeroic couplet" (284.10), for two zeros, "noughty times" (284.11), and "cooefficient" (284.12), with its doubled *o*. Whereas an explicit statement, such as "zeroic couplet," would work in either medium, most of these expressions are visual only. Many more passages like those above occur in the discussion of the geometric figure later in the "Night Lessons" chapter. The creative significance of these is summed up in lines full of puns and visual images of buttocks, genitals, and their intersecting:

> Gyre O, gyre O, gyrotundo! Hop lala! [ALP backwards, *o,* and the missing *h* of *humpty*] As umpty herum as you seat! O, dear me, that was very nesse! Very nace [nates] indeed! And makes us a daintical pair of accomplasses! You, allus for the kunst and me for omething [the *s* of *Kunst,* part of a pun with *Handel* on "art" and "trade" also belongs to *omething*] with a handel to it. *Beve!* Now as will pressantly be felt, there's tew tricklesome poinds where our twain of doubling bicirculars, mating approxemetely in their suite poi and poi, dunloop [Dunlop tires and *loop*] into eath the ocher. (295.23-33)

The exchange of *t* and *c* between *each* and *other* is a visual manifestation of the interpenetration discussed.

In the variety of this visual imagery, Joyce manifests clearly the extent to which his style reflects not only his times and background but also his celebration of the power and versatility of his artistic medium, language. In so far as *O* is not only a letter but also a number and a general symbol full of nuances, we see in part what was meant by Joyce's assertion that "Every letter is a godsend" (269. 17). But *letter* is also an ambiguous word—such is the nature of language. Joyce made much of such anomalies and so may we, for with letters we are back where we began, with language as man's basic means of communication, bringing people together yet also splitting them apart. *Finnegans Wake* demonstrates in its own way how difficult communication is, yet how rich the resources of our language are: "how minney combinaisies and permutandies can be played on the international surd!" (284.12-14).

Notes

1. *Books,* p. 15.
2. William York Tindall, *A Reader's Guide to "Finnegans Wake"* (New York: Farrar, Straus and Giroux, 1969), p. 171.
3. *Books,* p. 54.
4. Eugene Jolas, "My Friend James Joyce," *James Joyce: Two Decades of Criticism,* ed. Seon Givens (New York: Vanguard Press, 1948), p. 13.
5. Lewis Carroll, *Alice in Wonderland,* ed. Donald J. Gray (New York: Norton, 1971), p. 163.
6. Jonathan Swift, *Journal to Stella,* ed. Harold Williams (Oxford: Oxford Univ. Press, 1948), Vol. II, p. 493. All references to the *Journal* are from this edition.
7. Swift, *Journal,* I, p. 208.
8. Swift, *Journal,* II, p. 519.
9. *Ibid.,* p. 549.
10. Givens, p. 13.
11. *Books,* p. 127.
12. *Letters,* I, p. 255.
13. Carolyn Wells, ed., *A Nonsense Anthology* (New York: Scribner's, 1916), p. 81.
14. *Letters,* III, p. 4.
15. *Letters,* II, p. 93.
16. Givens, p. 14.
17. "Artificial Languages," *A Wake Digest,* ed. Clive Hart and Fritz Senn (Sidney: Sidney University Press, 1968), pp. 56–58.
18. Jared Harper and Charles Hudson, "Irish Traveller Cant," *Journal of English Linguistics,* 5 (1971), 78–86.
19. *Scandinavian Elements of "Finnegans Wake"* (Evanston: Northwestern University Press, 1965), p. 4.
20. *Secret Languages,* p. 73.
21. *Scandinavian Elements,* p. 14.
22. For a fuller discussion of the relationship between *Wake*-syntax and "normal" English, see Strother B. Purdy, "Mind Your Genderous: Toward a *Wake* Gramar," *New Light on Joyce from the Dublin Symposium,* ed. Fritz Senn (Bloomington and London: Indiana University Press, 1972), pp. 46–78.
23. John Gross, *James Joyce* (New York: Viking Press, 1970), pp. 79–80.

". . . but where he is eaten": Earwicker's Tavern Feast

Book II

chapter iii

Edward A. Kopper, Jr.

Many critics have implied that Earwicker's Tavern Feast is the most important chapter in Joyce's saga. Mr. Hart finds that chapter eleven is "the central expressionistic development of themes, on to which Joyce made his material converge and toward which he himself worked during the process of composition."[1] Mr. Benstock justly sees the chapter as, in part, an anti-war statement, a commentary "upon the stupidity of war, upon the common heritage that would ordinarily unify all mankind. . ."[2] Unfortunately, the chapter contains perhaps the most difficult prose that Joyce ever wrote; and, while Mr. Tindall finds the second half of the feast fairly lucid, he feels that the stories in what he calls the first two sections "are the obscurest part of the *Wake*."[3]

Sometimes, however, criticism tends to make even murkier the convolutions of Joyce's style. Tindall states in connection with the Butt-Taff Episode that Joyce "invented" television, that in his use of it he was being a prophet: "What matter that there was no TV at the time of Earwicker's dream or Joyce's writing?"[4] Hart, writing six years earlier than Tindall, found the Butt-Taff television skit to be a microcosm of *Finnegans Wake*. He cites Budgen, who informs us that Joyce never saw any television, but then adds that Joyce always took a keen "interest in any new scientific or technological advance and [that] he had both read and heard about the early telecasts with considerable enthusiasm."[5]

Another difficulty in approaching an explication of *Finnegans Wake* is the almost masochistic urge to see only the problems and obstructions in the text. In this paper I have tried to avoid this trap by discussing what I think can be known at this time about the *Wake*. The difficulties are spelled out in abundance by previous critics, including myself, and I do not think that this is the place to elaborate them.

In this essay I have analyzed in detail the first fifty pages of the Tavern Feast, which contain the first two parts of the five-part structure that I have imputed to chapter eleven. I have dwelt at length on the role of nineteenth century Irish politics in the first twenty-nine pages of the chapter and on the Battle of Balaclava in the Butt and Taff exchange of the "second" part.

Of the remaining pages, the "third," "fourth," and "fifth" parts of the Tavern Feast, I have said little. These pages, 359.31 to 382, seem to repeat motifs already secured in the preceding pages of the chapter; and they have perhaps been over-scrutinized by Joycean exegetes. In addition, the last parts of the chapter come as close to being self-explanatory as anything Joyce wrote in the *Wake*. However, I have said a few words about Joyce's use of Christian tradition in these final three parts.

The feast in Earwicker's Tavern, then, divides, with some Procrustean cutting and stretching, into five sections, the last being really a denouement rather than a separate part of the chapter. The first part (309.1–338.3) is unified by Earwicker's several mergings with and departures from the Norwegian Captain. Both are picaros, both invaders, both sinners, both troubled by women, both men whose clothing does not fit, i.e. who do not live in harmony with their surroundings. This part ends with Earwicker's protestation of his innocence before the jury of his customers and with his judges' insistence that the skit of Butt and Taff will provide new evidence for the trial, will disentangle Earwicker's deeds from the Captain's.

Part two (338.4–359.29) is built around the Battle of Balaclava in the Crimea, in which Buckley shoots the Russian General, who of course has traits of HCE. Buckley is composed of Butt and Taff (Shem and Shaun), and these children of Earwicker come together twice in the section. The pages are unified by the contrast between things of the body, sex, urination, and defecation; and the battle over Sebastopol, which becomes a bloody manifestation of suppressed physical needs. The section ends with Earwicker insisting that although the Butt-Taff episode proved nothing, a banned book which he has will clear his name. The patrons tire of his story and call for songs and merriment, and in the last lines of the section we discover that the preceding production has been called "The Coach With The Six Insides."[6]

118 / A Conceptual Guide to *Finnegans Wake*

The third part of the Tavern Feast (359.30–369.5) begins with a musical interlude but quickly turns into a review of Earwicker's purported foibles. The center of the section is Earwicker's Apology (363.20–366.30), which is close to the heart of *Finnegans Wake*. It begins with an allusion to the *felix culpa* and ends with a reference to "Fall stuff." Earwicker is partially exonerated since his faults can be traced to the Garden of Eden; and, besides, it turns out that his crime (at this juncture at least) was "just a feel" (365.30). His confession is a contrast to the commentary of the Four, which follows immediately and which reflects a sterile Schoolman ethic. No wonder that Earwicker sneaks in another drink at the end of their diatribe and that the other customers bury their noses in their pints.

Part four of the chapter (369.6–380.6) evokes more successfully than the previous sections the drunken mist which has descended upon the pub. Sigerson, Earwicker's bar boy, slams the shutters closed amidst rumors that a rann singing lynching party is gathering to accost HCE. At this point we hear echoes of the prankquean since Grace O'Malley was another denied hospitality. In the second part of the section HCE is the sacrificial victim as the remaining patrons receive his body and blood. Allusions to the twentieth century Mass and to the ancient Church practices abound in these pages, which shortly after are referred to as a Last Supper (380.15) and HCE's finest Holy Communion (380.10).

Section Five (380.7–382.30) pictures Earwicker alone at last (with the exception of the sound asleep Sigerson). Earwicker is compared to Roderick O'Connor, the last high king of Ireland. The Host weaves back and forth, feels sad, and then finishes off the remnants of his customers' cups and bottles. Here of course he resembles the priest after the Communion of the Mass, who drains his chalice so that none of the now consecrated wine is profaned. Earwicker is seen to "suck up" the liquor, and one is reminded of St. Patrick's baptismal name, Succat. At any rate HCE will sleep until St. Kevin's hen wakes him at dawn, Book IV of the *Wake*. Earwicker and his pub are ready to float into the next episode, where in deep sleep HCE will see himself cuckolded. His pub will turn into a chapel completely as Joyce draws upon the Latin derivation of the nave of a church, *navis* or ship.

Through all these permutations and perambulations Joyce gives the reader just enough physical details, concrete statements, and psychological realism to keep him going. These lucid moments are the ones that allow us to see that on some occasions the author is almost as frustrated by his task as the reader. It is reassuring to hear Joyce poke fun at the overworked motif of hesitancy, whether it be Parnell's or Lord Lucan's in the Crimea: "And be the seem talkin wharabahts hosetanzies, dat sure is sullibrated word!" (379.6–7). Or to hear the Four justify their scathing attack agains Earwicker and his family on the grounds that they have been in the midst of the tangles from the start, or at least through chapters nine, ten, and eleven: "And was theys stare all atime? Yea but they was. Andoring the games, induring the studies, undaring the stories, end all." (368.34–35).

These brighter moments break through the fog of alcohol and through the darkness caused by the gunpowder used in the Crimean War, which evoked a smoke so thick that in a heavy skirmish one would think it were night. From the beginning of the chapter a plot blinks through, and the first line establishes the dramatic irony of the piece: the customers, who will vilify their Host, probably couldn't care less about his guilt or innocence or even about the lineaments of his tale.

Also at the start the popping of the patrons' bottle corks helps recreate the stultified political atmosphere which Joyce had created in "Ivy Day in the Committee Room." The customers act out John Kells Ingram's injunction in "The Memory of the Dead" to drink a toast for the brave rebels of 1798: "But a true man, like you, man,/ Will fill your glass with us." (310.23–24, 28). These customers become menacing as they drop their voices to whisper about HCE "sottovoxed" (313.18).

Earwicker's picture emerges clearly at a few specific points in the Chapter. Wondering just when the altercation between the hunchbacked Norwegian Captain and the tailor who couldn't fit him took place, Earwicker picks his ear—to jog his memory, to help his hearing, and to remove the earwig of guilt (311.10–11). HCE often keeps the action moving and frequently cups his ear to pick out orders for drinks. When he is called to bed, he remains at his till, like a publican or a dedicated sailor; and, in fact, keeps the pub open so late that he is in danger of losing his liquor license.

In the last few pages of the chapter we find out several interesting items about Earwicker. In the past he has had dizzy spells (373.27), and we are not too surprised when he passes out at the end of the chapter. He has a sinus headache (like Cain's) and is offered help by the Four. Also, he is getting heavier from too much food and drink, a danger for a man in his early to middle fifties.

But the ostensibly valuable advice which is tendered to him by the patrons has an ulterior motive, and the customers try to the bitter end to dress him in clothing which he has rejected. Late in the chapter their pretext is that he needs to be disguised to escape from a mob (377.8–11). The patrons are Free Staters, "frayshouters" (378.26), and it is difficult to outlast their insistence.

Earwicker is helped, or hindered, by his curate or Man Servant, Sigerson. Perhaps the helper is a parody of Dr. George Sigerson, who was prominent in the Irish Revival and who claimed that Homer named Ireland Ogygia in *The Odyssey*. The bar boy plays a lead role early in the Chapter when Earwicker finds that he has soiled his clothing. He blames Sigerson for losing his alternate pair of trousers and complains about the curate all the way to the outhouse. Sigerson avers that the pants are behind the outhouse as Earwicker puts the curse of Olaf on him, the customers all the while laughing until they cry. Sigerson's first cousin, Earwicker claims, is an invalid or a worthless inn valet in the United States (320.1–17). Sigerson is fired, and Kersse takes his place, as Earwicker allows the Caddish enemy into his employ. Taking Sigerson's place, Kersse enters the pub from the back door and is told three times to remove his white hat.

Throughout the *Wake*, Sigerson is portrayed as a clod, and the "tout that pumped the stout" is of little use to his employer, even though he is assigned the honor of closing the pub for the night. He does this by tossing out a Last Blessing of the Mass over the heads of the bleary eyed customers (371.1).

Kate the Maid, too, helps pin the chapter down to physical reality. At one point a discussion of Earwicker's ancient meeting with the Cad in the park is interrupted by her appearance. A door is opened, and it is not Jerry—or Kevin?—but a woman (333.3), Anna Livia's maid or "slavey" (333.4–5). Kate maneuvers through the drunkards like Grace O'Malley in her pirate ship dipping through the ocean, or like the early proprietress of the Wellington-Napoleon Museum.

Kate brings the message past these "corkedagains upstored" and pours it into the porch of the publican's ear. Fortunately, HCE does not receive the same message as Hamlet's father did. Instead he is merely summoned to bed and of course rejects the plea.

Other isolated spots of clarity stand out, like buoys in a bay of shallows, and give the reader enough confidence to see the chapter as a structured entity and then hopefully to go on to its elusive symbolism. As Butt signs the sentimental "God Save Ireland," Taff points to Butt's open flies. Later, the Four Old Men become so terrified by reports of an approaching gang that they are paralyzed into playing "Hide and Seek" and then take out their fears on Earwicker. And it is refreshing to hear Joyce admit at one point that like "the hen in the storyaboot we [must] start from scratch" (336.17-18).

Before analyzing the individual parts of the chapter, I should like to suggest that one might do well to look more closely for elements of *Ulysses* at the Feast, as well as for points of narrative mentioned above. Joyce seems to have modeled much of the chapter on his previous book, once again extrapolating from a past work whatever best suited his purposes in a later one. Many of these references are subtly woven into the text and help to support the more obvious and important themes that are common to *Ulysses* and *Finnegans Wake*.

Some of the most lyrical passages in the chapter describe ALP and HCE as they were in their youth, and one is reminded of a coltish Molly Bloom and a suaver Leopold. With the help of *The Rubaiyat*, "O wanderness be wondernest and now," Joyce evokes that illuminating day in the wilderness when Molly passed on the seed cake of life to her lover: "Him her first lap, her his fast pal, for ditcher for plower, till deltas twoport" (318.12-17). The physical acuity of Molly, which led her to describe the male phallus in *Penelope* as stark and unlovely, is reflected in Anna Livia's exclamation, "I'll tittle your barents if you stick that pigpin upinto meh!" (331.12-13). Molly figures prominently in the indictment of Earwicker, and once HCE inadvertently reveals his love making with "Missmolly" (360.28), and possibly with Maud Gonne, "abroad by the fire."

The tone of these encounters, alternately passionate and pastoral, is reinforced by Joyce's use of the Sirens Episode during the musical interlude which follows the Butt and Taff fracas. Here the singing is done by nightingales, "to you! to you!" (359.31-32), including a Florence who helps relate the section to the Crimean War. References to the untuned piano player (and piano) set the piece squarely in *Ulysses*.

The antics of the Norwegian Captain seem drawn from the blasphemies of Buck Mulligan and the wheedling, mincing, sycophancy of W. B. Murphy in *Eumaeus*. The Captian fits well into the company of the tavern denizens, whose roistering resembles the drunken palaver of the medical students in *Oxen of the Sun*. At one point the pagan Captain must be instructed in Christian doctrine before he can marry. The start of the catechism, his Sign of the Cross, is a liquor filled cruet; and, like Mulligan in *Telemachus,* he blesses the waters that bring Norwegian seafarers from port to port (326.5–6).

The meal which the Captain sits down to (but doesn't eat) before his conversion resembles the abstinence breaking repast which Shaun does consume before his *Via Crucis* and suggests what might have been offered in the cabman's shelter during *Eumaeus* were the teetotalers' funds not so tight. The Captain makes the Sign of Thor over the food provided by the ship's husband; and the Eucharistic Feast consists of roasted St. Denis of Paris (who was burned at the stake before his beheading), Kennedy's bread, and an appropriately Christian fishball.

In the chapter, too, Earwicker's personality is defined by Bloom's. At one point the gossip of the patrons compares HCE to Bloom as he enters the Holles Street Maternity Hospital (369.18–23); and, another time, Earwicker is told that since soon he will be "Nomon" at all (374.23), he should listen to the strictures of *Ecclesiastes* concerning man's morality. Earwicker, it seems, cannot enter a park (or Sandymount Strand?) without bringing an umbrella, i.e. a prophylactic (373.20–21), and his doings might appear in *Titbits.*

Finally, the ending of the Chapter and the beginning of the next resemble the close of *Oxen of the Sun* and the start of *Circe.* Now thoroughly intoxicated, Earwicker is prepared to enter a world of deep slumber and ever increasing fantasy. In this section even the cries of the enticing gulls are heard over the canopy of Tristram and Isolde.

The chief butt of Joyce's satire in the first section of the Feast is political fumbling. The customers celebrate the glories of Fenianism, the Phoenix Park Assassinations, and especially the rise and fall of Daniel O'Connell, who in his blustering, temporizing, scurrilous way is a fine analogue for the sometimes ingratiating Earwicker. Of Fenianism Joyce did not have to add much to what he had already said in the Cyclops Episode. Nevertheless, Henry Cardinal Manning is at the Feast (311.26–28), for the Cardinal once observed, " 'Show me an Irishman who has lost his faith and I will show you a Fenian'."[7]

The demise of O'Connell is an excellent correlative for Earwicker's fall. O'Connell received his death wound not from the privations of Richmond Prison, which he entered on May 30, 1844, but, according to Gavan Duffy, from his infatuation for a girl whom he courted while in prison. The precocious lass was young enough to be his granddaughter and, worse still, was a Protestant. The girl rejected Dan many times while O'Connell's family expressed constant alarm at his choice of a person who "differed from them in race (*sic*) and religion,"⁸ but who would be placed above them socially. Duffy attributes O'Connell's final ludicrous acts to softening of the brain. In the chapter this January–May theme is the desire of the Liberator, the "liberaloider," to "feel to every of the younging fruits" (336.24–26).

The Phoenix Park Assassinations provided Joyce with a good amount of source material, which he used widely outside of *Eumaeus*. Whole parts of the *Wake* are structured on the deeds of the secret band that was betrayed by the Cad, James Carey, who informed on his cohorts during the Assassination Trials of 1883.

The trial of Joseph Mullett, one of the killers, began on Thursday, May 10, and Mullett may have been as ardent a follower of Thor as the Norwegian Captain. Mullet was hard to miss in a crowd, being hunchbacked, less than five feet tall, and sporting a blue serge suit: "the Northwiggern cupteam. . . . Or he was in serge?. . . . bufeteer blue" (511.2, 4–5, 10). The evidence against Mullett included a letter from his brother James—Shem?—and a number of receipts signed by Mullett under his code name, Salmon. Mullett's letter was read to the court by Mr. Porter, the chief prosecutor. The letter singled out a traitor in the Emmet Band and included the following transcript: " 'The Emmet suit on him; you will take it off him and send it home; it cost a lot of money'."⁹ Certainly, this letter is one source for the Captain's dealings with Kersse, whom he cheats.

In this chapter Mullett appears in the "Serge Mee, suit!" (322.17); and Skin-the-Goat Fitzharris, in an important allusion, one linking the three who spied on Earwicker to the Phoenix Park band, is seen in "Same capman no nothing horces two feller he fellow go where . . . . as three as they were there. . ." (322.25–28). Once the salmon pseudonym is associated with O'Connell as Joyce links together the destructive blarney of all Irish politicians, "old damn ukonnen . . . the lord of the saloom" (323.26–27).

Joyce had many reasons for disliking O'Connell, the Shaun-like blusterer, who placed Catholic Emancipation over national unity and sovereignty, even though he did admire the Liberator's lampooning ability. Malcolm Brown says of the Agitator: "O'Connell had raised sarcasm to a national voice, and his saucy epigrams, taunts, and rejoinders, along with those of Swift, Tone, and John Philpot Curran, were a sort of folk poetry recited at cabin hearths."¹⁰

Joyce's satire of O'Connell in this chapter revolves around three issues: his drinking, which was accented by his family's famous distillery; his red herring issue, the Repeal of the Union; and the great victory at Tara followed shortly by his defeat at Clontarf, where, under pressure from Peel, he called off a planned "monster meeting" scheduled for October 8, 1843. After Tara, O'Connell turned "chicken," as Joyce implies in his allusion to "tarrapoulling" (320.3).

One of these monster protest meetings was held at Mullingar and thus fits into the *Wake*. Seumas MacManus in *A Lad of the O'Friels* (1903) cites the cottagers' opinion of O'Connell after 1842. The young protagonist, Dinny O'Friel, has just told his Uncle Donal about the Mullingar gathering, which was attended by 150,000 partisans. Donal has grown impatient with O'Connell's promises to repeal the Union of 1800, for " 'it's what he didn't do that I despise Dan for .... Dan is still ferryin' petitions across the water, and wastin' the breath of him in a foreign Parliament. . .'."[11]

The references to O'Connell's drinking are spread throughout the chapter and are important for what they imply about pub bravado. At one point the patrons confuse O'Connell with the Sinn Fein movement: "Our svalves are svalves aroon! We rescue thee, O Baass, from the damp earth and honour thee. O Connibell, with mouth burial!" (311.17-19). Here O'Connell becomes both Finn MacCool, who will rise from the grave when summoned, and a cannibal who devours his own nation. Elsewhere O'Connell is seen merely as a swaggering drunkard and beer taster, "aleconner" (319.4), and "oelkenner done, liquorally no more powers to their elbows" (321.1-2).

The Repeal issue ended O'Connell's influence since it brought into the Irish Nationalistic movement the Young Ireland Society of Thomas Davis, the group of idealists who were to take over the country's political reins. In the *Wake* the three informers support repeal of the Union, "repeat of the unium!" (317.29).

O'Connell's abdication after Tara affected Joyce strongly. Tara marked the summit of the Liberator's powers, and the *Nation,* always conservative about numbers, estimated the attendance at one million. Brown describes the forty brass bands which greeted O'Connell with martial music and the ten thousand members of the Repeal Association, all on horseback, leading him to the platform. The gathering stretched solidly "three miles back from the speaker's platform."[12] But O'Connell feared his peasant army and refused to capitalize upon this vast display of manpower.

Joyce scathingly portrays the temporizing demagogue as a double dealer and a trickster. He is the Man Servant, Sigerson or Pukkelsen, who pukingly and puckishly hides Earwicker's "courting troopsers" (319.22–25). In betraying his master, Earwicker's curate becomes a "double dyode dealered . . . wallowing awash swill of the Tarra water," as O'Connell and Sigerson take their places in Joyce's rogue's gallery of traitors.

Given this view of Irish political history, with its cross purposes, its false boasts, its unfinished schemes, and its betrayals, it is easy to understand why Earwicker can merge with a Norwegian Captain, why Kersse becomes Sigerson, why the drunken customers mix up the principals, why a radio becomes a ship-to-shore transmitter, then a television screen, while maintaining its function as a conductor of stories about inverted sex, with its "valvulous pipelines" fastened securely in HCE's ear.

In Joyce's scheme, the Captain is the invader of Ireland and the tailor the small Irish tradesman who is only too eager to welcome the Viking. By his feasting the invader devours the Emerald Isle, facing only token resistance—and winning some acclaim—from the ostensibly patriotic patrons, who so much resemble Gaelic Americans sipping their pints and murmuring pious I.R.A. songs.

The first section of the chapter is a lesson in futility. Earwicker foolishly invokes Shaun, "lord of the barrels," and his wife (and nightmare), "Ana." When he first learns that he has been charged with the Captain's crimes, he forgets that these two people are the least likely to help him. Earwicker is flattered by the drunken politicians' praise picture of him as a combination of O'Connell and Moses (313.4–6) and feels that he can explain his life to them. HCE depends on Kersse for assistance, and this traitor makes a halfhearted attempt to defend his father (and O'Connell) but really would like to pierce HCE's side (313.7–8).

Filled with such helpful enemies of Earwicker, the pub becomes a "Thing," a Danish Parliament, and the Host is put on trial. The fall from the ladder is the prime bit of evidence, with Earwicker attempting to blame the customers for removing planks, i.e. political positions. They simply aver, however, that the publican gave the orders for the removal. The seventh thunderclap is heard, and Earwicker is once again condemned by the ubiquitous three (314.12), who say that he was in heat when the crime occurred. Over the radio comes the news that it was not really a ladder that Earwicker fell from, but a gibbet.

Momentarily buoyed up again by the easy praise of his customers, Earwicker becomes Noah and gathers up two of every species before the flood. He is also dubbed Adam and the Ancient Mariner by the group (324.7-8), and on his junket he carries a potato in his pocket, imitating Bloom (323.17).

From beginning to end of this section HCE allows the worst gossip about his marriage to circulate and then gives in to his patrons' insistence that the skit of Butt and Taff will clear his name.

The Norwegian Captain is made of sterner mettle, even though, like the pubkeeper, he can never complete a meal, i.e. never find fulfillment. The brusque visitor is first seen demanding of the ship's husband where he can buy a suit. This agent directs the Captain to his best friend, the tailor Kersse, successor to Ashe and Whitehead (white hat). The Norwegian seems pleased with the work of Kersse and leaves with his clothing for a forty day trip; but, like other exploiters of Ireland, he does not pay his bill.

The Captain at times becomes a parody of the "man's man," although this chameleon can also appeal to the transvestites in the tavern. Once when Earwicker leaves the pub to relieve himself, the Norwegian Captain enters with his phallus in his hand to show that he is one of the boys. Then he dances a sailor's hornpipe in the relaxed "Tam o'Shanter" atmosphere of the pub (315.24-25) and discusses with the captivated audience how Ireland has always repelled the proud invaders, "prowed invisors" (316.2). The Captain manages to survive all difficulties: he even escaped being butt-ended on one trip home by the tailor, who would have sewed on a purple patch.

The Captain's astuteness is most clearly seen in his escape from the marriage net which the tailor and the customers wanted to cast over him. Once the "nowedding captain" (325.27) was about to be hanged. Under threat of martyrdom he was to meet his doom at Trinity Church and be in the end "Cawcaught. Coocaged," like the stuttering Earwicker. The arrangements were made and the trap set by the tailor, the would-be spinner of the Captain's fate. The tailor wanted to combine all the principals of the story in one marriage: "gentlemens tealer" with "generalman seelord" (325.16), i.e. a captain, a teller of tales, and a tailor. But the Captain slipped away and enjoyed the All Saints Day wedding reception, even though the teetotaling Father Mathew Theobald was there, and left Earwicker with his hostages to fortune. This was no mean task for the Captain, since in preparation for the proposed marriage, he took complete courses in Christian doctrine, studying the lives of such saints as Brendan (327.2), Joseph, the Master of the Good Life (328.8, 329.6), and Elizabeth (328.36).

The Captain is the alter ego of the beleaguered Earwicker. He is unattached, able to travel, able to fascinate a group, and capable of committing sexual crimes without redress. HCE is simply a scapegoat, chained to his till with the world's burden on his shoulders. Only in this sense is he the Ancient Mariner.

The Battle of Balaclava for the possession of Sebastopol, of which the Charge of the Light Brigade is the most famous episode, forms the basis of "Butt-Taff"; and its events fit splendidly Joyce's over-all designs for *Finnegans Wake*. The disaster was caused mainly by a Captain Nolan, who issued an ambiguous order to Lord Cardigan, commander of the Light Brigade. Instead of charging the Causeway Heights—shades of Finn MacCool!—the Brigade marched directly into the Russian guns. The entire Light Division was under the command of Sir George Brown, a wonderful coincidence, which could not have escaped Joyce's attention.

Balaclava represented an application of the domino theory to Britain's interests, with the English needing to keep secure from the Russians their gateways to India. Sebastopol also involved possessions in the Holy Land, with the winner earning the right to custody of the Key to the main door of the Holy Sepulcher (343.5). The British army was placed under Lord Raglan; and the Light Brigade under Cardigan, whose supervisor was Lord Lucan, Cardigan's brother-in-law and bitter enemy. Their opposition, which helped to occasion the travesty of the celebrated Charge, becomes one of the brother battles in the *Wake*.

England's role in the Crimean War was complicated by its soldiers' disgust with the Turks, with whose forces they were once allied; and by homefront newspapers, which insisted that a mired and stalled British army give the Czar of all Russians, Nicholas, a "few good licks" before returning to England. During the Sebastopol battling Lord Scarlett (339.12, 352.6) commanded the Heavy Brigade, and especially at the Alma River lived up to his name.

The final debacle was effected by an order of Lord Raglan as difficult to decipher as the Letter of the *Wake*. Raglan seemed to order an attack by Lucan, but did not say where it should start or when. Nolan, an intrepid but vainglorious underling, badgered the harried Lucan into beginning the assault. When he saw that the commander was heading the wrong way, he galloped towards Lucan to warn him but was shot by the Russians as he approached the hapless troops.

The buffoonery of the Balaclava principals matches the twisted machinations of the politicians in the first section of the chapter. The colorful bunglers of the Crimean War were equal to the Invincibles and the Fenians, and Nolan's antics rivalled O'Connell's frustrated plans and wasted energy.

The cast at Balaclava reads like something only Joyce could create, as the military fiasco was carried out by an army which wore for the final time the picturesque red uniforms with the gilt trimmings that led Joyce to refer to Earwicker over and over again as a lobster.

Lord Raglan relates Balaclava to Wellington's campaign against Napoleon, for legend holds that he lost his arm by the last shot fired at Waterloo. A raglan sleeve, then, is sometimes an empty one. Lord Lucan, too, takes his questionable part in the *Wake*'s ship of fools. Because of his hesitancy—a key word in the annals of Balaclava—at the Alma, he became known as "Look-On" Lucan; and Joyce knew of his nickname, calling him "Look at Lokman!" and "locked at" (367.1, 371.16). Both men were appropriate executors of the over-all plans of the campaign, for Palmerston decided to send Raglan against Sebastopol after a cabinet meeting in which half the members were in a drunken sleep. Speaking of Russia, he felt that " 'the eye-tooth of the Bear must be drawn'."[13]

The events preceding the battle were typically mock heroic. Once, the British luckily captured a Russian baggage train because its captain was too drunk to move. The booty included ladies' underwear and scrofulous French novels. On another occasion the British shot a cow, mistaking it for a Russian soldier. Again, legend holds, the nearsighted Scarlett saw " 'funny pointed things'," Russian hats, then received the report that they were merely " 'thistles'."[14] The fact that these troops drilled in Phoenix Park to prepare for the battle with the Czar's men helped to form the basis for the horseracing interlude in "Butt-Taff." And perhaps the British were disturbed that throughout the Crimean campaign echoed the Turks' frightened cry: " 'Ship! . . . ship!' " and " 'dok [too many] Rus!' "[15]

Captain Nolan, however, is the prime fool of the piece. Nervous, obsessed with the superiority of horses in any fray, the author of two books on the cavalry, Nolan was the son of an Irish farmer. He believed Lucan was " 'all hesitation,' "[16] and the arrogant thirty-five-year-old lost control when he saw Lucan pausing while the Russians apparently were unprotected. Lucan could not withstand the diatribe of this young Persse, or Kersse, and ordered the outrageous and disastrous Charge.

The framework in *Finnegans Wake* which houses references to these antics is, once again, one of intoxicated ribaldry, as the customers share experiences not at all their own. In their drunkenness, reality for them merges with dreams of glory. Their demands for an "Order, order, order, order!" (337.35) are calls for more grog, not military commands. They resemble O'Casey's partisans, who bring the flag into a pub in *The Plough and the Stars*: "A public plouse. Citizen soldiers" (338.4); and more clearly than ever they remind the reader of the Citizen in *Cyclops*. In their reveries they are willing to accept as absolute truth a newscast that places O'Connell, a tired horse, in the Crimea: "Emancipator, the Creman hunter" (342.19–20); and adding to their frenzy is the patriotic music which swells through the tavern during this section of the chapter.

In the Crimean episode the characters of Butt and Taff are carefully limned and differentiated. Butt or Shem is firmly grounded in the physical. He is open and honest and freely confesses his secret desire to destroy his father. He has a lingering affection for his country and cannot bear to see it insulted. Butt points out the true battlefield horrors of Balaclava and insists that sensuality is better than war. He mourns his many lost comrades, the noble fusiliers. Butt's destruction of the Russian General follows a long hesitation, and even then the imminent assassination leads him to exaggerate his own flaws, to compare his eccentricities to Oscar Wilde's. Joyce put a good deal of his own relationship to his country and to his father into this private.[17]

Taff, of course, is the pompous and cliché-ridden Shaun, the accepted one, who is related explicitly to the St. Kevin of Book IV by his cry, "Yia!" (344.7). He is patronizing, and his reassurances are misleading. Taff takes pleasure in pointing out flaws; he reprimands Butt for not shooting the General sooner, as he applies his own simplistic code of battlefield ethics to his aide-de-camp, urging Butt to do what Taff would like to implement had he the courage.

Butt opens the section standing in a cesspool and looking through the roof of a Carmelite monastery, while at the same symbolic time scouting a battlefield near Sebastopol. Butt confesses that he has dreamed of his father being surrounded by all the important generals of the Crimean War (339.9–12) and suddenly points out the prime representation of the Russian Bear (339.27–28), the General himself. Laced through his dialogue are descriptions of the real terrors of Balaclava.

Butt goes on to describe the stench of the General's leavings, that

130 / A Conceptual Guide to *Finnegans Wake*

insult to Irish peasantry and then admits that he was still unable to fire. Burdened with ever increasing guilt, Butt lives up to his name, explaining that like Oscar Wilde, the Great White Caterpillar, he has confessed to buggery before the Old Bailey Court (350.10–15). He has had a belly full of Turkish delights (350.21–22), i.e. candy or taffy, anal sex, and the Crimean War.

Butt maintains that his experiences have made him unsuited for civilized warfare. Even in his halcyon days as a raw recruit, before he received his dogtags (351.20), he could take care of himself (and his privates!), but rarely showed respect for generals. For example, as a noncom (352.2), he was nonchalant when he saw the "urssian gemenal," Butt's only flaw being his Billy Budd-like stutter.

Nevertheless, Butt did shoot the General, when his posterior was raised above the ground like a grasshopper's, an "aceupper" (352.12), and the offense to Ireland became even greater when the Russian General used a shamrock to wipe himself (353.16–17). Butt simply had to gain vengeance and fired his gun as St. Patrick might have used his crozier on King Leary's Druid priests.

From the start Taff is as unctuous as taffy, or a Welsh Taffy. He tells Butt not to mind an occasional nocturnal emission, since dreams are forgotten by daybreak (338.29–31). Taking on his father's stutter in spite of his dislike for him, Taff proves himself to be the derivative and platitudinous stage Irishman, who relegates everything to the past (340.13–16). It is Taff who insists from the beginning that Butt tell his tale. He certainly qualifies for the role of Postman, living vicariously, like Shaun, through the adventures of others.

Butt and Taff merge twice in the section, and on both occasions their union is effected by false agents: the Roman Catholic Church and Irish politics. Obviously both institutions can bring about merely an ephemeral amalgamation. Thus at one point Taff is a bishop offering Communion, Butt a prospective communicant (344.8–9), and the Russian General both a recipient of Baptism and a penitent about to be shriven (344.16–17, 32). Happily, Taff's attempts to make Butt a soldier of Christ fail; and even though Butt does accept Communion from Taff's hands, the outcast considers the Eucharist a communion of sense.

Religion, Joyce feels, is beside the point. Butt describes the true nature of the march over the Causeway Heights as a *Via Crucis* (343.7–8). Indeed it seems at times that Balaclava is only Clongowes Wood College, with pupils like young Stephen fighting the War of the Roses (348.21, 28) in a religious atmosphere.

Butt and Taff's other unification is effected by the fluff of drunken political talk (354.6–7). The two exchange a handshake common to the band of Fianna, as the despotic slave owner and the serf are combined in Ireland's giant: "Faun MacGhoul!"

With the skit ended, Earwicker is no better off than before. He must once again protest his innocence before returning to the bosom of Anna Livia (355.19–20). The skilled felon of the fallen scaffold (355.27) insists only that the preceding anecdote, about Sebastopol, contained no truth, that indeeed truth is impossible for man, even with lie detectors (355.35–36). Once again, Earwicker is mauled by his customers, who make sure, however, not to harm his maypole. Since the innkeeper is tit for tat the same old "dustamount" (359.12), the patrons tire of his story and call for songs.

Of the interruptions that blare through the Butt and Taff dialogue, the first is the most problematic (341.18–342.32). It is the account of the horserace which is heard by the two principals and presumably by Earwicker's customers. It seems likely that the newscast is received by both the two at Sebastopol and those back home. If the horseracing description is the *only* newscast, then the tale of Butt and Taff is being told by Earwicker himself; and I do not feel that this is the case. I think, though, that in this digression Joyce may have strained verisimilitude a bit too much.

"Butt and Taff" was truly Earwicker's last chance to clear his name. During the final three parts of the chapter the remaining customers refuse to listen to anything HCE says and instead devour the Host, as Joyce weaves several Holy Week allusions into the last twenty-two pages of the Feast. Earwicker's Apology takes on as much dramatic significance as Polonius' platitudinous advice to the departing Laertes or as Andrea del Sarto's outpouring of emotion to a wife who smiles at all the wrong times while waiting for her lover. Earwicker is flogged, eaten in a Eucharistic meal, then crucified. Some aspects of the Holy Week services have not been explicated by previous critics, and these I shall dwell upon.

After the musical interlude, the Holy Week Sequence, the customers return to their favorite topic, Earwicker's guilt, even though the witching hour is fast approaching, the hour when Holy Thursday will become Good Friday. We learn that the stuttering Earwicker may have tried to disguise his criminal intentions by using ventriloquism. The "nurses" (361.14), the nightingales in the pub, decide against him and continue his *Gesta Romanorum*. Intolerable as it may seem (to both the reader and the Host), all of Earwicker's past is again brought forward to convict him: his initial hanging in Persse O'Reilly's Ballad, evidence garnered by a female detective, some of Lord Northcliffe's books sold by newsboys. Even the theological validity of his marriage is called into question.

Earwicker begins his defense by insisting that he is incapable of corrupting small girls, or any girls. Like the Russian General he was merely looking for a piece of turf when he came upon the urinating ladies (369.25–26). Or, on one occasion, he was merely dodging a chamber pot carelessly tilted out of an upstairs window. In fact, he will dismiss from the mind of God anyone who bears such false witness against him (364.1–2).

Earwicker maintains that he is simply a henpecked husband and a legitimate Christian, who has renounced the Devil and his pomps (365.1–4). He is really another Parnell, averring that no man may put a stop to the march of a nation (365.26–27). Like Stephen, Earwicker appeals against the light (366.2) and asks mercy of his patrons before they "go to mats" (366.8), the Mass of the Pre-Sanctified since no Host can be consecrated on Good Friday.

All comes to naught, however, as the bemused publican ends by confessing his guilt in a Freudian slip: "the lilliths oft I feldt" (366.25), Christ's lilies of the field, an African veldt, and HCE's two girls. He then realizes that this Ides of March is a good time for his execution, as well as for defecation: "thit thides or marse makes a good dayle to be shattat" (366.29–30).

The four enigmatic Old Men, the "avunculusts" (367.14) are tired of hearing Earwicker's protests and the three parables which help to define his personality and perhaps that of his Deirdre, Anna Livia: the "threestory sorratelling" (367.15). With their wearying precepts the Four try to add a fourth dimension to the events. They warn Earwicker to avoid the marketplaces of Jerusalem (368.8–9) and never to receive Communion, Christ, the sardine, while in the state of Mortal Sin: "never to ate the sour deans if they weren't having anysin on their consients" (368.21). The Old Men live up to their reputation as authors of the Synoptic Gospels, for they "see" everything and sin, especially in the next chapter, with their eyes.

Earwicker's crime is still mired in the Crimean War as well as in the Garden of Eden and Phoenix Park; and he is seen as a drunken O'Connell playing the part of a bishop at Sebastopol (365.9). After the fatal Charge, Lord Lucan-HCE simply returned to the grocery business, his "grossery baseness" (367.1–2). Earwicker is still being censured for his use of "back excits" (368.18–19); and, though he desires to put away his appurtenances, Irish slang (in some parts of the isle, I am told) for testicles, he will never be granted eternal rest: "attomed attaim arrest" (367.30).

What Earwicker fears is that he may be cuckolded by a wayfarer, perhaps one like Stephen, as Molly receives her wafer God, Christ, "herwayferer gods" (365.1); and one is reminded of Molly's fantasy of fellatio with young Dedalus. But Earwicker's crucifixion is the central matter of the last pages, and the Sequence sung by the naughty nightingales prepares us for this sacrifice (359.31).

As I suggested in a previous article, Joyce may well have based the last two chapters of Book One on the Sequence of Easter Sunday, the short prayer which follows the Gradual and directly precedes the "Munda Cor Meum."[18] The start of the Sequence glorifies Christ as the Paschal Victim, leading fallen humanity back to the Father. In chapter seven Shem is portrayed as the crucified artist who lures men away from the established hierarchy. The second half of the Sequence is addressed to Mary Magdalen in her role as eyewitness of the Resurrection. It begins with words closely resembling those spoken by Joyce's Washers at the Ford: "Tell us, Mary, thou our herald be,/ What in passing thou didst see?" Joyce writes, "O/tell me all about/Anna Livia . . ." (196.1–3).

In this Chapter the discussion of Earwicker's married life by the Four (363.12–16) strongly suggests the conversation recorded on the first page of Chapter Eight, which I feel incorporates the Sequence: "You know that tom. . . . Is their bann bothstiesed?" The "tom" of course is doubting St. Thomas, as "toms will till" (196.22) and the "bann," both the announcement of an upcoming marriage and the bands of the risen Christ's burial clothing. The concern of the Four Evangelists over whether HCE and his wife have been redeemed (363.13) places the fourth part of chapter eleven in the heart of Holy Week and prepares the reader for the worst that is to come.

The structure of part four (369.6–380.6) mirrors a stage of late drunkenness, with its sporadic stops and starts and occasional glimpses of profundity. The remaining customers resemble the very ancient Greeks, who drained their toasts to Bacchus before devouring their king, a doughty deed performed each day in Roman Catholic ritual.

HCE's last drink probably pushed him over the edge, yet he resumes his tale even though now it is broken into more frequently than ever. Possible clarification might be found in Belinda, Joyce's bird of creativity, fashioned upon Pope's heroine, whom Earwicker is accused of having raped. However, the famous Letter that she inspired Shem to write contains as usual only chatter. Earwicker's one retort is that all his patrons are in the same boat, united in dream machinery, "Treamplasurin" (370.18), if nothing else.

When the patrons suddenly realize that Sigerson is shutting the doors, they ask Earwicker in vain for another round of drinks, another Mass Host (371.9). Seen as Finn MacCool, St. Boniface (patron of innkeepers), and the Russian General, Earwicker drives out most of his customers with bombs in a scene reminiscent of the battle of the Alma River.

As Sigerson closes the shutters, the Prankquean appears with her riddle since in the legend she too (as mentioned before) was denied a room for the light. Learning that a lynching party singing a rann against HCE is gathering to invade the pub, the Four become entirely disoriented and, with their celluloid donkey (373.4), a product of the reel world, decide to stay in the pub. They excoriate Earwicker in one of the most extensive condemnations of the *Wake*.

In the midst of the speech we discover that Persse's lynching party passed through the alley outside the pub but was denied entry by the porter (373.32–33). The Four resume their scurrilous attack, made under the guise of giving advice and consolation. Earwicker is a guilty Good Shepherd (373.13–14), a drunk, and a misshapen Richard III, who is said to treat Anna Livia as Richard treated Lady Anne. Before long HCE will face his twelve jurors, and he is urged to confess and kiss the Bible: "So yelp your guilt and kitz the buck" (375.15–16).

HCE is compared to the love sick boy of "Araby," and the remaining customers feel free to give him advice on methods of sexual intercourse (375.21, 26–30). Although his wife is no beauty, Earwicker might bring her around with his ability as a "lupsqueezer" (376.20). The big Dane would make a good protagonist for "The Rape of the Lock": "And he shows how he'll pick him the lock of her fancy" (376.20–21). Perhaps Joyce had in mind the assault of Lord Petrie (pee-tree?) on Arabella Fermor.

The Four—or Twelve—mention that a hearse has been drawn up by crucifiers, who are casting lots to decide which one of them will obtain the seamless garment of the crucified Earwicker-Christ and, above all, who will tell his Sorrowful Mother the bad news. As the customers receive the Eucharist, HCE sleepily sways above them, on the Cross of their gossip, "for his good and ours" (377.36–378.1), though he is the meal being consumed: "To pass the grace for Gard sake!" (377.30-31). Unfortunately, they never did understand his message (378.22-23) and simply try to make him drunk.

Joyce explicitly establishes the fact that the Tavern Episode takes place on Holy Thursday night and the earliest part of Good Friday morning. With Earwicker's death comes the end of a cycle, and Joyce sets things up firmly for the next Viconian era, "all's set for restart after the silence" (382.14). He takes great pains to expand HCE's symbolic importance, for as the spokesman of a new age he must assume gigantic proportions. Not only is he the last high king of Ireland, Roderick O'Conner, but Almighty God Himself, "old *Mighty*" (378.35). His death is the death of God on this "tootorribleday;" and, as he approaches his Golgotha almost stark (381.21), he realizes that he has "a terrible errible lot todue todie," with the suggestion of a *Te Deum*, which is prohibited during Lent.

Earwicker is a modern god, however, a victim of the bureaucracy, an alien who is hounded by the Foreign Office (374.24-25), that is interested only in his offal. Like Joyce wrangling over passports, HCE is a modern version of the Tarot pack's Hanged Man: "Hang coersion everyhow!" (378.27). Found guilty by crooked jurors and by Jesus Christ—the real one—his only escape from the burden of sexuality is the celibate life of the priesthood; and even this is a kind of execution: "Slip on your ropen collar and draw the noosebeg on your head" (377.8-9). But HCE can never get away from religion; and the same detective work exercised upon the *Book of Kells*, which concerned another hanged Man, helps bring about his conviction (374.8-11).

In these final two parts of chapter eleven, HCE's pub becomes a chapel, with the cry to "Shatten up ship!" (370.34-35) suggesting that the nave of the church is to be emptied soon in preparation for the most solemn day of the liturgical year, Good Friday. The customers leave, flooded by nautical imagery (372.17-21); and Sigerson is obviously the sexton of the church, "sockson," as he locks the door and shuts up the shutters, "shoots the shopper rope" (372.5).

Joyce reinforces all of this liturgy by specific allusions to Holy Week customs and legends. The reference to St. Hubert and his Way of the Cross, "*chemins de la croixes*" (376.6-7) fits the Good Friday pattern well, while suggesting that Earwicker has yet to face many crosses. One Good Friday morning the carefree Hubert went hunting—like Chaucer's monk—instead of attending church services. As he pursued a large deer, he suddenly saw a crucifix wedged between its antlers.

If Shaun had repented, as this young man did, he would not eat so much meat in chapter fourteen before starting his own *Via Crucis*. Joyce alludes in another instance to the Holy Thursday custom of the Pope's washing the feet of thirteen people, a reenactment of Christ's gesture of humility when he washed His Apostles' feet before the Last Supper. One pope, while performing this service, found a thirteenth person in the group, Christ Himself: "We dinned unnerstunned why you sassad about thirteen to aloafen, sor, kindly repeat!" (378.22-23). Here the grocery store publican has a baker's dozen of people to care for.

But for all his humility Earwicker does not succeed in winning the allegiance of his patrons any more than Christ did. He is still "Mocked Majesty in the Malincurred Mansion" (380.4-5), ridiculed by followers as drunk as Freddy Malins or perhaps just "bad boys." The brand of Cain still mars his brow (374.32-33), and the Protestant is still considered a devil by the partisans, indeed, as Lucifer himself: "Loose afore!" (378.17). He is unable to effect a reconciliation of Ireland's warring factions, to bring about "one flock and one shepherd": "One fledge, one brood till hulm culms evurdyburdy" (378.4-5). The inspiration of Belinda, Joyce's Holy Ghost and bird of peace, stops short of such a *détente* in this "Easterlings" season; and not even in dreams can the Danish Charon, the "traumconductor," succeed.

The last sections of the Chapter are unified in part by the flogging administered to Earwicker as he anxiously awaits the hordes of people marching down the turnpike as though they were headed for a Mullingar monster meeting: "Mullinguard minstrelsers are marshalsing" (371.34-35); and by the sound of the clapper (379.27-30) used during the Consecration of Holy Week Masses in place of the joyful church bells. Throughout it all Earwicker is the poor Fish, or Christ figure, eaten traditionally during the Easter season: "The fish fried was Christ that died." Here the consumption of the fish is related to the "Agnus Dei," a prayer which follows the Consecration and comes immediately before the Communion: "Fisht. . . . But of they never eat soullfriede they're ating it now. With easter greeding. Angus! Angus! Angus!" (376.34-377.1).

Earwicker is whipped as was Christ before the *Via Crucis;* and these sections are filled with references to various types of whips: a quirt (376.4), a birch rod (376.25), an echoing pandy bat (378.36-379.1), just to name a few. All of these are delivered as part of Earwicker's "twelfth correctional" (375.11); a shouting mob races to demand his death, as did Christ's detractors.

With the clapper one can legitimately wonder if Joyce had in mind more than this sacramental. The clapper certainly suggests thunder, which in Christ's time ended a millennium; and with sufficient free association the clapper might be imagined to refer to venereal disease. Joyce seems to use the word this way when he writes, "she clapped her charmer on him" (376.17–18).

The last few pages of chapter eleven leave us with a picture of Earwicker that tells a good deal about Joyce's own fears and doubts. As the Host stumbles about the pub, lapping up drinks with his "venerated tongue" (381.31–32), his bar boy and retainer, Sigerson, sleeps in the corner. The clock is set for Eight O'Clock Mass, and Earwicker is left alone to his fate, with an assistant who could not "watch and pray" with him. Only the hope of Pentecost, with its power to speak in "diversed tonguesed" (381.20), prevents the evening in Earwicker's pub from being a complete disaster.

Perhaps in the new age the bird of peace will set things straight.

Notes

1. *Structure and Motif in Finnegans Wake* (Evanston, Ill.: Northwestern University Press, 1962), p. 131. See also Nathan Halper's "James Joyce and the Russian General," *PR*, XVIII (July, 1951), 424–431.
2. *Joyce-Again's Wake, An Analysis of Finnegans Wake* (Seattle: University of Washington Press, 1965), p. 172.
3. *A Reader's Guide to Finnegans Wake* (New York: Farrar, Straus and Giroux, 1969), p. 188.
4. Ibid., p. 197.
5. Hart, p. 158.
6. For one source of this title see J. Mitchell Morse, "The Coach With The Six Insides," *A Wake Newslitter*, VIII, new series (June, 1971), 46–47. All quotations from *Finnegans Wake* are from the 1968 Viking Press printing.
7. Malcolm Brown, *The Politics of Irish Literature* (Seattle: University of Washington Press, 1972), p. 33.
8. Sir Charles Gavan Duffy, *Young Ireland, A Fragment of Irish History 1840–45*, vol. II Final Revision (London: T. Fisher Unwin, 1896), 81.
9. Edward A. Kopper, Jr., "Some Elements of the Phoenix Park Murders in *Finnegans Wake*," *A Wake Newslitter*, IV, new series (December, 1967), 117.
10. Brown, 54.
11. *A Lad of the O'Friels* (New York: The Devin-Adair Co., 1947), pp. 47–48.
12. Brown, p. 70.

13. W. Baring Pemberton, *Battles of the Crimean War* (New York: The Macmillan Company, 1962), p. 23.
14. *Ibid.*, p. 83.
15. *Ibid.*, p. 78.
16. *Ibid.*, p. 92.
17. Adaline Glasheen, *A Second Census of Finnegans Wake* (Evanston, Ill.: Northwestern University Press, 1963), xliii.
18. "Some Additional Christian Allusions in the *Wake*," *The Analyst*. no. XXIV (March, 1965), 5–22.

Love that Dares to Speak its Name

Book II
chapter iv
Michael H. Begnal

—As stage to set by ritual rote for the
grimm grimm tale of the four of hyacinths

The fourth chapter of Book II of *Finnegans Wake* is dominated by Mamalujo: Matthew, Mark, Luke, and John in all their various guises. Among others, they are the four old sailors who drink nightly in HCE's pub, the four Evangelists, the Four Masters of the Irish Annals, the Four Master Waves of Erin, the four evil advisors who forced King Mark of Cornwall into marriage (according to Joseph Bedier, whom Joyce advised Harriet Weaver to read for Tristan and Isolde), and four seagulls who hover above the ship which is carrying the lovers away from Chapelizod and back to Cornwall. Basically, however, they appear as four old men, reminiscing about their faded youth in contemporary Dublin, wandering through the tricky canyons of memory in search of the past: "and all wishening for anything at all of the bygone times" (386.6). They are the center and focus of this mythological sea journey.

In Joyce's Viconian scheme of things, this fourth chapter serves as a recorso or waiting period for another cycle to begin. Its balanced structure might be capsulized as:

Poem
Narrator's Introduction
Johnny's Speech
Mark's Speech
Luke's Speech
Matt's Speech
Narrator's Conclusion
Poem.

On its surface level the chapter has no narrational tie to the plot or to the characters of *Finnegans Wake*, as the omnipotent narrator retells a bit of mythic history. As well as having Bedier and Richard Wagner in mind here, it is interesting to wonder, as does Herbert Howarth,[1] whether Joyce might not have been responding in part to a challenge voiced by T. Sturge Moore in his essay on the uses of the Tristan and Isolde story in modern literature. There Moore states that: "However highly we laud the modesty of those who refuse to measure their work beside acknowledged masterpieces, behind such talk there glows some perception of the courage and logical soundness of those who dare."[2] One might be fairly sure that had Joyce read these words, as he quite probably did, he would not have been at all abashed. He was certainly not one to worry overmuch about the competition of his predecessors or contemporaries, having already redone the work of Homer in 1922.

Joyce composed first drafts of the two sections "Tristan and Isolde" and "Mamaluju" which were to become this chapter in 1923, his beginning of the construction of *Finnegans Wake*. As he wrote to Miss Weaver on October 9th of that year: "I work as much as I can because these are not fragments but active elements and when they are more and a little older they will begin to fuse of themselves".[3] This fusion was formally to take place in 1938, the result being the integrated chapter which we have today.

Like many of the other sections of *Finnegans Wake*, the chapter is basically dramatic in its presentation, and allusions abound to the works of Dion Boucicault and Shakespeare. The Four are in many ways like the audience at a play: "listening in, as hard as they could" (383.23), or a Greek chorus, while the poems which begin and end the section may serve as prologue and epilogue. Never privy to the thoughts or feelings of Tristan and Isolde, we as readers must view them as characters on a stage, listening instead to the observations of Mamalujo, another part of the audience. Thus we receive a second-hand account of what goes on. We are treated to "the gratifying experiences of highly continental evenements" (398.13), but we are consistently distanced from the action. This stage, however, rather than being the conventional room with one wall removed, is instead the deck of the ship which carries Isolde to Mark, her betrothed. And, as the physical encounter of the two lovers unfolds, there is occasionally a voyeuristic element to the situation which is heightened by the presence of the Four Old Men. Though, as was said, the Four appear as seagulls and waves in the sea, strangely enough it often seems that they are not always overtly interested in the romantic proceedings. Though Luke may emerge with "his kingly leer" (398.22), for the most part Mamalujo are relatively uninvolved in the shipboard drama, and would rather think about their own times gone by: "in the good old bygone days of Dion Boucicault, the elder, in Arrah-na-pogue" (385.2). They will prove more attentive in the bedroom of the Earwickers.

Since the chapter ends with: "So, to john for a john, johnajeams, led it be!" (399.34), we might be reminded of Hamlet, who calls himself: "A dull and muddy-mettled rascal, peak,/ Like John-a-dreams" (III,i, 594). Like Hamlet's play "The Mousetrap," it is possible to see the Tristan and Isolde action as a play within a play, a miniature drama which is meant to aid in the elucidation of the themes of the larger. In the speech mentioned above, the Dane says: "Hum, I have heard/ That guilty creatures sitting at a play/ Have by the very cunning of the scene/ Been struck so to the soul that presently/ They have proclaimed their malefactions." Yet, ironically enough, the Four remain unmoved, though their malefactions are more insensitivity and meddling than murder, but again we are reminded of the downfall of a kingly father. Since the play of Tristan and Isolde does not catch the conscience of Mamalujo, it seems quite probable that it is meant to work upon the feelings of the reader. Hamlet has just commented on the feigned or assumed passion of the players, and certainly the reader is intended to see that the lovemaking is but another mock-up. Rather than commenting on the myth itself, the interlude points instead to the tawdry and brazen nature of love in the contemporary world. Hamlet's player is "in a fiction, in a dream of passion," as are Tristan and Isolde, and so, by implication, are the citizens of this new age.

On another level the chapter functions as the presentation of a conflict in which youth supplants age. Following naturally from the previous section in which HCE has drunk the dregs of the pints left in his pub and collapsed: "our wineman from Barleyhome he just slumped to throne" (382.25), the interlude implies that the father is past his prime and must give way to the younger generation. The Four undoubtably serve as a surrogate HCE here, are consistently described as old, and they too are passing out, moving from: "now pass the fish for Christ sake, Amen" (385.15) to: "pass the teeth for choke sake, Amensch" (397.22). And this is perhaps why the chapter is followed by the four watches of Shaun, scion of a new age. King Mark of Cornwall is replaced by the virile Tristan; as Johnny describes it: "Where the old conk cruised now croons the yunk. Exeunc throw a darras Kram of Llawnroc" (387.36). Isolde serves as a surrogate Issy, the Earwicker daughter herself perhaps having usurped her mother's role since Anna Livia is not present, and typically the girl seems concerned with little more than her appearance. She may be an Irish princess, but she certainly lacks the charm and grace of her mythic counterpart: "a strapping modern old ancient Irish prisscess, so and so hands high, such and such paddock weight, in her madapolam smock, nothing under her hat but red hair and solid ivory . . . and a firstclass pair of bedroom eyes, of most unhomy blue" (396.7). Described as a mare prepared for breeding, she is fit and ready for a revel in purely physical sensuality, the physical experience of adulthood. Isolde is no doubt, in her description here, somewhat reminiscent of the lusty Queen Maeve of Celtic mythology, and the two will require no love potion to stimulate their encounter.

Tristan is a matching, mindless mythic companion for his Isolde: "the hero, of Gaelic champion, the onliest one of her choice, her bleaueyedeal of a girl's friend, neither bigugly nor smallnice, meaning pretty much everything to her then" (384.23). He is compared, among others, to Roland, Oisin, Galahad, and Gawaine, and the epic description should certainly recall Finn MacCool. As well, he probably embodies within himself a combination of Shem and Shaun. Much as the twins came together in the Burrus and Caseous fable to accomplish the seduction of Margareena and as they united as Buckley to assassinate the Russian General, they are here metamorphosed into a single individual. Tristan's "sinister dexterity, light and rufthandling . . . fore and aft, on and offsides" (384.26) would seem to point to such a Brunoian fusion of opposites. The sons assume possession of the daughter by natural right, and momentarily at least they are free from the threat of parental intrusion. In contrast to the Dave the Dancekerl episode, where the twins were at odds over the possession of the female, this hazy, dreamlike setting provides them a moment of success. As is perhaps fitting in a recorso, the way now appears prepared for the dawning of a new age of youth.

It might be noted also that the lovemaking here described is in direct contrast and thematic parallel to that of Earwicker and Anna Livia Plurabelle in III,iv. The sexual involvement of the elders is presented as flawed and incomplete: "Withdraw your member! Closure. This chamber stand abjourned. . . . Humbo, lock your kekkle up! Anny, blow your wickle out! Tuck away the tablesheet! You never wet the tea!" (585.26). The Earwickers must return to sleep unfulfilled, as dawn slowly breaks over Chapelizod. Yet, in Joyce's comically graphic description Tristan proves himself the true knight which Isolde expected him to be: "they [Mamalujo] could hear like of a lisp lapsing, that was her true knight of the truths thong plipping out of her chapellledeosy, after where he had gone and polped the questioned. Plop" (396.30). There seems little doubt that something of importance has happened.

In further parallel, HCE's symbolic defeat as Jarl von Hoother at the hands of the Prankquean is recalled by these "parkside pranks of quality queens" (394.27), though here the situation is reversed as Tristan triumphs: "the lad on a poot of porage handshut his duckhouse" (395.28). (The father's humiliation as the Willingdone in the Museyroom may also be alluded to as Tristan is exhorted during the lovemaking: "And now, upright and add them!" [396.4]). Humphrey and Anna Livia, past their prime, have no choice but to give way to the young who are capable of passion, if nothing else, and this is a fact which Anna Livia will contemplate bitterly in the final chapter of the novel. For better or for worse, one generation has pushed to the fore over another, and the young must come face to face with the same reality which badgered and beguiled their parents. In an objective, amoral, Viconian universe, one must contemplate events rather than rueing them.

Joseph Bedier's account of the Tristan and Isolde story is charming, graceful, and perhaps a little sentimental, and it is just this last characteristic which Joyce often plays with. As well as beginning and ending the chapter with poetry, snatches of quasi-Tin Pan Alley lovesongs are sprinkled throughout the text: "in the fair fine night, whilst the stars shine bright, by she light of he moon, we longed to be spoon, before her honeyold loom" (385.27). In parodic verse, Isolde is seen as: "Fulfest withim inbrace behent. As gent would deem oncontinent" (388.4), and Johnny implores: "O weep for the hower when eve aleaves bower" (389.20). The scene had been set initially by: "All the birds of the sea they trolled out rightbold when they smacked the big kuss of Trustan with Usolde" (383.17). In many ways this is an ironic, modern redoing of mythic love, stripped of its pretension and utopian unreality, though the satire cuts mainly at the somewhat ignoble behavior of our contemporary lovers. This is not to say that the parody is heavyhanded or weightily moralistic, since the keynote of this chapter is its humor, yet Joyce chooses to substitute the farcical for the romantic. Summed up, from a reversed perspective: "Wehpen, luftcat revol, fairescapading in his natsirt. Tuesy tumbles" (388.3).

Though the narrator, with tongue in cheek, reminds us occasionally of the high seriousness of all this, a reader probably remembers more readily the maudlin strains of "Auld Lang Syne," ironically pertinent for a new year, which Mamalujo sing throughout. Another important effect of such lyrical doggerel is again its distancing, since we are not really supposed to take this whole thing all that seriously. The threat of Mark is virtually nonexistent. The unfolding of historical and archetypal cycles places all actions upon the same level for the most part, soon stripping them of melodrama or cosmic significance. Our emotions in reaction to the goings-on become as artificialized as the story itself. In order to see clearly one must strip the cobwebs of sentimentality from one's eyes, and this is just what this comic coupling accomplishes.

Despite the presence of Tristan and Isolde, however, the core of the chapter is the four dialogues of Mamalujo. As was mentioned, they seem little interested in the lovemaking itself, and instead, like the Four Masters, they attempt to recover the historical truth of the past. For the most part their musings are rambling and disconnected, as, for example, Johnny mixes memories of nineteenth century Dublin with "how our seaborn isle came into exestuance" (387.12) and "the official landing of Lady Jales Casemate, in the year of the flood 1132 S.O.S." (387.22). The reminiscences of the Four are spotty and sketchy and jump irrationally from disconnected point to point—essentially they tell the same meaningless story over again four times with variations. Just as Giambattista Vico in the *New Science* dates modern history from Noah's Flood, the Four, as befits old seadogs, seem to specialize in memories of floods and sea battles: Johnny's "the drowning of Pharoah and all his pedestrians" (387.26); Mark's "the Flemish armada, all scattered, and all officially drowned" (388.10); Luke's "poor Dion Cassius Poosycomb, all drowned too" (391.23); Matt's "tyred as they were, at their windswidths in the waveslength" (394.16). Typically for the Four, they never extend their symbology into baptism or resurrection. Never sure of their facts or their timespans, they argue and interrupt each other continually, and, significantly perhaps, this is one of the few places in the *Wake* where they speak in a confused order: John, Mark, Luke, Matt.

One of the salient characteristics of these dialogues is that, not only are they confused and confusing, they are not really even very interesting. It is no accident that the act of recapturing memory in each of the four speeches is described as "remembore," with the emphasis on the final syllable. Just as myth has become sordid, history has become garrulous. And here certainly one begins to see an underlying thematic function of this chapter: the interplay and relationship between history and myth. We might have noted throughout *Finnegans Wake* that history is of little help in understanding the past, for the more we learn of the conjectured backgrounds of Earwicker and Anna Livia and of the former's sin in Phoenix Park the more we remain at sea. History remains inseparable from humorous story, rumor, and malicious gossip.

In their roles as historians, Mamalujo state confidently: "that now was how it was" (387.32), but certainty was long ago lost in the mists of their imagined facts. History is reduced by them to: "the past and present . . . and present and absent and past and present and perfect *arma virumque romano*" (389.17), for, as Joyce stated earlier in *Ulysses*, primarily through Stephen Dedalus, it is all too easy to interpret history to suit the historian. Repeating, repeating, history repeats itself to no purpose, for we have lost our comprehension of it. History, as Vico said, used to be myth, but it is so no longer, and myth is no longer history. Everything has been reduced to a story which might be told over the bar in a pub, perhaps reduced to a tale told by four idiots which signifies, in itself, nothing. The Four are as untrustworthy as any other historians, since actually they sentimentalize and glorify their pasts. There is no objectivity to their "dear prehistoric scenes" (385.18), their "dear byword days" (390.20), their "dreams of yore" (393.36)—a long series of events which Mark platitudinously sums up as: "the good go and the wicked is left over" (390.29).

If we were not convinced of these things ourselves, the narrator takes it upon himself to set things straight in his final and concluding statement. In contrast to their supposed assurance of their facts, he says that: "they used to be so forgetful, counting motherpeributts (up one up four) to membore her beaufu mouldern maiden name" (396.35). He seems solicitous of the Four, albeit somewhat condescending to their quasi-senility, but he does decide that this is: "like another tellmastory repeating yourself" (397.7), that we are "all repeating ourselves, in medios loquos" (398.8). Obviously Mamalujo are not to be trusted, not to be taken seriously, and they are finally reduced to something of a ragtime band, Irish style: "The Lambeg drum, the Lombog reed, the Lumbag fiferer, the Limibig brazenaze" (398.29). Ironically enough, they bray about love and romance as Tristan labors upon Isolde, and thus they substitute their own imaginative created reality for what really exists. If they do nothing else, they serve to underline further the point that history is a mismarked yardstick for measuring human experience. This chapter is not HCE's dream—nor is it anyone's dream—it is a vignette presented by the narrator to elucidate further some of Joyce's speculations on myth and history.

As early as his first essay on James Clarence Mangan (1902), Joyce had realized that: "history or the denial of reality, for they are two names for one thing, may be said to be that which deceives the whole world." Time and memory are the keys to both history and myth, but it is the difference between historical and mythical time which causes the problem for Western civilization. The modern world has opted for scientific, historical, empirical time, and is thus locked in to a basically linear conception of experience. This position is Christian as well, recording history from the Creation or the Garden of Eden, and looking forward to the Last Judgement. Though Christ is a momentary pause in this linear thrust, and His sacrifice is ritually recelebrated in the Mass, the basic perspective is forward looking rather than backward.

Mythic time, in contrast to this is cyclic, and continually returns to its beginnings. It is concerned much more with how we have arrived at where we are than with where we are going. Mythic time, in Joyce's view, does not posit a cessation to being—this is usually just not considered—and thus mythic time is affirmative and optimistic, in human terms, in opposition to Christian history which is awaiting man's destruction. On this level the past becomes an integral part of the present, for it is always a part of man's consciousness, and thus an effort of memory is not required to return to the beginning.

Obviously Mamalujo are historians, not mythographers, and they have had little practice in recapturing the past. They record long gone events, mixed up and mismatched, rather than recognizing archetypal patterns, and this is the reason for their faulty memories. They are not at all schooled in the backward look, so that their results are faulty and even self-gratifying. They deceive themselves by substituting historical reality for mythic reality.

Following Vico, then, we might turn to myth and fable as true accounts of universal history, expressing within themselves the consciousness of a race. But here also we are to by stymied, for myth in contemporary civilization has lost its potency and ability to illuminate. In his rendering of the Tristan and Isolde story, Joyce points out that myth has come to be treated as either a lie or a joke, that stories from the past can no longer help to explain the present, especially when they are distorted in ways such as this. Such tales at best may entertain, but they are: "all puddled and mythified, the way the wind wheeled the schooler round" (393.32). When Joyce in the *Wake* makes use of Finn MacCool, he rejects the folkloric retellings of Yeats, Lady Gregory, and the Celtic Renaissance, and instead revitalizes the mythic figure by making him an integral part of the present. But the simple resurrection of bygone times and heroes, as here in this chapter, will not do, since myth must spring from the innermost consciousness. Ultimately this retold romance is a sham, a poor joke which reveals the barrenness of contemporary tradition and perhaps looks forward to a new.

Mamalujo's song or poem at the end of the chapter inadvertently points this out most clearly, since Isolde the Beautiful becomes "*Lizzy my love*" (300.11). The poem is an ode to the Irish princess, but the Four have converted her to modernity with a vengeance, much in the way that the narrator's version had done. Lizzy's encounter with love takes place following her ironing on a Friday evening, and she handles the fact of her lover's anonymity with perfect aplomb: "*By the cross of Cong, says she, rising up Saturday in the twilight from under me, Mick, Nick the Maggot or whatever your name is, you're the most likable lad that's come my ways yet from the barony of Bohermore*" (399.25). The reader's only possible reaction can be that of the narrator—snorts of laughter—and all seriousness, tenderness, or mythic significance has been once and for all destroyed. Much as, in the opening poem, King Mark is jeered as: "*the rummest old rooster ever flopped out of a Noah's ark*": (383.9), and Tristan is reduced to: "*Tristy's the spry young spark*" (383.11), the whole affair now seems almost the subject of a bawdy music-hall comedy.

Thus, as well as signifying the overthrow of a father-figure and the death of an old order, the chapter documents the end of the usefulness of a method. If the old myths have no relevant value, it is time to look elsewhere, to recognize the myths of today which may grant insight into the present and the future: "for the seek of Senders Newslaters and the massacre of Saint Brices, to forget the past" (389.36). Book II has been called the Book of the Children, but it is certainly an inconclusive one, since the youngsters posit no viable answers to the questions posed by their parents. Ultimately, the chapter is no end point or solution, and we must go on. It documents a societal process—the succession of one generation by another—but it describes no true physical or spiritual regeneration, and we must wait for the Anna Livia of Book IV.[4]

Notes

1. *Notes on Some Figures Behind T. S. Eliot* (Boston: Houghton Mifflin, 1964).
2. *The Criterion* 1922–1939, I, Ed. T. S. Eliot (London: Faber and Faber, 1967).
3. *Letters,* I, p. 204.
4. A helpful study of this chapter is David Hayman's "Tristan and Isolde in *Finnegans Wake*: A Study of the Sources and Evolution of a Theme," *Comparative Literature Studies,* I, 2 (1964), 93–112.

10

Shaun A

Book III
chapter i

James S. Atherton

The first two chapters of Book III were continuous in the early versions. Even when this is remembered it does not seem helpful to quote Joyce's description of the passage to Miss Weaver: it is "a description of a postman travelling backwards in the night through the events already narrated. It is written in the form of a *via crucis* of 14 stations but in reality it is only a barrel rolling down the river Liffey." But reality in *Finnegans Wake* is merely the name of one of a large number of levels, and for the moment it is more helpful to concern oneself with the reality presented by the words on the pages before us. So let us turn to page 403 and consider what signs are afforded, as Stephen Dedalus advises, interpret the work "by the signs which the artist affords."[1]

A clock is striking midnight while an indefinite number of people count its strokes in various languages. "Tolv two elf kater ten . . . sax." 12, 2, 11, 10, 6—in Danish, English, Dutch, Gaelic, English, Swedish. Then "Hork"—"Listen" in German—followed by more counting in various languages, including Welsh this time. Surely we are being told that a number of people, of varying nationality, are listening to the clock. My own interpretation, with which many would disagree, is that this and the rest of *Finnegans Wake* is being dreamt—or observed—by what Yeats called in "The Tower," "the Great Memory," a phrase he used earlier in his essay on "The Philosophy of Shelley's Poetry": "the Great Memory is also a dwelling-house of symbols, of images that are living souls."[2] As Joyce knew, the concept is extremely old. It is first mentioned, perhaps, in the 10th chapter of the *Book of the Dead* where "the deceased . . . is taken in charge by the great Khu-soul of the Other World and to be identified with him. He was thereby enabled to cleave the horizon and the heavens and pass through the earth."[3] Many other sources for this idea could be cited, Jung's "Collective Unconscious" for example. But I will leave it now and continue my examination of "the words on the page."

The numbers seem to be spelled so as to avoid the ambiguity which Joyce seems to seek in the rest of this chapter, and usually elsewhere in *Finnegans Wake*. Presumably "pimp" or "pump" and "sex"—more conventional spellings for the numbers—would bring in unwanted overtones. Only "kater," a phonetic version of the Gaelic *ceathair*, produces in German a tom-cat and a hangover, both perhaps allowable at this hour. Then comes an undistorted English sentence. "And low stole o'er the stillness the heartbeats of sleep." It is not a quotation, but the line is a hexameter with a classical form suggesting that another organizing intelligence is presenting, or commenting on, the scene.

So far the experience has been purely auditory; now it becomes visual. A "fogbow" encircles the vision, a colorless rainbow to symbolise synthesis, or perhaps failure to analyze. The night-scene is "wobiling" (403.10) before us with many diverse and seemingly irreconcilable elements. In the "arch embattled" which serves as frame or proscenium arch, are we to see warring figures or has it a crenellated upper surface? Or both? And is there a reference to the rainbow promising peace? More questions arise than can be stated, let alone answered. It is difficult to distinguish the figures in the silvery sylvan scene; is it a gorse-cone or a Gascon? The savage male figure who seems to be *recubans sub tegmine fagi*, "resting beneath the beech tree's shade" like Tityrus in the line that begins and ends Virgil's *Eclogues* and is so well-known as to be the archetypal tag to evoke the atmosphere of pastoral peace. Virgil's name might have been expected in the context as a typical Joycean "key" but instead it is Publicus Ovidius Naso, whose *Metamorphoses* seems appropriate to the shifting scene who is named to be rejected, "nought like the nasoes." Perhaps we are being told that it is Virgil who, according to Macrobius in his *Saturnalia*, from which Joyce took the names of his four "watches of the night,"[4] was "of rustic parentage and brought up in the brush,"[5] whereas Ovid was city bred. The resting figure has a big nose and an erect phallus ("hornhide" 403.14), as well as a thick skin. The female, "his Anastashie" is Byzantine, Russian or Dutch/German, with her "aal [Heel or Dutch/German for "eel"] in her dhove's suckling," unexpectedly but appropriately bringing in *Midsummer's Night's Dream* and Bottom roaring "like any sucking dove." The serpent and dove symbol is obvious, but the dove is also the Gaelic *dubh*, "black" which reverses the symbol's meaning. All critics have agreed that the couple are HCE and ALP. Fritz Senn has suggested that the reference to Rembrandt ("Remembrandts" 403.10) alludes to Joyce's experience of watching hundreds of Dutch people "eating silvery raw herrings by moonlight,"[6] but there is fire (*brandt*) here as well. All the images slip away like fish in a stream.

The paragraph ends with a series of exclamations: "Apagemonite!" which must refer to the "Agapomene" established by H. J. Prince and briefly notorious before the first World War. One of the surprises of Frank Budgen's *Myselves When Young* was that it influenced his own boyhood,[7] and he is likely to have mentioned it to Joyce. Perhaps we are being told that we have started on the wrong topic. Are we perhaps continuing with the parents when we should have proceeded to the son? "Black!" could say that it was evil; that we should obliterate it; and it also evokes a theatrical ambience which is supported by "Switch out!" and is carried on throughout the next three pages.

All this, except the opening striking of the clock, was added four years after the bulk of the chapter had been drafted. It forms a shimmering, shifting, moonlit prelude before we hear voices announcing the arrival of Shaun. The two washerwomen have left some "garments of laundry" behind. On the literal level it is the Liffey near Chapelizod and upon the surface of the water some objects are drifting. One of these is the empty Guinness barrel which the dreamers envisage as Shaun.

On the family history level this is the uncreative but seemingly highly moral brother, always at-outs with Shem the Penman, who has already appeared at several points in the story. Now, beginning at "some glistery gleam" (403.36)—a phrase that has survived with only one letter altered ("glittery" to "glistery") from the first version—the light grows brighter, voices cry "Shaun! Shaun! Post the post!" Gradually we are shown the figure of a character from Dion Boucicault's play *Arrah-na-Pogue*. This play has already been used at some length as typifying "the dear prehistoric scenes" (385.08) "in the good old bygone days of Dion Boucicault the elder" (385.02) which are in *Finnegans Wake* chronology identical with those of "Twotongue Common" (385.04) or Tutankhamun. Joyce's attitude to Boucicault is ambivalent. He is an old-fashioned playwright whose works were revived annually in Dublin in Joyce's youth; he is one link in that chain of brilliant Irish dramatists that runs from Sheridan to Shaw.

Shaun, "Whom we dreamt was a shaddo," (404.13) is basically a stage-Irish "jarvey jaunty" (407.06), a comic driver with a whip in his hand, wearing the traditional costume for the part and with a lamp hanging from his belt. The smattering of theatrical jargon, "hand prop" and "prompt side" (404.16) indicates this aspect of his character. The scraps of songs are heard because Shaun in the play sings "The Wearing of the Green" (408.30; 411.25, etc.), "Open the Door Softly" (427.05) and scraps of popular Irish songs were often added to the part by the various singers who played it. Some of the song references are oddly distorted. "The Rose of Tralee," for example, becomes "the lees of Traroe" (405.19). Joyce's language reproduces the confusion of a dream shared by many sleepers of an object rippling like the waters. There may seem, in linguistic terms, to be more noise than signal, but in fact it is all signal. Words suggesting animals, wild things and sea creatures are interwoven with words suggesting food and words evoking the theatre. "Mereswin" (404.19) is Old English for dolphin or porpoise (literally "sea-swine"). The word "sparable" means "with heavy studs in the soles" but is derived from "sparrow bill," alluding to the shape of the metal studs. We are looking at a kind of mosaic, a complex pattern by which the picture of Shaun is built up out of many conflicting details.

One of Joyce's favorite hunting grounds for material was the 11th edition of the *Encyclopaedia Britannica*. In the article on "Vision," under the heading "Visual Sensations are Continuous," there is the statement: "Suppose the image of a luminous line falls on the retina, it will appear as a line although it is placed on perhaps 200 rods or cones, each of which may be separately excited so as to cause a distinct sensation." The phrase "by the hundred and sixty odds rods and cones of this even's vision" (405.12) is probably referring to this. The encyclopaedia article goes on to say that the physical basis of perception is "a kind of mosaic," which is just what Joyce is here creating.

But the majority of the tesserae is Joyce's pattern have more than one significance. Even the "eatwords" that form so marked a feature are divalent. A "maltsight" (405.20) is a drink in one language and a meal (*Mahlzeit*) in another. "Kitzy Braten's" (406.09) is *Kitzenbraten*, roast goatmeat, looking like a restaurant. Shaun has "gigot" (403.31), or leg of mutton "turnups" to his trousers which go nicely with his "twentytwo carrot" seeming buttons. The non-logical aspect of his character is shown in his "beamish brow" (405.16) which connects him with the "beamish boy" who is the hero of "Jabberwocky."

But, again the word is performing a double function, for Beamish is the Christian name of the hero of *Arrah-na-Pogue*, an Irish gentleman who is the head of the sept of O'Grady. Sean the Post, in the play, is of the sept of MacCoul—one of Finn's people. His first speech in Act I begins: "There's lashings of mate inside and good liquor galore—" and ends, as he invites them all to the feast, "cead mile failte"—Gaelic for "a hundred thousand welcomes." It is this scene that underlies the opening pages of Joyce's Shaun 1, and the "hundred thousand stewed letters" (403.36) refer us to it.

All kinds of objects are arranged around the verbal picture, too many to enumerate. Shaun's playing-cards form one of the many sets of articles that serve to present his character: "clubs" (404.25), "hearts" (405.29), "spadefuls" (405.30) and "Lawzenge" (405.24) or slipped over the page to "diamond" (406.16). Each is something else as well. The spades are tools for shovelling food into Shaun's mouth; the clubs may be gold-clubs or shillelaghs; the diamonds share a word with Dublin's patron saint. Other Irish saints, surrounding saintly Shaun, are similarly used to convey plural meanings. St. Patrick as "Haggispatrick" (404.35) mutates the Greek for saint into a Scottish meat pudding, while "Huggisbrigid" suggests Shaun's amatory activities. Several tenors are brought in. Caruso, who was famous for his appetite, is a "carusal" (406.13). "Mario" (407.16) was the stage-name of Giovanni Matteo de Candia who is mentioned again as "the pincipot of Candia" (408.11). Michael Kelly, the Irish tenor who was a friend of Mozart, is mentioned in "Michaeleen Kelly" (407.16). Simms Reeves is named in "what Sim sobs todie I'll reeve tomorry" (408.21). The picture, and the identity, of the "softbodies fumiform" (413.31) is constantly changing, although it remains recognizably Shaun throughout the chapter.

We appear for a moment to be told the identity of the narrator: "I, poor ass, am but as their fourpart tinckler's donkey." (405.06) It may be, as some critics believe, that the donkey belonging to the four old men is about to cross-question Shaun. One of the objects literally present is undoubtedly the "ass them four old codgers owns" (214.33), but a close inspection of the passage before us leaves me uncertain whether this can be taken as anything but metaphor here. The donkey may be supposed to be telling this part of the story, but a few pages later we find Shaun himself seemingly addressed as the donkey: "salve a tour, ambly andy" (409..31). This is complicated by "salve a tour" which seems to say *Salvator*. It has been said that

Joyce is describing the donkey as Christ, but it seems more likely that this is Shaun who is, one must remember, performing a *via crucis*. He is also being called Handy Andy, the comic hero of the Samuel Lover novel of that name, which adds another fictional persona to the two already mentioned. It seems likely that the passing reference to *Huckleberry Finn*: "those pedestriasts Top, Sid and Hucky" refers to the chapters at Aunt Sally's when Tom was Sid and Huck was Tom. Identities are constantly changing so that it is no wonder that Shaun has difficulty trying "to isolate i from my multiple Mes" (510.12).

The way in which the voices reach us is like the way, "as softly as" (407.20), the radio signals cross the Atlantic. The allusion is to the Marconi radio communication stations set up, according to the *Encyclopaedia Britannica's* 11th edition[8] on 17th October, 1907, between Clifen (407.20), Connemara and Glace Bay, Nova Scotia. One of the difficulties in reading *Finnegans Wake* is recognizing figures of rhetoric. Here the metaphor comparing the quasi-psychic communication with radio communication can be misleading, especially as it includes the cry of an Australian bird combined with a reference to Moor Park where Swift first met Stella: "more pork" (407.19).

All these details are late additions which seem at first embroideries or ornament, but so thickly clustered around the original narrative that they mask its outline. In the first version we are told that Shaun is "simply clothed, as you perhaps see, in one of Guinness's registered barrels."[9] In the final version this does not appear till (314.08): "I am as plain as portable enveloped, inhowmuch, you will now parably receive, care of one of Mooseyeare Gooness's registered andouterthus barrels." In the early versions the barrel rolled out to sea and vanished—"spoorlessly disappaled and vaneshed" (427.06)—somewhere about Delgany, on the coast about ten miles south of the Liffey. In the final version it seems to be ending up "on the spits of Lambage Island" (410.13), presumably Lambay Island about as far north as Delgany is south. One has a feeling that the barrel is not as important as the decoration surrounding it. That the stories surrounding his passage are more important than the journey. So I will go back to the paragraph following the reference to Marconi.

Before Shaun's first speech we are given messages in two other modes: gesture and music. The gestures—"His handpalm lifted . . ." (407.23) and so on—are probably taken from a diagram in Bell's *Standard Elocutionist*, a book in Joyce's "working library."[10] This shows fourteen positions of the hands to be used by elocutionists as they recite. The ones Joyce chooses for Shaun mean, according to Bell, negation, affirmation, cautioning, supplication, violent repulsion and, finally, apathy or prostration. The total impression being that Shaun is going insincerely through a series of mechanical mimings. The music that follows gives the same impression, for Shaun simply sings the names of the notes of an octave in sol-fa: "Does she lag soft fall" (407.27), which is Do-si-la-so-fa-me-re-do. Unlike the passage analyzed by Jack Dalton,[11] this conveys no message except that Shaun is showing his paces. The later example of solemnization repeated, as Dalton pointed out, the letters HCE. They do occur in this passage, disguised as "has-say-ugh" (407.30), as part of Shaun's complaints about his father and things in general, including the food such as yesterday's hash and the day before's pigeon-pie, and Tuesday's champagne. Three of the phrases complain about the lack of success that the theatrical performance is having: "the rag was up" is actor's slang for the last-performance notices having been posted outside; "a houseful of deadheads" adds that none of the present audience have paid to come in, which is repeated by the word "billpasses" which means bearers of complimentary tickets. Shaun moistens his teeth and sits down to rest. The phrase "weight of his iosals" (408.06) includes, in its last word, *Iosa,* the Gaelic name for Jesus, and *iseal,* the Gaelic for "lowly," as well as, probably, the old English word *jossa* or *iossa,* meaning "down there." The phrase conceals the third station of the Cross, "Jesus falls the First Time." The second station, as several critics have already pointed out,[12] is at "My heaviest crux," and is "Jesus receives His Cross." The first station is named in "it was condemned on me" (409.34), which is "Jesus is Condemned to Death." The postman Shaun/Christ is, as Joyce said, "going backwards through the events," but it is with "his highly curious mode of slipashod motion" (426.35).

But "while me and yous and them we're extending after us the pattern of reposiveness" (408.14), while we are all asleep and re-creating a copy of archetypal dream, Shaun wishes that it had been his brother who had been sent on this journey. "It should have been my other with his leickname," however, suggests that Shem is a corpse (*Leichnam*). They were friends, he says, "we lofobsed os so ker" (408.19), in which "lofobs" is Volapuk for "we loved," and *os saa kær* is Danish for "us so dear."[13] Scraps from a dozen songs are sung; two recognizable places are named: Badeniveagh and John's Lane. Both are connected with drinks for the first is one of the great houses of the Guinness family and the second is the address and original site of Powers Distillery. The whiskey is followed by an Irish toast, *Slainte,* mutated to include the Sanscrit *Shantih* quoted in Eliot's *Waste Land.*

In the first version Shaun simply said that he was unworthy to carry the letter. The additional material, occupying roughly thirty times as much space as the original, seems mainly to add other personalities to Shaun's, but Shaun's remarks seem to say that there is only one extra person, "that other of mine." (408.25). Shaun includes all the tenors, and writers such as T. S. Eliot and Wyndham Lewis and Ezra Pound; the other is the group composing Shem.

It is a third group, represented by the Donkey who now cross-question Shaun. There are fourteen questions, perhaps to match the fourteen stations of the *via crucis*. Shaun's answers vary greatly in length.

1. Who gave you the permit?

Shaun replies that he had it from St. Colum-Cille's Prophecies. The work in question is a poem in Gaelic suposedly addressed by the saint to St. Brendan. It begins:

> The time shall come, O Brendan,
> When you would feel it painful to reside in Erin;
> The sons of kings shall be few in number,
> And men of letters shall be deprived of dignity.

It goes on to predict a time when everything will decay in Ireland, particularly the "men of letters" for "The descendants of the sages shall become ignorant;/They will be continually sneering at each other."[14] The editions of this so-called "Prophecy" usually include another spurious book, the "Prophecies of Malachy," which Joyce used both in *Finnegans Wake* and *Dubliners*. The reference to "beliek" (409.24) is probably naming Belleek, a small town in Northern Ireland famous for the delicate porcelain it produces. The "How are you to-day, my dark sir?" motif which is repeated in many languages throughout *Finnegans Wake* is given here in Italian: "Comb his tar odd gee sing your mower O meeow?" (409.14) *Come sta oggi, signor moro mio?* No doubt it is addressed to one of the tenors. Shaun says good-bye.

2. Salvator, Ambly Andy, you might be so by order.

Here Shaun seems to be addressed as combining the identities of Christ, the Donkey, and Handy Andy, the comic-hero of a novel by Samuel Lover about a wild Irish boy who turns out to be heir to a fortune and a title. Shaun replies that the instruction was given to him by the Gospels. The Eusebian Canons to which he refers are transcribed at the beginning of the *Book of Kells*. They are lists of parallel passages in the four gospels drawn up by Eusebius of Caesarea about the year 320. In the Studio Edition *Book of Kells* that Joyce gave to Miss Weaver, Plate I is a reproduction of a page of these Canons. They are ornamented with four evangelical symbols, Man/Angel, Calf, Lion and Eagle. The decoration on their wings has a resemblance to that on various wings in Ancient Egyptian art. It is only a vague resemblance, but I think that Joyce had noticed it, although the cyclic theory of history he adopts makes such a link unnecessary as he passes in the same sentence from the Eusebian Canons to the "book of breedings" (410.01).

The "Book of Breathings" is the title of a recension of the *Book of the Dead* written during the Graeco-Roman period and published in English translation, in the third volume of Budge's edition, in the "Books on Egypt and Chaldea" series published by Kegan Paul and E. P. Dutton. In my *Books at the Wake* I suggested a variety of sources for Joyce's knowledge of the *Book of the Dead,* but the late Frank Budgen assured me that Joyce at one time owned the three-volume translation by Budge and he had seen him studying it. By means of reading the "Book of Breathings" the deceased becomes "Osiris triumphant" to add a further one to his "multiple mes" (410.12). He is finding himself, he says, "like them nameless souls" (410.08). These, I suppose, are the souls mentioned in Dante's *Inferno,* Canto VII, 11.52–66, whose "life, which made them sordid, now makes them too obscure for all recognition." Yet they seem to be treated, not as condemned to struggle in one place, but to be like the souls in the fifth Canto which Joyce is recorded as reciting occasionally, the Carnal Sinners who circulate Hell endlessly "as the Cranes go chanting their lays"—"*come i gru van cantando for lai.*" But Shaun is, he says, "hopelessly off course."

3. We hear you will bear this letter. Speak to us.
I have the power—to speak
4. Where mostly do you work?

"Here! Shaun replied" (410.31). But he goes on to refer to Ancient Egyptian gods, Mark Twain's characters and the Czech national anthem, *Kde domov muj,* "Where is my home" ("Hek domov muy,"—411.18), and begins to recite the Lord's Prayer in Dutch. This is interspersed with various references to walking, one of which, "one housesleep there," etc. (411.06) is in the Melanesian pidgen that seems to follow references to *Huckleberry Finn* with as complete regularity as any feature of *Finnegans Wake*.

5. You are "tarabred" (411.22)

This says that Shaun is an Irish poet or perhaps royal person (Bred in Tara), or in Dutch that he is wheaten bread. The questioners go on to say that Shaun has painted the town green. Shaun's answer contains half-a-dozen snatches of song as he admits that they are right and says they made a "freudful mistake" (411.35).

6. They say that his songs smell sweet as honey but what is he trying to squeeze out of them?

The Latin travesties the Vulgate version of Psalm 80, line 4, which is A.V. *Ps.* 81, 1.3: "Blow up the trumpet in the new moon, in the time appointed, on our solemn feastday." They seem to be telling him to blow his own trumpet in Emania, which was the ancient royal palace of Ulster. But, O fair-haired boy (Gaelic: *a phaistin fionn*), what are you trying to take from us? The Bridge of Belleek could refer to the Ulster/Free-State Border; "Kisslemerched" (412.10) conceals a reference to "The Castle," the Irish term for the English government of Ireland; "*volumnitatis*" (412.09), which looks like veluminousness, could mean a velum or soft palate, a cellum scroll, a snake's coils. Whatever they said, they annoy Shaun. Perhaps the key to the passage is that Belcanto was one of the names that Wyndham Lewis used for Joyce in *Time and Western Man*. One meaning of "verdure" is taste, savour. If it vanished, or were like varnish, our wine might well be "verjuice" (412.17).

Shaun's reply with its Dublin "confoundyous" includes the information that he cannot read the letter which is "too much privet stationery and safety quipu" (412.28). It is private stationery which the tree names suggest is in Gaelic, the letters of which are named after trees, or in Quipu, the knot-writing of the Incas which nobody can read at all. Te quipu provides a Peruvian detail to allow Joyce to "Survey mankind from China to Peru" in the chapter. The Chinese details come later. The goats have been at it, Shaun says. It is *Colpa di Becco*, the sin of a Spanish he-goat, a fine game (*buona partits*), good appetite to them (*bon appetit*), but the goat is a scape-goat (Dutch: *zondebok*; German *Sundenbock*), being, in fact, the mascot of the Welsh Fusiliers, a regiment which really has a goat as its mascot. From the earliest versions we have it that the goats got into the post office, and that Shaun intends to write a book but his publishers, "Nolaner and Browno," seem to have opened a public-house and their *Nihil obstat* has become "Hopstout," although it is not clear whether they have sold out or are pricing it at five cents, one "Nickil" (412.36).

A letter is then commenced with a formal Latin-style opening. Perhaps it is Shaun's sense of decency which causes him to alter the last syllable of *Salutem dicunt* (They send greetings) to "dicint" (413.05), but he has his "i" in a queer place. The "shuft" (413.06). German: *Schuft,* scoundrel) talks about two sisters and the allusions take on a Swiftian tone. The Swift allusions are mainly from the *Journal to Stella.* Hester's legs in Joyce's spelling are also Easter eggs, "Easther's leggs" (413.08), perhaps from Swift's remark, in letter 24, that Irish ladies have legs "only to be *laid aside.*" (Swift's italics.) There is the word dean in "tottydean verbish" (413.10) as a key, and "ptpt," "Pepette," and "M.D.D.O.D." are all in the *Journal*. "Roggers" (413.25) repeats Swift's pun on "roger," the slang term in Swift's time for the penis, and the name of his clerk Roger. The letter was written by multiple deceased personalities, by "P.L.M." (413.14), "poor late Mrs" (413.12), which copies Swift's trick with initals in M.D. and so on. The author of the document is called Sanders or Shunders or von Anderssen—all mainly meaning simply the writer of the letter, presumably the one from Boston, Mass, which is also *Finnegans Wake* itself.

But Swift's entry into the passage seems to be part of a different *Finnegans Wake* phenomenon, the quasi-spiritualistic seance in which various voices compete for hearing in the stream of *Finnegan Wakes* narrative and dialogue. The voice of Swift comes in at first in single words and takes over completely at the end of Shaun's reply.

7. The interlocutors seize immediately on the identity of the new speaker. The dean is "cadenus" (413.27) and he is combined, tethered, with the goats and the women, who now are two in number. "Biggerstiff!" (413.29) tells us that the author of the Bickerstaff pamphlets and Shaun are both speaking. They ask him to tell the story of his cloudlike identity ("fumiform" 413.31). Let us pray replies Shaun, with a cheer there is none. The voice still is partly Swift's as he explains that he is in a Guinness barrel who livest and reignest with you, but manages to combine the Latin *Qui tecum vivit et regnat* with a suggestion of the *Accipite et bibite* ("Take ye and drink") of the Consecration. He is Christ as well as Swift.

8. So be it, they say—or Soviet. Sing us a song. Have Dutch Courage. (*Moed,* pronounced mood, is Dutch for courage.)

I would rather spin you a tale, replies Shaun, coughing a hundred-letter word to clear his throat. The word includes the German, English, Latin, Portuguese (or Italian) for "cough," then a couple of damns, then Gaelic, Chinese (cough and spit, this time), French, a language I cannot identify, Russian, again all meaning "cough." The whole word sounds extraordinarily abusive, as if it were a prolonged swearword or even a divine curse, and it ends with a distorted version of "cataract"—one of the eye diseases from which Joyce himself suffered.

Shaun announces that he will tell the Fable of the Ondt (Danish, "evil") and the Gracehoper. It is based on La Fontaine's first fable, *La Cigale et la Fourmi*. An interesting account of this by Clive Hart[15] points out that the fable

> hums, buzzes and flutters throughout. Apart from the names of insects, Joyce includes, in several languages, many other terms from natural history, with a strong bias towards bees and butterflies. The constant flow of biological terminology serves something like the same mosaic function as do the river-names in "Anna Livia" and the roads in III.4, but Joyce makes it do much more besides. As insects have always been closely associated with superstition and with primitive gods, Joyce raises earwigs, beetles, and other small creatures to divine status.

Hart goes on to explain the attention paid to the scarab in Ancient Egypt, where it was named "Khepera, the creator of the gods." As Hart explains, "Shaun tells his fable to denigate Shem but, in fact, by having already characterized him as a beetle he has allotted him the majestic role of the most seminal of the gods, and he even repeats the identification with the Great Beetle at 417.04: 'not a leetle beetle.'"[16] Hart sees this identification as explaining the interspersion into the text of the host of other gods that have at some time appeared in animal or vegetable form. I would suggest that a further reason is that all these images are, in Yeat's words, "in the great memory stored," and re-appear here as fragments of that memory. Whether this is so or not, I agree completely with Hart as to "the splendidly magical atmosphere created by this rich association of gods, insects and Elysian fields."[17]

The fable is also a dispute over philosophy. Amongst those named here are Spinoza (spinooze, 414.16), Kant (akkant, 414.22), Schopenhauer (schoppinhour, 414.33), Vico (417.06), Aquinas (aquinastance . . . summa, 417.08,9), Confucius (confucion, 517.15), Aristotle (aristotaller, 417.16). Grotius (Groscious me, 415.25) is famous for his work on international law. His first precept was that neither state nor individual may attack another state or individual. The Ondt, we find, has a "windhame" (415.29); that is, he represents Wyndham Lewis, who should not have attacked Joyce. In spite of being a "weltall fellow" (German: *Weltall*, "the Cosmos"), he was too busy "making spaces on his ikey" (416.06). "Ikey" means, according to Partridge's *Dictionary of Slang*, "smartly dressed," and "conceited." Richard Ellmann points out that the description of him as "chairmanlooking" (416.05) means German, as well as "chairman" and "suggests Lewis's Prussian aspect, and the ending of the fable, with the . . . fine ironic question,"

> *Your genus its worldwide, your spacest sublime!*
> *But, Holy Saltmartin, why can't you beat time?* (419.07)

Lewis might be a classicist and cling to sharp outlines, but he could not write a book which would live in its rhythm and conquer time, as Joyce had done."[18]

In a letter to Miss Weaver, Joyce once wrote that Lewis had offered to instruct him "in the art of the Chinese."[19] It is one of the hidden jokes in the fable that Lewis, if he is to understand Joyce's riposte, must know some Chinese, for amongst the pyrotechnic display of linguistic knowledge there are several puns in Chinese that Lewis was unlikely to recognize. The Gracehoper's house is named "Tingsomingenting" (413.23 and 416.27). The repetition of this name proves that Joyce was pleased with it. On the surface it says in Danish *En ting som ingen ting*, "a thing like no thing"—which is idiomatic for "a mere nothing." But there is also the Cinese, *T'ing-so ming . . . t'ing*, "listen to what you understand . . . listen." On the one hand the reader is being told it doesn't matter, on the other that he must pay attention. It has often been pointed out that Joyce delighted in the construction of phrases that meant two opposite things. Another example is the word "zeemliangly" (415.24). It means, of course, "seemingly," or seems to, but it combines the Russian *zemlya*, "land, earth," here to be taken as "Space," with the Chinese *liang*, one of the meanings of which is "Time." Joyce has summed up his Space-Time fable in one word which employs the language of the vast spaces of Russia for one aspect and Chinese with its immense antiquity for the other. Nothing could be neater, or more astonishing.

The Gracehoper as the specialist on Time is amusingly presented in the paragraph beginning "He had eaten all the whilepaper"

162 / A Conceptual Guide to *Finnegans Wake*

(416.21). The "lustres" are periods of five years (Latin, *Lustra*), "mensas and seccles" are months and ages (Latin, *Saecula*). He ends up by eating eternity itself, but "left home at Christmas when the buttlerflies had become chrysalids, till the grillies in his head and the leivnits in his hair made him thought he had the Tossmania" (416.29). The "leivnits" combines live nits, from the insect theme, with Leibniz who theorized about "nonspatial monads." To balance this we have "grillies" which obviously refers to the German *Grille*, "cricket"—near enough for a layman to a grasshopper. But there seems something missing in the trope. Another meaning is wanted for "grillies" to balance it, and the answer is probably to be found in that book by Plutarch entitled *Gryllus* but sometimes referred to in English as *Do Animals Think?* It is an interesting fable, set in Circe's island, in which a pig attacks the stoic doctrine that animals cannot reason, and provides a nice balance for Leibnitz in Joyce's trope.

As Clive Hart points out,[20] Shem's journeys go around the earth from north to south. From "Tossmania," or Tasmania, he travels to the island of Bora-Bora, in French Polynesia, where "the Boraborayellers" (416.34) live, then goes northwards to meet the Ondt, Shaun, who travels equatorially. The Bora wind, from which Joyce suffered in Pola and Trieste, is blowing so violently that it is "blohablasting tegolhuts" (416.35). A Russian flea (*bloha*) and a Dutch tile (*tegel*) complicate the issue in which everything is blown "to tetties" (416.35), a word which combines "tatters," *tettix*, Greek for cicada, and possibly *tetu*, Hungarian for louse. When the end of the world, "ragnowrock," (416.36) seems in sight he meets the Ondt. He himself is ghost-like: "spuk. Graussssss!" In German: "ghost. Horror!"

Like the other pages of this fable, p. 517 is crowded with the names of insects in many languages. For a sample I will give the butterflies: "smetterling" (1.4, German, *schmetterling*), "motylucky" (1.10, Russian or Czech, *motylek*), "babooshkees" (1.12, Russian, *babochka*), "farfalling" (1.13, Italian, *farfalla*), "marypose" (1.28, Spanish, *mariposa*). The Ondt's harem, however, consists of four: Floh (a flea), Luse (a louse), Bieni (a bee), and Vespatilla (a wasp) with whom he is "boundlessly blissfilled" (417.27) when *sans hantisse ne chouchou* ("sans mantis ne shooshooe," 417.34), without security or sweetheart, the hapless Gracehoper appears to him. It was too much for the gravity of his champions. "Let him be Artalone the Weeps . . . I'll be Highfee the Crackasider" (418.01). "Artalone" is the solitary artist who has lost his friends (or parasites) in Paris, and the Celtic hero Art the Lone. "Highfree" is the successful artist or writer, and Aoife, the Celtic heroine who bore a child to Cuchulain. She taught Cuchulain to use the *gae bolg,* a foot-spear which filled the enemy's body with darts, and so its user could well be named "the Cracksider." The phrase describing the Gracehoper as "sans mantis ne shooshooe" (417.34), as well as being French written like much of the French in *Finnegans Wake* as English, also brings in the mantis, an insect about which there are many superstitions. In the context here it refers to a passage in the *Book of the Dead* where the triumphant spirit says, "I have come to the house of the king by means of the mantis which led me hither.[21] The "house of the king" was at *Sekhet-Hetep,* the Fields of Peace, or Heaven, which the Ondt has already told us he knows: "May he me no voida water! Seekit Hatup! May no he me tile pig shed on! Suckit Hotup!" (4.5.34). The "voida water" quotes from Budge's Introduction to the *Book of the Dead*: "he voideth water, he enjoyeth the pleasures of his love, and he is the begetter who carrieth away women from their husbands. . . ."[22] The "tile" is from the same book, in which it is said: "thou shalt draw a representation of this upon a new tile moulded from earth upon which neither a pig nor other animals have trodden."[23]

Whether Joyce knew any Ancient Egyptian is doubtful. Twenty years ago I suggested that he might,[24] but I am still not sure. "Nefersen" (415.33) means "she is beautiful" and is not in Budge's edition. "Beppy's realm" (415.33) undoubtedly comes from Budge. It refers to the Pyramid text of Pepi II in which the words "shall flourish" recur 33 times, and on the page facing it in Budge's Introduction are explanations of the nine constituent parts of a man. They include the *khu* or "spiritual soul" the *sahu* or "spiritual body which formed the habitation of the soul" and was eternal, and the *Khaibit* or "shadow."[25] Joyce uses these without much regard for their precise meanings; "sahul" (415.25), "khul on a khat" (415.32) and "ba's berial" (415.31) may be examples with the *ba,* or "heart-soul," and *ka,* or "double." But Ba is, as Budge says, one of the gods of the eleventh hour, and Beria, may be part of the Soviet contingent who accompany the Ondt. The *khaibit* seems to be used in the sense of "night" in "anygo khaibits" (570.29) in another set of allusions to the *Book of the Dead,* for these recur frequently in *Finnegans Wake.*

A possible reason for the use of Ancient Egyptian details may be the belief of some Irishmen in the Middle Ages that Ireland was peopled from Egypt. This is considered and rejected by Edmund Spenser in his *View of the Present State of Ireland* (1956) as "a verye grosse ymaginacion that the Irishe should discende from the Aegyptians which came to that Ilande first under the leading of one *Scota* the daughter of Pharao."[26] The suggestion was also mentioned, and rejected, by Richard Stanyhurst. Joyce would have been aware of it, and it may have provided another reason for including Ancient Egypt in his all-inclusive book.

Clive Hart has explained that the Ondt and Gracehoper here become the warring brothers Horus and Set of Egyptian myth.[27] The "ant-boat," which has nothing to do with the English "ant," is here by *Finnegans Wake* logic the boat of Shaun, the Ondt. It carries the sun-god Kephera, who is here Shem, and it may be—as Hart says—that Shaun is leading his brother to perdition. The Ondt is addressing the Gracehoper who, he says, "sekketh rede" (418.06). In the first place this is Chaucerian English for "seeks help or advice." It is also the Egyptian *Sekhet-Aaru*, "Field of Reeds" which is a part of *Sekhet-Hetep*, with the second word translated into English. Horus acts as steersman to the boat, he is "lord of loaves in *Amentet*," for which Joyce substitutes "Amongded," making it doubtful whether he resides in Heaven or Hell. The phrase "the fleet is spindrift" cannot be from the *Book of the Dead*, but I do not know its source, if it is not Joycean invention, nor is it clear who is speaking. *Empfange du von meiner Weisheit*, transmuted into "impfang thee of mine widehight, means "receive thee of my wisdom." "Haru!" seems to combine "Harrow!"—the cry raised after the fox in the "Nun's Priest's Tale" with Hru, the last word in the title of the *Book of the Dead*, which means "by day" or "into day," or simply "day."

The verses that follow, beginning *"He larved and he larved"* are, as Padraic Colum first pointed out, in the rhythm of Goldsmith's "Retaliation," a poem which Joyce had parodied as a schoolboy.[28] As can be seen from the opening, it is as multivalent as any part of *Finnegans Wake*. The word "larved" means laughed, lived, loved and produced larvae. Some of the insects are Welsh: *"moregruggy"* (418.19) includes *morgrug*, ants; "Gwyfyn" and "Drwebryf" are a moth and bugs.[29] *"That Accident Man"* includes amongst its meanings Wyndham Lewis of *Time and Western Man* as the Occident man. He and the Ondt are wielding their baton or *Takstock* (German). The music apparently is Smetana's "Luisa's Polka" ("Luse polkas," 418.14). "Quileone" (418.26) combines the Latin for eagle, lion and north wind, and possibly, since it is so relevant to the text, the Ancient

Egyptian word *Aqa,* "the true one." It occurs in a passage in the *Book of the Dead* concerning the Ant-Boat: "Tell me my name, saith the Rudder; Aqa is thy name. Tell me my name, saith the wind . . . The North Wind which cometh from Tem to the nostrils of Osiris is thy name."[30] Joyce is displaying his command over the history and languages of the world. It is a good-humoured rebuttal of Lewis's attack, accepting Lewis as a genius, and refuting all his criticisms. The theme is continued later in *Finnegans Wake,* and is here a continuance of earlier replies to his contemporaries.

9. How good you are in exposition! How far-flung is your folk-lore and how all-embracing your vocabulary! the questioners say, with *velk,* the Russian for "big" and Volapük, the first artificial language, the name of which means "world language," entwined in their remark. But can you read the letter, Shaun?

Shaun's answer brings in many writers, all of whom he considers, as Oscar Wilde's ghost was said to have considered *Ulysses,*[31] "Puffedly offal tosh" (419.34). Oscar Wilde himself comes in as "Oscan wild" (419.25), Lady Gregory, whose maiden name was Persse, James Clarence Mangan, who claimed that his poems were translated "from the Ottoman" or "the Coptic," from Hafiz—and when questioned explained that the poems were "half his"—are the first. A reference to Poe's "Purloined Letter" and, perhaps, to Charles Peguy ("pay Gay," 419.31), the eighteenth-century Charles Lucan's pamphlets against the Irish government of his day, and the *Times* articles on Parnell that were entitled "Crime and Libel" follow on. Lewis Carroll, who made "a cat with a peep" (420.06), is combined with HCE and Joyce's father, who both met cads with a pipe. There is a general synopsis or series of samples of *Finnegans Wake* itself including another example of the misunderstanding between nationalities that is presented in the ALP chapter with "Fieluhr? Filou!" (213.14). The new example is "Comme bien, Comme bien!" which is misheard as *Combien* and answered "Feefeel! Feefeel!" (420.13), giving Shaun's ususal salacious undertone.

Shaun then explains why he has not delivered the letter. All the addresses are wrong addresses of houses in which Joyce lived in Dublin. The list of Joyce's addresses compiled by Richard Ellmann[32] enables me to give parallel lists of these, with their dates:

"29 Hardware Saint." (420.19)   14, Fitzgibbon St., 1893–4.
"13 Fitzgibbets."   17, North Richmond St., 1895.

"12 Norse Richmound."
"92 Windsewer. Ave."
"8 Royal Terrors."
"3 Castlewoos. P.V."
"2 Milchbroke . . . Traumcondraws."
"7 Streetpetres. Since Cabranke."
"60 Shellburn."
29, Hardwick Street., 1893-4.

29, Windsor Avenue, Fairview., 1896–9.
8, Royal Terrace, 1900–1.
23, Castlewood Ave., 1884-7.
2, Milbourne Avenue, Drumcondra., 1894.
7, St. Peter's Terrace, Phibsborough, Cabra., 1904.
60, Shelbourne Road." 1904.

I have not attempted to check these addresses in any way. A less complete, but much chattier account in Patricia Hutchins' *James Joyce's Dublin*[33] gives several of the same addresses with the unimportant variation of Richmond Street North for North Richmond Street. The address 8, Royal Terrace, Fairfield, is that given in *Letters,* Vol. I, as heading Joyce's letter to Ibsen, which perhaps accounts for the phrase "Dining with the Danes" which is near it. Stanislaus Joyce's *My Brother's Keeper* tells us that "a young clergyman named Love, a long-suffering Christian . . . who . . . makes a brief appearance in *Ulysses*"[34] was their landlord at 29, Windsor Avenue. This must be connected with the "Noon sick parson" that puns on "no such person" near that address. The last address, 60, Shelbourne Road, was, so Ellmann tells us, a house in which Joyce occupied one furnished room. Presumably he had to ask for the key from the landlady or somebody else named Kate. One can only conclude that the whole passage is an extreme example of self-indulgence on Joyce's part in building up such a complex structure on experiences which his readers could not be expected to know anything about. Nevertheless it succeeds in being rather amusing even if it is in a somewhat school magazine way. Younger Joyceans may need to be told that the old pail closets in Dublin, and elsewhere, had little doors behind them by which the pails could be removed for emptying. If a door came off then indeed it was a "Closet for Repeers," or if not closed for repairs there might be some peering at rears. The reader may be left to work out Joyce's other puns. For the narrative it is important that we realize that the letter is from Boston, Mass., from a divided personality.

10. Kind Shaun, we all requested, have you not millions of times used language as bad as your celebrated brother's? The question is complicated by words such as "sinscript" (421.18), which includes Sanskrit, Chinese, and sinful writing in its connotations, and the "hesi-

tancy" of Pigott, the forger, and the final "ahem" which involved Atem, the primordial god of the Egyptians, and the earlier mentions of Lewis Carroll.[35]

Shaun replies that notorious would describe Shem better. He mentions Shelta, but does not use it, and equates Shem with Swift of the Drapier's letters and a will o' the wisp (German *Irrlicht,* "irelitz" 421.27) that suggests "compulsory Irish," a disputed subject in modern Irish education. His news from Reuters and Havas tells him that Shem is on his last . . . . But he does not explain which last.

The first version of the reply was simply: "I doubt it, Shaun replied."[36] Like the Grand Inquisitor in *The Gondoliers,* Shaun is not the character to make a simple admission of such a nature, "Of that there is no possible doubt whatever." Shem and Joyce are conflated with other writers and insulted in various ways. Richard Ellmann points out, with a reference to "his prince of the apauper's pride, blundering all over the two worlds" (422.15), that the *Two Worlds* was the title of the magazine in which Samuel Roth pirated several chapters of *Ulysses,* which is here indicated by "unique hornbook." But this is also a Unicorn book, i.e., *Alice in Wonderland* by Lewis Carroll, and the *Revue des deux mondes* which published critical articles on Joyce's work, and Mark Twain's *The Prince and the Pauper,* and a "hornbook" which shows an ABC to teach children to read. The insults are many and varied with details of description such as the dalickey cyphalos" (422.07) which says, amongst other things, dolichocephalic, "Long-head"—one of the marked differences between James and Stanislaus being that Stanislaus's skull was squarish whereas James's was the long-headed Celtic type. The long-headedness is puzzlingly on his "brach premises." There is a Czech word *brach* meaning "comrade" and a German word meaning "fallow" as an adjective or "broke" as a verb. The whole seems to tie up with the word "Homo!" (422.11) which is, of course, the Latin for man, but Shaun seems to be hinting not at Homo Sapeins but homosexual. Almost imperceptible among the insults is a mention of Joyce's creation of "the mammy far" (421.35) who combines Molly Bloom and Anna Livia.

11. Explain it?

"Well it is partly my own," (422.23) answers Shaun varying Mangan's reply about Hafiz, and so claiming to be a writer. The rest of his answer combines a derisive account of Joyce's life and the characters of *Ulysses* and *Finnegans Wake.* "Wu*c*herer" (422.36) combines HCE and Bloom (German: "usurer," Jew). The writers brought in include MacPherson, Carcilaso de Vega (whose mother was an Inca), Swift ("the decan") and Proust ("Prost"). Books include *The Royal Divorce,* the *Tale of a Tub,* the *Pilgrimage of Childe Harold,* and "Chaka a seagull" (424.10) which is *Chaika* or *The Seagull.* There are distorted quotations from *Twelfth Night,* "no more Kates and Nells" (423.21), *When We Dead Awaken,* "Digteter!" (Combining Irene's "Digter!"—"Poet!" with Dictator.),[37] Horace's *Ars Poetica, in medias res*—"in muddyass ribalds" (423.18). The "idioglossary he invented" is, says Shaun, taken by the "imitator" Shem, from him. Shem's sex even is doubtful "With the smell of old woman off him, to suck nothing of his switchedupes" (423.19). For which, "to say nothing of his transvestism—or switch to jupes," is one possible meaning, but the final word includes the Russian for "knot-hole" (svisch),[38] and the Polish for more intimate and human orifices, *Dupa.* He is also medieval, possessed by the mid-day-devil, and tried to study the medieval medical texts by Galen at Cecilia Street. He should go, and leave his "libber to TCD" (424.11). His liver and his book (Gaelic: *leabhar*) to Trinity College, Dublin, to be studied by real medical students such as Gogarty, who went there.

12. Why?

For his root-language, replies Shaun. Then comes a thunder-word of 101 letters. As I find myself disagreeing with the previous explanations of this, I will put my suggestions down in full: "Ull"—Thor's stepson. "Hod"—the blind god who killed Balder. Mrs. Christiani explains the next element—"turdenweir"—as "Danish, *Tordenveir,* stormy weather."[39] The god Tyr's name may also be included, and *weird* is Fate. According to one version Tyr warned the gods of the coming of Ragnarok, and the danger from Fenrir the wolf. The next—"mudgaard"—is obviously based on *Midgard,* but here may refer to the Midgardsormr, or Midgardr, the "World-serpent." If "grignir" were Grimnir, it would give us a name for Odin, but I cannot see how such a change could happen. "Urdr" is the old Norse word for Destiny, which became the name of the eldest of the Norns; "molnir" is Thor's hammer *Mjolnir,* The Destroyer; "fenrir, the wolf; "lukkilokki" is Loki. "Baug" was the giant who helped Odin to steal the cauldron Odreri; the syllable "mand" adds the word Bogeyman to Baug-Odreri. "Surt," the fire-giant, fought in the final battle against the gods. Mrs. Christiani suggests that the next element may be formed from Hrimgerd, a giantess. The name of Garm, the great dog, may perhaps be there too, but I have no sure answer. Finally, the Norse *Ragna rokkr,* means "the twilight of the gods," not *Ragna rok,* "the end of the gods," as has been said.

13. Having admired the hundred-lettered word they ask: How?

For his penultimate answer, Shaun says they have missed his drift. "Thaw!" (424.35) he says, which is the same sound as the Gaelic *Ta,* "It is," and is as near as one can get in Gaelic to saying "Yes." Shem has stolen his tale.

14. The last question asks if he could not write it himself.

Shaun's answer is "Undoubtedly!" It is given at length in a voice that contains echoes of John Joyce ("one of these fine days, man dear"—425.25) and all the previous Shaun-types that exist "tame, deep and harried, in my mine's I." Every Tom, Dick and Harry says that he will be almost moved to put it in print. But the word is "ormuzd" not almost, and so brings in a new personality, Ormuzd, the Zorastrian Spirit of Good; and he says "Paatryk," which is Danish for "in print," so bringing in another person, St. Patrick. He won't put it in print because he is too much of an "hairyman" (425.34) which combines an old Dublin slang word for clever with Ahriman, the Zoroastrian Spirit of Evil. Being at the fourteenth question we are at a final stage corresponding to 111 in another set of sequences. The 111th Prophecy of Malachy refers, according to tradition, to Peter II, who according to superstition will be the last Pope. Shaun's "piop" (425.36) includes him and also Piobb, the editor of a French translation of the *Prophecies of Malachy* in Joyce's library.[40] It also provides a Peter to go with the Patrick to satisfy Joyce's love for tidy sets. The 111th Sura of the Koran, "Abu Laheb" or "Flames" is quoted: "will commission to the flames" (426.02), and the Ahriman named again.

Then to the tune of "Little Annie Rooney" (426.03) Shaun's songs take over "Mother Machree," "Erin the tear and the smile in thine eye" and an aria from *Maritana,* "Turn on, Old Time"—"those chimes, so softly stealing . . . the mansions of the blest." The scene divides. We can see a barrel rolling over in the water, and a man climbing up a tower. The second is Shaun as Boucicault's Shaun the Post again following the stage directions according to which, by means of a huge drum which slowly revolves, Shaun seems to be slowly and painfully climbing up the wall of an ivy-covered tower while remaining stationary in the spotlight. We hear an Irish song, "by Killesther's lapes and falls" (427.01)—"Killarney," with Swiftian mutations—then *"Open the Door Softly,"* which is the song Shaun sings that causes Arrah to exclaim, "It's that thief of the world, Sean. Or is it the auld cow that broke her sugain [straw rope]?" There is a similar doubt here "as the town cow cries" (427.03) but Shaun has disappeared—as Sean the Post did after climbing the tower.

We hear Moore's melody "How dear to me the hour when daylight dies," which was written to the old tune known as "The Twisting of the Rope," which we hear as well: "how dire do we thee . . . a twhisking of the robe" (427.17,19). The lamp has gone out, *es ist zu bedauern,* "it is to bedowern" (427.18)—it is regrettable. Or is he simply bedding down? It is doubtful where he has gone, to which of the "inds," and "Tuskland" might indicate Africa if it were not also the Norwegian for Germany (Tyskland). The words "gods and pittits" (427.29) mean the audience in the chapest seats in the theatre, those in the gallery ("the gods") and the pit. Shaun is "the salus of the wake," the health of the weak (Latin, *salus*) and the solace of the *Wake.* The twelve and the four old men will be waiting for his return.

A final group of songs begins after a reference to Mother Goose ("Mery Loye" 428.07). "Slyly mamourneen" is "Eily Mavourneen," a tenor aria from the *Lily of Killarney,* which is about the visioned return of the supposedly dead heroine. Following this is a parody of a line from "Tis sweet to think," one of Moore's melodies, which is followed in its turn by a reference to the name of the traditional tune to which Moore wrote it, "Thady, you gander!" It is a very suitable song for Shaun since its refrain is:

> And to know, when we're far from the lips that we love
> We've but to make love to the lips that are near.

Mere L'Oie and "yougander" (428.10) make a pair; so do "Tuskland" and Uganda. Obviously we are meant to be undecided where Shaun has gone, but the songs suggest that it is a happy affair: "Rolling Home" (428.11), "The Foggy Dew," "The Wind that shakes the Barley." So till Ireland is free, till Dun Laoghaire regains its right name from Kingstown and the good ship the *John Joyce*[41] takes over from the *Erin's King,* may Shaun be happy and prosperous.

Notes

1. *Stephen Hero* (London: Faber and Faber, 1959), p. 66.
2. (New York: Macmillan, 1961), p. 79. (First published in *Ideas of Good and Evil,* 1903.)
3. Sir E. A. Wallis Budge, *The Book of the Dead* (London: Kegan Paul, 1938), p. xciii., p. 59. (Note, "I have traversed the earth.")
4. See the present writer's "A Man of Four Watches: Macrobius in

Finnegans Wake," AWN, IX, 3, 39–40; and Macrobius, *Saturnalia,* I, 3, ad finem.
5. Macrobius, *Saturnalia,* V, 2, 1.
6. Rosa M. Bosinelli & Fritz Senn, "We've Found Rerembrandtsers," *AWN,* VII, 4, 62–3. *Letters,* I, p. 256.
7. F. Budgen, *Myselves When Young* (London: Faber and Faber, 1970) pp. 19–22.
8. And see Jack Dalton, ' . . . ', *A Wake Digest,* pp. 69. 70.
9. MS 47482 b, 5. British Museum.
10. "Principal Positions of the Hands," *Bell's Standard Elocutionist* (London: D. C. Bell, 1892), p. 30.
11. Jack Dalton, "Music Lesson," *A Wake Digest,* pp. 13–6.
12. W. Y. Tindall, *A Reader's Guide to Finnegans Wake.*
13. See M. J. C. Hodgart, "Artificial Languages," *A Wake Digest,* pp. 56–8; and 11th ed. *Enc. Brit.,* article "Volapük" in which "Lofob" is the first word in the brief example given. As Hodgart says, Joyce had other sources. The Danish is translated by Mrs. Christiani in *Scandinavian Elements in Finnegans Wake.*
14. See Adaline Glasheen, *A Second Census.*
15. Clive Hart, "His good smetterling of entymology," *AWN* IV, 1, 14–24.
16. *Ibid.,* p. 14.
17. *Ibid.,* p. 15.
18. Ellmann, *James Joyce,* pp. 608–9.
19. *Letters,* I, p. 167.
20. *Structure and Motif,* pp. 116–128.
21. Budge, *Book of the Dead,* p. 247, and footnote.
22. Budge, p. lxviiii.
23. Budge, p. 377.
24. J. S. Atherton, "Lewis Carroll and *Finnegans Wake," English Studies,* Groningen, XXXIII, 1 (February, 1952), 200.
25. Budge, p. lxiii.
26. Edmund Spenser, *The Prose Works,* ed. Rudolf Gottfried, (Baltimore: Johns Hopkins Press, 1949), p. 104, and editorial comments with further details, p. 335.
27. Clive Hart, "His good Smetterling of entymology," *AWN,* IV, 1, 23.
28. Padraic and Mary Colum, *Our Friend James Joyce,* (London: Gollancz, 1959), p. 147.
29. Clive Hart, "More Entymology," *AWN,* IV, 3, 57, from material provided by Nathan Halper. This provides a typical example of the pooling of information by *Finnegans Wake* fans nowadays, and gives me an opportunity to add that most of the linguistic information set out in this article comes from the pages of *AWN* or the various 'lexicons' to *Finnegans Wake.* See n. 39 below.
30. Budge, p. 300.
31. J. S. Atherton, *The Books at the Wake* (New York: Viking Press 1960) p. 48. The quotations from the Ottoman etc. come from Joyce's essay on Mangan. See *Critical Works,* p. 76.
32. *Letters,* II, p. lv.
33. Patricia Hutchins, *James Joyce's Dublin* (London: Grey Walls Press, 1950), pp. 27, 37, 41, 42, 80. The text is largely reproduced in her later *James Joyce's World* (London: Methuen, 1957), but with fewer illustrations of Joyce's Dublin homes.
34. Stanislaus Joyce, *My Brother's Keeper* (London: Faber and Faber 1958), pp. 90–91. For *Ulysses* see the "Wandering Rocks" chapter.

35. *Books at the Wake,* pp. 124–136, and the "Lewis Carroll" article mentioned at n. 24 above.
36. Hayman, *First Draft Version,* p. 224.
37. Christiani, *Scandinavian Elements,* p. 190.
38. Petr Skrabanek, "355.11 Slavansky Slavar, (Slavonic Dictionary)," *AWN,* IX, 4, 51–68. All my Polish and Russian words are taken from this article.
39. *Scandinavian Elements,* p. 190.
40. Connolly, p. 31.
41. See Ellmann, p. 718. The *John Joyce* was a tender given, by coincidence, the name of Joyce's father.

11

Growing Up Absurd in Dublin

Book III
chapters ii–iii

Hugh B. Staples

In a discussion of postmen, one may as well start with a letter. Concerning the chapters under discussion, which had been sent by the author in manuscript in 1926, Ezra Pound replied:

> Dear Jim: MS arrived this A.M. All I can do is to wish you every possible success.
>
> I will have another go at it, but up to the present I can make nothing of it whatever. Nothing so far as I can make out, nothing short of divine vision or a new cure for the clapp can possibly be worth all the circumambient peripherization.[1]

Pound lived to see the latter of his desiderata accomplished, and, let us hope, has by now experienced the former. One may excuse the keenest critical mind of his time for such a judgment because he had not then the advantage of seeing the *Wake* "weather," in Clive Hart's phrase, nor could he see the passage in the context of the whole work. Though the "circumambient peripherization" remains, the best contemporary readers of Book III see it as one of the most "accessible" sections of the *Wake*. Generally speaking, this is true: "what happens" is relatively clear and generally agreed on.*

As this essay has for its scope nearly a quarter of the text of the whole *Wake*, there is not space here for the kind of close reading that enables David Hayman, for example, to devote nearly twenty pages

---

*See discussions in Benstock, Campbell and Robinson, Adaline Glasheen, Clive Hart, Tindall, *et al.* Of these, the most succinct and accurate summary is in Benstock, xii-xiii. Complete information about works cited in this chapter appears in the bibliography at the end of the chapter.

of analysis to a single sentence.² Instead, it will consist of speculations of a biographical kind, and considerations of thematic patterns, with perhaps an occasional divagation down the primrose path of explication. Throughout, my intention is to be suggestive, not definitive.*

First, however, one must attempt to clear away a roadblock thrown up (unintentionally, I believe) by Joyce himself: the supposition that the *"via crucis"* is a structuring device. The allusion is contained in the well-known letter to Harriet Weaver of 24 May, 1924:

> I am sorry that I could not face the copying out of Shaun, which is a description of a postman travelling backwards in the night through the events already narrated. It is written in the form of a *via crucis* of 14 stations, but in reality it is only a barrel rolling down the river Liffey.³

This casual pronouncement, wedged into a much longer discussion of such problems as book storage, the ways of Drs. Rosenbach and Borach, and so on, though *ipsissima verba,* leaves a lot to be desired. For one thing, one would like to know exactly what is meant by the phrase "in reality." In my view, elements of such a matrix are at best vestigial, and I think, unimportant. As David Hayman has shown, this part of the *Wake* underwent very considerable modification before reaching its final form.⁴ In this case, the later changes seem to have nearly obliterated Joyce's original intent, as stated in his letter. Christian formulae with their precise ordering are always a temptation to Joyce scholars, especially in view of the importance of the liturgy in *Ulysses,* but such applications to the *Wake* need to be done cautiously. For me, Shaun/Jaun/Yawn cannot be a Christ-figure, whatever else he may be.**

The Shaun of III,1 wants to be thought of as a man-about-town, a snappy dresser, a glutton and a gourmet. He is possessed of a musical voice and he is a braggart. He is treated most courteously by his inter-

---

* I would like to acknowledge here my debt to Adaline Glasheen, whose patient efforts seem to me (along with Clive Hart's *Concordance*) the most useful contribution to *Wake* scholarship that we have. This indefatigable lady, in her *Census,* has come in for some (often rude) criticism. But I say to her critics—which of your books on the *Wake* shows more wear?

** On the important (but to me tedious) question of Joyce's later religious attitudes, and on the question of Catholic imagery in the *Wake,* see Benstock, 68–107. Benstock admirably discusses much of the earlier criticism on these points, and comes to conclusions with which I am mainly in agreement. For me, the Christian elements in *Finnegans Wake* remain for the most part decorative, rather than structural.

rogators, who are either reporters or the public in general. He is not happy in his work, which is that of a messenger or a postman; he would prefer to be a priest. Oddly, he is a writer (or at least says he is), and claims to have a patroness who has suffered on his account. He is given to *sententiae* of dubious purport (though not nearly to the extent of Jaun in III, 2), and he tells a good story. Nevertheless, he is jealous of his brother Shem, whose literary work he deprecates, and whose character he slanders.

His language is vernacular, his diction slangy, and his sentences tend to be short and emphatic. He has a little Latin—mostly tags that he likes to throw out to impress his audience. He appears half-educated, and prefers to express himself in concrete terms rather than in abstractions; it is evident that he is immersed in the quotidian rather than the intellectual experience. His reading, judging from the relative paucity of literary allusions, is scanty and rather childish; what appeals to him are writers like Grimm, La Fontaine, Maeterlinck and Edward Lear.* The general impression is one of late adolescence, with its insecurities and gaucheries; but for all this, Shaun retains the affection of society. His public is sorry to see him leave, and is anxious for his return. For his part, he appears unhappy at the prospect of setting forth.

Commentators on the biographical and autobiographical elements in the *Wake* have sometimes made rather dogmatic assertions to the effect that "Shem is James," "Shaun is Stanislaus," that the former is the Gracehoper, the latter the Ondt, and so on. But these same critics admit that the picture gets confused, so that some such formulas as "Shaun here seems to turn into Shem," or "HCE here replaces his sons," becomes necessary. For my part, it makes for a more satisfactory reading to regard Shaun, at least in Book III, as a composite figure—a mixture of the character and temperament not only of the two older brothers, but of the youngest, Charlie Joyce, as well.

As no one, to my knowledge, seems to have considered Charles Joyce to have any place at all in the canon, perhaps it might be well briefly to consider what little we know about him. Most of this information comes from Stanislaus Joyce, in *The Complete Dublin Diary* (a document we know James Joyce, with his brother's consent, read carefully),

---

* The exception to this observation is, of course, to be found in the elaborate list of philosophers embedded in the fable of the Ondt and the Gracehoper. This kind of knowledge seems out of character for Shaun, and seems to me explained by the fact that this 'set-piece' was written separately and interpolated into the text well after much of III,1 was composed. See Hayman, 36–37.

and in *My Brother's Keeper*. Here is the picture that Stanislaus paints of his younger brother:

> Charlie is an absurd creature. He is foolish, a vain and stupid boaster and very sentimental, and has a habit of imitating people he knows. He likes to hear himself talk big and, like his kind, thinks himself shrewd. He is lively and talkative, though rather stupid. He is courageous, too, and against authority spirited. He is an amusing clown when boisterous but rough and loud-voiced and naturally very strong. . . . . .He has the gift of writing though practically uneducated, and writes verse. He occasionally expresses himself well, gets a musical effect or a graceful phrase, but is possessed of a love of grandiloquence. One can see by him that he, too, is troubled by that familiar, self-consciousness, which keeps constantly telling us what we have done and why we did it, and which does not flatter.[5]

In short, I suggest, at least a partial prototype for the Shaun of III,1 and even more for the Jaun of III,2. According to Stanislaus, whose self-portrait is that of a rather dour, censorious puritan, Charlie shared his oldest brother's predilection for drinking and whoring, though he was also popular with respectable girls, which Stanislaus, to his chagrin, was not. These qualities are those which also lend a kind of spurious authority to Jaun's sermon. And how else are we to account for Jaun's appointment of the Dionysian Dave the Dancekerl as deputy to rule in his absence? A question of elective affinities would seem to rule out an identification of Jaun and Stanislaus at this point.

In III,2, the dandy has turned into a character out of Beckett, with the obligatory tattered clothes and worn-out shoes. Like Watt and the others, he has problems of locomotion—a poor lookout for a postman, and it is no wonder that during most of this chapter Jaun wags his tongue to give his feet a rest. He is "amply altered for the brighter, though still the graven image of his squarer self as he was used to be" (429.13–14). His innate didacticism, already prefigured by the moralistic fable of III,1, now attains a more sophisticated kind of expression in the form of a lecture/sermon to the twenty-nine schoolgirls. Consonant with this maturation, the mood of his audience has changed from one of mere respect to one of adoration. He is becoming the "most purely human being that was ever called man." (431.11). For his part, he is filled with love for his sister, Issy. He is given to such Americanisms as "tarnelly easy," "Gee whedge!," "tammany," and so on, perhaps a reflection of his readings in American authors (Oliver Wendell Holmes, James Fenimore Cooper, and "Uncle Remus") and an indication that his journey is to America.[6] (Interestingly enough, Charlie Joyce was the only one of the three brothers ever to go to America. After marriage in 1908, he emigrated to Boston, but after failing to prosper, returned to Ireland in 1912, and subsequently took a job in the Post Office).

Jaun's sermon implies that he knows a lot about the ways of a man with a maid (and vice versa). His advice, though pruriently motivated, is practical. His text, it seems, might have been borrowed from Lily, the caretaker's daughter: "The men that is now is only all palaver and what they can get out of you."[7] It is evident that he has a smattering of theology and tag-ends of liturgy, picked up, no doubt, from Father Mike, his "orational dominican and confessor doctor." Stanislaus Joyce had much of the preacher in him (and consequently became a college professor) but nothing of the priest. Always more anti-clerical than James, it was he who first fell into apostasy. About Charlie's religiosity, he has this to say:

> Charlie's Catholicism is intolerable. He is the spoiled priest to his finger tips. His talk is all of Father This-body and Father That, and this Church and that Church, what he said to the Missioner and how the people were all looking on. He likes to hear himself criticising priests. Of devotional exercises he talks dogmatically like one who knows all the tricks of the trade.[8]

At a somewhat later stage, Charlie thought that he had found his "vocation in life" and entered a seminary, as Stanislaus tells us:

> Still another flitting, not the last, but the last that Jim took part in, deposited us at 7 St. Peter's Terrace. . . .We were now reduced in numbers, for Charlie, as I have said, had entered a seminary, and on Sundays his admiring sisters had the pleasure of seeing him, complete with soutane, biretta, and prayer book, filing down the Clonliffe College with the other clerical students to high Mass at the Pro-Cathedral in Marlborough Street.[9]

But for "Buck Jones, the pride of Clonliffe" (210.18), ambition was not matched by ability, and Charlie left the seminary after a year to become clerk to a wine-merchant, whose amusement it was to get him drunk, much in the manner of Bloom's treatment of Mrs. Riordan's nephew.*

This conjectural excursion into the biographical elements in III,2 will, I hope, illumine the meaning of the passage in itself and in its context. I take the Shaun passage to be drawn upon the Joyce family in the period (1895–1905) when the children were becoming adolescents, but before the consequences of adulthood, though foreshadowed, had become seriously apparent. There is still a certain amount of fun to be had; the "message" takes the form of a childrens' fable instead of a sermon. The mood is one of irresponsibility; hopes for the future are high. But in the sibling rivalry, there are premonitions of family disintegration and preparations for leaving home.

In III,2, this process is intensified—the emphasis is on growth ("at this rate of growing our cotted child of yestereve will soon fill space and burst in systems . . .") (429.11–12), and on maturity and the problem of responsibility. Jaun's preoccupations are typically adolescent: what career to take up in life—singing? civic reform? business? the Church? But the grand question is sex: how to reconcile animal lust with romantic idealism.** Those who see Jaun as a transposition of (Don) Juan are right insofar as both figures are obsessed with the intensity and the ambivalence of the sexual drive; wrong insofar as either is thought of as a great lover; for like both the Mozartian and Byronic version of the hero, Jaun remains fundamentally incomplete, adolescent and sometimes even infantile in his relationship with women. This fact explains the radical shiftings in tone that characterize Jaun's address to the rainbow girls, and it underlies his unresolved feelings for his sister.[10]

Jaun's first effusions are couched in language so sentimental as to remind us of "Nausikaa":

> . . . for he knew his love by her waves of splabashing and she showed him proof by her way of blabushing nor could he forget her so tarnelly easy as all that since he was brotherbesides her benedict godfather and heaven knows he thought the world and

---

* Cf. *U*, 300. It is perhaps superfluous to point out that the character of "Mrs. Riordan" ("Dante" in *A Portrait*) is based on the lady who was in real life Charlie's "aunt."

** This problem, as it is found in the Joyce canon, is dealt with at length in Darcy O'Brien's *The Conscience of James Joyce*. See especially 225–226.

his life of her sweet heart could buy, (brao!) poor, good, true, Jaun. (431.15–20)

and his present affection, as it is expressed in the following paragraph, arises out of childhood memories. From this sentimental preamble, however, Jaun abruptly modulates to the cynical tone of the hardened libertine, and this remains the dominant mood of his sermon. Underneath the homily, of course, lies the darker substratum of lust and incest; Jaun's warnings about the dangers of sex have the effect of exciting himself to the pitch of sadism, and the language of Gerty MacDowell gives way to the rantings of Bello Cohen:

If ever I catch you at it, mind, it's you that will cocottch it! I'll tackle you to feel if you have a few devils in you. Holy gun, I'll give it to you, hot, high and heavy before you can say sedro! (439.3–6)

Perhaps frightened by the intensity of his own emotion, Jaun briefly pauses to get his Id under control:

I feel spirts of itchery outching out from all over me and only for the sludgehummer's force in my hand to hold them the darkens alone knows what'll who'll be saying of next. (439.22–25.)

Jaun is aware that he has a rival—perhaps his brother, perhaps an older man "about fifty six" or so (the age of John Stanislaus Joyce in 1905), and he reacts with warnings (445), further attempts at endearment (446), by boasting of his plan to improve Dublin if she will join him (446–448), and by sketching in an idyllic future. After passing his exams (450), and having become successful in business (451), they will share happiness "on the electric ottoman in the lap of lechery, simpringly stitchless with admiracion, among the most uxuriously furnished compartments. . . ." (451.30–32).

Issy's reply to all this is affectionate but narcissistic; she cannot refrain from teasing Jaun with the details of her intimacy with her latest boy-friend, to whom she has accorded gestures not unlike those with which Molly Bloom favored Lieutenant Mulvey: " . . . I shouldn't say he's pretty but I'm cocksure he's shy. Why I love taking him out when I unletched his cordon gate. Ope, Jack and atem!" (459.25–27). Issy, it seems, corresponds to the Joycean view of Ireland: fickle, always ready to be disloyal to her own; always ready to receive the foreign invader.

Finally, Jaun appears resigned to the irrationality of sexual impulse, and can only recommend to his flock a policy of hedonism before "Bouncer Naster raps on the bell with a bone and his stinkers stank behind him with the sceptre and the hourglass." (455.14–16). The audience is enjoined to eat (455–456), drink ("with Jollification a tight second") (455.12) and be merry (under the direction of Dave the Dancekerl) (461–468), who has completed *his* term of exile on the Continent "absintheminded, with his Paris addresse" (464.17).* Jaun's own return is prefigured, and in the meantime, he is encouraged to pursue his own destiny ("Work your progress") as the chapter ends. The return is accomplished, however, not by any one of the three brothers, but by Yawn, who is not a character in the sense that he has unique human attributes, but a symbolic entity in whom the family conflicts have become projected into the conflict of Irish history.

On The Brocken

In III,3, as the scene opens (the phrase, though trite, is apposite, since the structure of this chapter is scenic and disjointed), Yawn is discovered recumbent on the Hill of Uisneach, the ancient *omphalos* of Ireland. Like the Martello Tower, this mound has vatic qualities, and Yawn is the more or less unconscious medium through which various prophecies and historical interpretations issue. The larger themes of this chapter are for the most part variations on these already presented earlier in the *Wake*: the fall and resurrection of HCE; a reworking of the by now somewhat tiresome details of the "incident in the park" and of the relations between HCE and ALP.

A number of thematic problems invite attention here: playing-card imagery, geographical exploration, the "P/K split" Irish weather, radio/television/seance as media, the Tree, horse-racing, fishing and many more. A major theme, HCE as city-builder, has been adequately treated by most of the major commentators. The balance of the present

---

* I believe that Joyce's inspiration for this name for his self-portrait came from a remark made by Frank Budgen after one of Joyce's terpsichorean displays: "You look like David leaping and dancing before the ark." (Budgen, 190). And as Joyce told Budgen at a later date: "When you get an idea, have you ever noticed what I can make of it?" (Budgen, 327). For a longer, and certainly much more learned, explanation see E. L. Epstein, *The Ordeal of Stephen Dedalus*, 114–141. Professor Epstein does not, however, cite Budgen.

essay will concern itself with three major themes: The Four (and their donkey), Yawn as St. Patrick (and the Triptych Vision), and war (and the events in Ireland between 1916 and 1923 in particular).

The Four

The Four Old Men, because of their collective nickname (Mamalujo), have usually been identified with the four evangelists, and because of their accents and from other geographical hints, with the four provinces of Ireland. To interpret the Four as the gospel-makers in this chapter raises more questions than it answers. Their presence around Yawn's "cubical crib" is more suggestive of the Adoration of the Magi than of the men who were to become Christ's disciples. After all, there were only three of them, and it is hardly adoration that the Four display. Besides, they are so stupid; one can easily imagine Joyce to be satirizing hagiolatry, but not hagiography. It is true that the first four books of the New Testament can be seen as different versions of the life of a single man, and that the collective biography is intended as a universal paradigm for all mankind, just as the figure on the hill of Uisneach, in his successive avatars, is a symbolic presentation of man's fate. But tempting as a religious interpretation of the Four may be, I prefer to retain my secular bias.

The best solution to the problem that has been advanced seems to me to be that they represent the Four Masters—the 17th century quartet of chroniclers, though as usual, it is well to be wary of too precise identifications.[11] In a larger sense they represent the collective efforts of all historiographers; their attempt is to assemble, through research, a reasonably accurate record of "history as her is harped" (486.6), or the "map of the souls' groupography." (476.33).* That this is an enterprise doomed to defeat is indicated by the very imperfect communication between Yawn and the Four, and by the consequent confusion of the "inquest." (That we are dealing mainly with Irish history here is implied in the word "harped"; that it is always a bore, by the name "Yawn"). They are, after all, "traversing climes of old times gone by of the days not worth remembering." (474.34–35). But whatever else they may be, the Four are Irish—all too Irish, perhaps.

This brings us to the vexed problem of the donkey—a problem that is solved dogmatically by those who identify him with Christ, and

---

* A good way to describe Jung's theory of the "collective unconscious."

somewhat less grandly, by those who see in the burro the figure of Joyce himself. The latter choice is rendered more plausible by the fact that the Four refer to him as "our interpreter, Hanner Esellus." This fits both Joyce as interpreter of history in the *Wake,* and it is also in accord with the pattern of self-depreciation established earlier in the book (most notably at 179 *et seq.*). More generally, I would like to suggest that the donkey is a symbol of the artistic imagination, here stubbornly opposed to the procedures of scientific historical inquiry. The Four are represented as face-cards, emblems of constituted authority, but the ass is "the odd trick of the pack"—the joker, presumably wild. It is not facts, records and dates the donkey listens to, but rather to "the harp in the air, the bugle dianoblowing, wild as wild, the mockingbird whose word is misfortune, so 'tis said, the bulbul down the wind." (475.36–476.2). In short, the donkey prefers the Vico Road of symbolic, poetic interpretation, not the Roman Road of the archivists. But he is no match for the "brand-new braintrust," and he has nothing to say for himself, unless, indeed, he is the narrator of the entire proceeding.

The first twenty pages of III,3 are a mish-mash, but certain patterns may be discerned. As soon as the inquest begins, the Four make out that the giant infant is alive, and they prepare to catch him in their "nets"—a motif that looks forward to the capture of the "Human Conger Eel" later on in the chapter.* He is alien, they sense, "his wind's from the wrong cut"—and indeed he is soon to prove by his outlandish speech that he contains in him aspects of the foreign invaders of Ireland: the Christian missionaries of the fifth century, the Danes of the ninth and tenth, and later, as HCE ("Enwreak us wrecks")—Henry II, who planned and consummated the Norman invasion in the twelfth.**

Yawn/Patrick

Yawn's first concern is for his "Typette." A man of letters, like Leopold Bloom, he apparently wants "smart lady typist to aid gentleman in

---

* Cf. the "nets" of nationality, language and religion that are flung at an Irishman's soul in Stephen's famous declaration of independence in *A Portrait.*

** Cf. Joyce's typically casual remark to Harriet Weaver in a letter of 25 April, 1925: "Dr. Sigerson's statement about the Norse in Ireland before S. Patrick justifies my precipitate jumbling of the fifth and tenth centuries in the last phase of Shaun ('Norske He raven flag etc.')"—*Letters* I, 227.

literary work" (*U* 157), but on this subject the Four offer no help, nor do hints that he is St. Patrick ("the woods of fogloot") (478.34) evoke any intelligent reaction at first.

Yawn's speech, beginning "Fierappel putting years on me . . . ." (483.15) seems to be his first attempt at converting Ireland; there are references to the Gospels here. His sermon ends with the pronouncing of his Britonic name: Succat. The Four are not used to having their authority challenged, and one of them, probably Matthew, who often takes the role of spokesman, replies in anger, accusing Yawn/Patrick of being the son of HCE ("the twicer, trifoaled in Wanstable") (485.24–25).* Surprisingly, he replies meekly in pidgin English, perhaps because this is in character for a missionary, perhaps because he is over-awed by the druidical Four. In effect, St. Patrick, like the Normans, is successful in his mission, but becomes assimilated into the native Irish culture.**

If this is so, then the riddle and the Triptych Vision of 486 can be read as parts of an initiation ceremony. First comes the challenging question: "Are you roman cawthrick 432?" and the riddling answer:

—Quadrige my yoke
Triple my tryst
Tandem my sire   (486.3–5)

What does this mean? Some conjectures: 432 is of course the legendary date for the beginning of Patrick's mission to Ireland. It can also mean that Yawn is acknowledging the sovereignty of the Four, as composite Ireland. "Quadrige" = Cothraige = Paudrigue.*** He is three persons (the three brothers, Shaun, Jaun and Yawn, who together make up one person, HCE). He has been a pagan Briton, a Christian missionary, now to become an Irish druid. "Triple my tryst" also suggests the Triptych Vision, which is to occur shortly. "Tandem my sire"—he

---

* "twicer" refers to HCE's capacity for re-birth (in terms of Patrick's mission, a reference to the Resurrection); "trifoaled"—an allusion to the trefoil, or shamrock, which Yawn/Patrick has already used as a symbol of the Trinity (478.21), combined in the One, "foaled" in a stable.

** This point is made by Benstock, 96. No one seems to have pointed out the significance of what seems to be (but is not) a mistake in Joyce's letter to Harriet Weaver of 2 August, 1923: "I send you this as promised —a piece describing the conversion of S. Patrick *by* Ireland."—*Letters* III,79. (Italics mine)

*** For details of this complex linguistic transformation, see Brendan O Hehir, in his discussion of the "P/K split," 403–405.).

will be, *at length,* his own father, and in fact he soon does become HCE, the "twicer."

Reading over the *Tripartite Life of Patrick* and J. B. Bury's *Life of St. Patrick,* both of which, as Atherton and others have shown, are source books for the *Wake,*[12] one gets an impression of St. Patrick rather different from the stereotype of a kindly old gentleman whose main feat was to rid Ireland of snakes. Here for example, is what Bury has to say about St. Patrick's visit to the Hill of Uisneach:

> But if the bishop was in danger from a son of Niall at Taillte, he is said to have fared worse at the hands of a grandson of Niall at another place of high repute in the kingdom of Meath. The hill of Uisnech, in south-western Meath, was believed to mark the centre of the island, and was a scene of pagan worship. Patrick visited the hill town, and a stone known as "The stone of Coithrige"—perhaps a sacred stone on which he inscribed a cross—commemorated his name and visit. The stone has disappeared, but the traveller is reminded of it by a stone enclosure which is known as "St. Patrick's bed." While he was there, a grandson of Niall slew some of his foreign companions. Patrick cursed both this man and Coirpre, and foretold that no king should ever spring from their seed, but that their posterity would serve the posterity of their brethren. Tradition consistently represents Patrick as finding in malediction an instrument not to be disdained.[13]

Granting all his acts of mercy and conversion, and his undoubted success in putting the existing Christian establishment on a much sounder basis, there is another side to St. Patrick that suggests a kind of superior druid. After cursing various places for their lack of fish (so that they remain barren today), he set out to visit his former master, Miliuc. The latter, at the approach of St. Patrick, was so frightened that he immolated himself with all his treasure, for which act Patrick invoked an eternal curse of damnation on Miliuc and his posterity. In an effort to convert Loegaire, Patrick forces a confrontation with Lochru, the king's chief wizard:

> Each, then, asked tidings of the other, namely Patrick and Loegaire. Lochru went angrily and noisily, with contention and questions, against Patrick; and then did he go astray into blas-

pheming the Trinity and the catholic faith. Patrick thereafter looked wrathfully upon him, and cried with a great voice unto God, and this he said: "Lord, who canst do all things, and on whose power dependeth all that exists, and who has sent us hither to preach Thy name to the heathen, let this ungodly man, who blasphemeth Thy name, be lifted up, and let forthwith die!" When he said this, the wizard was raised into the air and forthwith again cast down, and his brains were scattered on the stone, and he was broken in pieces, and died in their presence. The heathen were adread at that.[14]

As well they might be. Later, St. Patrick arranges for 12,000 of Loegaire's men to die in a single day. Loegaire, a sensible man, eventually yielded to *force majeure,* though St. Patrick had no more luck with converting him than he did later on with Oisin. Something stubbornly pagan about the early Irish leaders, apparently.

The Triptych Vision

Campbell and Robinson have some interesting things to say about this curious passage, including the comment that "As they change the position of this symbol [the T-square of burial jade], it sounds deeper and deeper levels," so that the parts of the vision progressively recede backward in time through the Christian, pre-Christian and primitive periods of Irish history.[15] This is arguable. It has not, I think, been observed that the first word in each of Yawn's responses to the ritual questions (i.e. "pious," "purely," and "bellax") echo Vico's phrase for religious wars: *"pura et pia bella."* With this observation at a clue, we may see in the Triptych Vision a recapitulation of the Viconian theory of history upon which the whole *Wake* is based, namely, the three successive ages: the theocratic, the aristocratic, and the democratic stages of civilization. Viewed in this light, the first vision:

—I see a blackfrinch pliestrycook . . . who is carrying on his brainpan . . . a cathedral of lovejelly for his . . . *Tiens,* how he is like somebodies! (486.17–19)

represents a religious ritual, such as the offering of the Host in the Mass (possibly Yawn/Patrick sees himself as celebrant), but, as in the

Viconian scheme each cycle of history has its own deity to appease, it can refer to pagan forms of sacrifice as well. Each of the three questions is put in reference to a different mode of apprehension; here the operative word is: "Do you *see* anything, templar?" This is consonant with the Viconian theory of language: the mode of communication in the theocratic stage is "a divine mental language by mute religious acts or divine ceremonies".[16] The symbol of the "lovejelly," appropriately carried on the "brainpan" reinforces the mental character of this language, and since it is mute, it can only be apprehended by vision.

The second vision, corresponding to the heroic age, suggests, both in the question and the answer, the courtly romance. In the question, "What sound of tistress isoles my ear?" there is, of course, a clear allusion to the high romance of Tristan and Isolde, and this is framed by the questioner's comment on the answer by the reference to Swift and Vanessa. In this part of the ritual, the respondent is asked to *feel*, and the reply is couched both in the imagery of the romance, and in the language appropriate to the heroic age: that of "heroic blazonings, with which arms are made to speak:"[17]

> —I feel a fine lady . . . floating on a stillstream of isisglass . . . with gold hair to the bed . . . and white arms to the twinklers . . . O la la!*   (486.23–25)

By the third part of the vision, civilization has reached the stage of "articulate speech" which of course depends on hearing. As the T-square of burial jade is laid upon Yawn's breast, what he hears partly is his own heart beating:

> —I ahear of a hopper behidin the door slappin his feet in a pool of bran.   (486.30–31)

The language is appropriately "vulgar"; the image is one of a peasant ("a race of clodhoppers" Stephen calls his countrymen)—a ballocks. What is foreshadowed is warfare (*bella*)—the necessary catastrophe that must occur before the new cycle can begin again.

   * This part of the vision looks forward to HCE's apostrophe to his wife later in the chapter, in which she appears in his "serial dreams of faire women" (532.33). (One wonders, incidentally, whether this phrase partly suggested the title for Beckett's unpublished *Dream of Fair to Middling Women*—Tennysonian and Chaucerian overtones notwithstanding?)

Bloody Wars in Ballyaughacleeahbally

Even before the Triptych Vision, there are many references to war in III,3, though sometimes they appear to amount to little more than decorative embellishment, as, for example, the double allusion to the Crimean War and World War I at 474.16–17: "When, as the buzzer brings the light brigade, keeping the home fires burning. . . ." More important are such foreshadowings of the Irish civil war: "shanator Lyons, trailing the wavy line of his partition footsteps" (475.24–25), "dogumen number one" (482.20) and the confrontation between Ulster and the Republic at 482.26–30. After Yawn/Patrick's vision of the "bellax," however, martial imagery becomes more frequent, and denser. For example, from 492.13 to 493.15 there occurs a rather incoherent passage in which ALP attempts to defend her husband on the grounds that he was confined to quarters for an intestinal complaint at the time of the alleged indiscretion. Woven into matters pharmaceutical and abdominal* are a whole series of allusions to the British conquest of India, centering around the episode of the Black Hole of Calcutta (1756), and the defeat of Tippoo Sahib by Lord Cornwallis at Seringapatam (1792). Some insight into the manner in which Joyce constructed his palimpsest may be gotten from comparing the original version of the passage (as reconstructed by David Hayman) with the final form. Here is the original passage:

> —I beg to travers above statement (inasmuch) as my revered was confined in barracks by Doctor Finncane (entailing a laxative tendency and him being forbidden fruit) when my reputed husband # took a drink *out of* the said . . . *bottle* and he showed me a poker (which was (here) produced) with the remark: This is for Sneak # 18

This simple early draft, which I believe has autobiographical overtones,** may be taken as Joyce's original idea for the "plot-line" (which itself is cribbed out of *Genesis*). The question then arises: why does he later on embellish it with all the complicated oriental and martial imagery of the final version? Two possibilities occur to me. First, Joyce is inflating the character of the "revered mainhirr" by an extended trope that compares HCE's humiliation by the three sol-

---

* Hoses, syringes, and so on.
** See my note, "Finucane Lives" in *AWN*, X, 2 (April, 1973), 23–24.

diers with the panorama of man's inhumanity to man that was the conquest of India by British Imperialism. At the same time, and typically, he is deflating HCE through the farcical and scatological details of his digestive problems, and also by reference to the amusing fraud perpetrated on the burgesses of Dublin by "Doctor Achmet Borumborad" in the 18th century.*

This trope is extended for several more pages, as various international tyrants "pay their firstrate duties before the both of him" [the twicer] for his "five hundredth and sixtysixth borthday."** with the result that he is "reduced to nothing" at the top of page 499 and mourned by cries of "death" in many languages.

But, sure enough, "there's leps of flam in Funnycoon's Wick" (499.13), and the struggle of antinomies begins again. As this section is to end with HCE's triumphant account of the founding of Dublin and modern Ireland, it is perhaps necessary that the long chronicle of internecine strife that is the history of Ireland be recited first. At any rate, the watchers immediately hear ancestral voices prophesying war:

>—Oliver! He may be an earthpresence. Was that a groan or did I hear the Dingle bagpipes Wasting war and? Watch! (499.28–29)

Irish history at best is a somewhat cloudy business, but in spite of faulty radio transmission, against the background of martial noise (I take the repeated "Zin-zin" to represent the clashing of cymbals, or perhaps swords), certain slogans associated with Irish wars are heard:

Clan of the Gael! (500.2–3): Clan-na-Gael, a 19th century Fenian organization.

Dovegall and finshark (500.4): Dubh-gall and Fine-gall: "black foreigners and fair foreigners": Danish and Norwegian invaders.

Crum abu! (500.6): ancestral war-cry of the Fitzgeralds (the earls of Kildare).

Cromwell to victory! (500.6): Cromwell never lost a battle.

---

* For details of this story, see my *Ireland of Sir Jonah Barrington*, University of Washington Press, 1967, 159–167.

** Cf. the entry for 566 A.D. in the parody of the Annals of Dublin in *Thom's* at 14.9–10: "Bloody wars in Ballyaughacleeaghbally."

O widows and orphans, it's the yeomen! (500.10): The yeomen were native Irish troops loyal to the government in the rebellion of 1798.

Redshanks for ever! (500.10–11): "redshanks—a Celtic inhabitant of the Scottish highlands or of Ireland;—in derisive allusion to their bare legs." (Webster)

Up Lancs! (500.11): The Lancashire Regiment. Also, with preceding item, a reference to another civil war—that of the Roses.

Slog slagt and slaughter! Rape the daughter! Choke the pope! (500.17–18): Unhappily, this is the class of sentiments still to be heard in Belfast.

Sold! I am sold! (500.21): As elsewhere, this motif refers to Parnell's betrayal, and to his sardonic advice: "When you sell, get my price."[19]

The next forty pages of the *Wake* have varied thematic emphases: Irish weather (the war of the elements) (501–504); the events of *Paradise Lost* in an Irish setting (504–510); the Fall is followed by an account of the 'ballay at the Tailor's Hall'—a recapitulation of the ballad of "Finnegan's Wake;" domestic-civil strife ('Twas womans' too woman with mans' throw man.') (511.23); ending on Armistice Day ('the uneven day of the unleventh month of the unevented year. At mart in mass.') (517.33–34). But 1918 was only the beginning of further hostilities in Ireland; it was as if:

> —They did not know the war was over and were only berebelling or bereppelling one another by chance or necessity with sham bottles, mere and woiney, as betwinst Picturshirts and Scutticules, like their caractacurs in an Irish Ruman to sorowbrate the expeltsion of the Danos? (518.19–23)

From this point to page 523 (where the—to me—incomprehensible digression on fish begins), Ulster and Eire, Protestant and Catholic, bicker with each other, exchange insults, and generally get ready for the hostilities that were to follow De Valera's rejection of the Treaty in 1922. As usual, the details of these preliminaries are confused, but the general portent is clear. In the paragraph beginning: "This is not guid enough. . ." (519.16 to 519.25), the voice is the voice of Ulster, betrayed by its Scotch accent and by the fact that he refers to "the grand jurors of thathens of tharctic."* This northern allusion is balanced at the end of the paragraph by reference to "your Corth examiner" ("court examiner" and *Cork Examiner*—a principal newspaper of the southern city). This Ulsterian interrogator is replied to by the title of "Robman Calvinic"—a concise epithet that combines both the religious and economic aspects of the hostilities—then and now. On page 521, in a passage studded with allusions to Irish drink—itself a not insignificant factor in Irish troubles—the quarrel almost reaches a climax:

>   —Will you repeat that to me outside, leinconnmuns?
>   —After you've shouted a few? I will when it suits me, hulstler.
>   —Guid! We make fight! Three to one! Raddy?
>   —But no, from exemple, Emania Raffaroo! What do you have? What mean you, august one?** (521.28–33)

According to the evidence of *A First Draft*, all this was added at a later date, and though it sounds (and is meant to sound) like Tweedledum and Tweedledee getting ready for their battle, it in fact looks back to the near-rebellion of the Ulster Volunteer Force in 1916 and forward to the Troubles that have lasted down to our own time.

As even some Joyceans appear confused about the principal aspects of the conflict in Ireland between 1916 and 1923, perhaps a brief summary is not out of place here. Although the Home Rule movement seemed likely to succeed in its aim of moderate self-government after the conclusion of World War I, the more radical nationalists, such as the Irish Volunteers and the Citizen Army and, to some extent, the I.R.B., wanted complete separation from Great Britain. This movement reached its first climax in the events of Easter Week, 1916—a

---

* This must be another item that Joyce picked up from Brewer, who, in his Sassenach way, informs us that Belfast is "The Athens of Ireland." (Brewer, 72).

** The Battle of the Boyne, which sealed the fate of the Catholic cause, was fought on August 1, 1690 (O.S.).

glorious political victory, though a military defeat. Part of the failure of the Rising arose out of mistrust, and out of failure of communication among the leaders (MacNeill and Pearse), and between the capital and the provinces (the tragic farce of Sir Roger Casement is only one example). Anglo-Irish negotiations for Home Rule (including partition of Ulster) dragged on, and Lloyd George might have had his way, had not the British Government foolishly threatened military conscription of Irishmen in the spring of 1918. This action tended to unite all shades of political opinion in Ireland, and in the general election following the Armistice, the Sinn Fein (nationalist) party, with Eamon De Valera at its head was elected to Westminster by a sweeping majority. But they refused to take their seats. Instead, they tried to maintain a *de facto* Dail in Dublin, backed by the guerrilla army of the I.R.A. These troops the British attempted to control with three paramilitary groups: the "Black-and-Tans" (veterans of the British Army), the regular Royal Irish Constabulary, and the "Auxiliaries" ("Auxies"). Normal government became impossible, and partly for this reason, and partly on account of international pressures, mainly American, the British signed "the Treaty" (as it is always called), in December, 1921. This document made Eire a self-governing dominion; the question of the partition was to be settled later. But De Valera would not accept the treaty signed by his own plenipotentiaries (Griffith and Collins). He resigned, and Ireland was divided into two camps: pro-Treaty and anti-Treaty, Free State troops and "the Irregulars." After protracted hostilities, including the occupation and burning of the Four Courts in 1922, the Free State forces, under Collins, won out and the Republic of Ireland came into being.

It was a troubled period for everyone: Catholics versus the Protestants in Ulster; Irish nationalists against the British in the South; Irishman versus Irishman, after the Treaty, sometimes referred to as Document Number One. It was a time of mistrust, sabotage, disloyalty, confusion, and suffering. It was also a time of personal heroism and martyrdom. In addition to the heroes of the Rising, (among whom may be named Joyce's close friend Sheehy-Skeffington, shot by a mad British officer) later heroes included George Clancy, Mayor of Limerick ("Davin" in *A Portrait*), murdered by the Black-and-Tans; Terence MacSwiney, Mayor of Cork, dead of a hunger-strike in a British jail; Michael Collins, shot in ambush near Cork. Nevertheless, in spite of continuing tensions, the Irish had at last achieved a kind of independence.

What were Joyce's reactions to all this? Judging from the published letters, and other evidence, he took no interest in the political and military events in Ireland during the period. What little he has to say is entirely related to himself and his family: he shows natural concern for Nora and the children, who were visiting in the West of Ireland in the Spring of 1922;[20] the hunger strike of Terence MacSwiney is the inspiration for a jingle in which he compares the mayor's fate with his own comic-opera altercations with Sir Horace Rumbold;[21] years later, he refers to the death of George Clancy only to explain that "Davin" had been the only person ever to address him by his first name.[22]

A reflection of Joyce's attitude towards the troubles in Ireland—and in my view, towards history generally—is to be found in the long paragraph that extends from 528.26 to 530.22. In its original version, which seems to have been composed late in 1924, it is simply a series of questions about various alleged infractions of the law on the part of HCE and the Three, but there is nothing specifically Irish about the passage. Essentially, it is a continuation (by radio) of the inquisition into the character of the alien invader (Yawn metamorphosed by now into HCE, who will shortly emerge as Haveth Childers Everywhere). The voice is that of Leinster, more specifically that of nationalist Dublin, and its first admonition is to the other three provinces to stay in line. He then addresses himself to the "chatty cove"—evidently the British overlord, with whom he differs about partition. Leinster has already given proof of its opposition, and there's more to come between Munster and Connaught. The pro-Treaty forces have won in the first instance, but the fight isn't over yet. What follows is a series of complicated, idiotic questions couched in modern bureaucratese. The purpose of the questioning is to enable the "brandnew braintrust" (presumably the new leaders of the Republic) to comprehend the odd and sinister events that have transpired in Dublin. It is the intent of the "braintrust" to show that the outsider, HCE, is behind it all. Was the flour of this "raw materialist" adulterated? Did Martha and Mary, those *agents provocateurs,* have proper credentials? How did that son of a bear get hold of the liquor? What was he doing in the Coombe, when he might have been living in comfort? Where were the three soldiers "when confronted with his lifesize obstruction"? When did he stop robbing the poor? Is he the owner of a sideshow, and did he complain to the police about women who had seen his picture in the paper? Did he get his son to go after some porter, while he and his paramours were living it up on the town? Where is the G-man who reported this whole business? There is then a cry to recall "Seckesign/Sickerson/Seckerson/Sackerson" (the Sassenach), whom we last saw serving as a support for Jaun on page 430. His remarks at that point were in Danish; now they echo the Dano-Norwegian of Henrik Ibsen:

> You provide the flood for the world-field
> I (shall) gladly put a torpedo under the Ark.[23]

All this seems an unlikely scaffolding upon which to dramatize the events of modern Irish history (with occasional glances backwards to earlier times), but that is what Joyce used this passage for. In the hope of making some sense out of his method, there may be some value in glossing some allusions in the passage—nearly all of which were added to the material in Hayman's *A First Draft*.

—*Dis and dat and dese and dose!* (528.26)
   Here Joyce is having his cosmopolitan Dubliner make fun of the provincial accents of the rest of Ireland. Cf. *U* 39, where Simon Dedalus mocks the accent of his despised in-laws: "O weeping God, the things I married into. De boys up in de hayloft."

—*2 R.N.* (528.27)
   The call letters of Radio Belfast in the early days of radio. R.N. stands for Royal Navy (?).

Longhorns Connaught (528.27–28)
   Probably a reference to Radio Athlone, now Radio Eireann. Cf. same allusion at 324.18. Also the proverb "Cows in Connaught have long horns." Cf. *U* 322 and Thornton's gloss on same.

You've grabbed the capital and you've had the lion's shire since 1542. (528.28–29)
   By the Treaty of Windsor (1175), Roderick O'Connor yielded sovereignty over Leinster to Henry II, while retaining his own authority in Connaught, but it was not until 1542 that Henry VIII first took the title "King of Ireland." (1542 seems to be the only "authentic" historical date in the entire *Wake*.)

borderation (528.30)
   "Botheration"—and the question of the border between Eire and Ulster, not settled in the Treaty.

The leinstrel boy to the wall is gone (528.30–31)
>   Of course an echo of Thomas Moore's "The Minstrel Boy" and a reference to the fact that the principal thrust of revolutionary activity in 1916, and later, took place in Dublin (Leinster).

there's moreen astoreen (528.31)
>   "The Minstrel Boy" is set to the tune of "The Moreen." For the Gaelic here, see O Hehir, 281.

With the tyke's named moke (528.32)
>   Reference to the Valley of the Black Pig, traditionally prophesied as the place where the overthrow of Ireland's enemies will take place[24] ("tyke" = dyke; "moke" = *muic,* "pig" in Gaelic). Cf. "Black Pig's Dyke" (517.14), and also a note by Adeline Glasheen, *AWN* III, #3, 65.

Doggymens nimmer win (528.32–33)
>   The treaty was referred to as 'Document Number One.' ("nimmer" = "never" in German.)

skullabogue (528.36)
>   Scullabogue was, like the Black Hole of Calcutta, the scene of an atrocity committed against the British. D'Alton has this to say about the fighting that raged around New Ross in the rebellion of 1798:

>> "Those who had at an early stage of the fight run away from New Ross brought the news to Scullabogue, at the foot of Carrick-byrne Hill, that the English were victorious, and were murdering all the Irish prisoners in their hands. In revenge, they showed an order from one of their leaders commanding that the prisoners detained in Scullabogue barn should be instantly executed. The guards refused to obey the order—in reality it was forged—but they were overpowered and the barn set on fire. A few of the prisoners emerged into the open but were at once piked; the remainder were roasted alive. Gordon puts the total number murdered at 200, Hay at less than 80; and the latter account is the more probable, as the barn was but 34 feet long and 15 wide."[25]

>   This allusion is unclear to me, but the suggestion of "skull and bones" together with the imagery of intense heat seems relevant.

six disqualifications (529.7)
>The six counties of Ulster, which remain a barrier to the union of all Ireland.

Committalman Number Underfifteen (529.8–9)
>Committee Room 15 in the House of Commons was the scene of Parnell's rejection by his party in December, 1890. This action, of course, inspired Joyce's first work: "Et Tu, Healy."

nose money (529.10)
>The tributes exacted by the Formorians from the Dedannans were paid annually at the Hill of Uisneach. Those who did not pay had their noses cut off in lieu of gold. Later, the Danes were said to have exacted "nose money" in this fashion.[26]

Misses Mirtha and Merry, the two dreeper's assistents (529.11–12)
>The two partially undraped ladies on each side of the coat-of-arms of Dublin.[27]

J. H. North (529.13)
>"North, James H. J. P. county Dublin, T. C. house, land and estate agent, auctioneer and valuator. .110 Grafton Street" (*Thom's,* 1891, p. 1805). I suspect that John Stanislaus Joyce may have made use of this gentleman's services in his eternal changes of residence.[28]

O Bejorumsen . . . Mockmacmahonitch . . . Fauxfitzhuorsen. (529.16–20)
>All variants of "false son of a bear" in various languages.

Butt and Hocksetts (529.17)
>Not a firm, but "butt and hogsheads" = wine barrels.

this hackney man in the coombe (529.19)
>This a previously unnoticed motif in the *Wake,* earlier instances of which occur at 255.21–22, 390.31–32, 423.23–25, 506.11–12 and 516.13. The Coombe is a slum area in South Dublin. Joyce likes to play on the word, relating it to "comb" and to "hairs". As usual, erotic overtones. Another instance of Joyce's raid on Brewer is at 390.31–32: "As the holymaid of Kunut said to the haryman of Koombe:"
>>"Holy Maid of Kent (The). Elizabeth Barton, who incited the Roman Catholics to resist the progress of the Reformation, and

pretended to act under direct inspiration. She was hanged at
Tyburn in 1534."[29]

Nora was from Connaught; Joyce from Dublin, here as Ahriman, Heremon etc.

his ark, of eggshaped fuselage and made in Fredborg (529.21)
Reference to the Zeppelins with which the Germans bombed Great Britain in World War I. They were built in Friedrichshafen.

Glassthure cabman (529.23)
A reference to J. M. Synge? Cf. *U* 197: "The tramper Synge is looking for you, he said, to murder you. He heard you pissed on his halldoor in Glasthule."

hearts of steel (529.25)
Name adopted by peasants organized for agrarian rebellion against their Ulster landlords in the early 1770's.[30]

Hansen, Morfydd and O'Dwyer (529.25)
The three soldiers mocked. The trio echo the name of a principal bakery in Dublin: "Johnston, Mooney and O'Brien."

R.U.C'S (529.27)
The Royal Irish Constabulary metamorphosed into the Royal Ulster Constabulary.

trench ulcers (529.27)
Trench-coats—the favorite garb of the I.R.A., with "ulsters," a kind of overcoat made in Belfast.

Paterson and Hellicotts (529.30–31)
Paterson and Co. are the only company listed under "Match Manufacturers" in Thom's for 1891.

a hengsters circus near North Great Denmark Street (529.34 et seq.)
For "hengsters" see Glasheen, *Census* under "Hengler." The principal edifice in Great Denmark Street, in North Dublin is (still) Belvedere College. I take what follows as a jibe against Joyce's old prep school. For the incident in which Joyce parodied the Rector in a school play during his senior year, see Ellmann, 56–57.

St. Patrick's Lavatory (530.10–11)
A public lavatory, as described by Tindall;[31] Professor Tindall, however, does not explain that St. Patrick's Purgatory has reference to an island in Lough Derg (in Co. Donegal, not the one

in Clare, Galway and Tipperary), where St. Patrick is alleged to have had a vision of Purgatory. Possibly also here a reference to St. Patrick's Oratory, in the monastery of Armagh.

Morgue and Cruses (530.13)
J. P. Morgan, the modern Croesus.

Prepare the way! (530.17)
Translation of the ancient Gaelic war cry: *"Faugh a ballaugh."*

Where's that gendarm auxiliar, arianautic sappertillery (530.17–18)
The armed forces: police, "Auxies" (liars), Irish Navy (non-existent), aeronauts, engineers and artillery.

Morse-erse wordybook. (530.19)
Morse code and Irish dictionary (*Wörterbuch*).

trunchein up his tail (530.19–20)
Truncheon up his tail/trumped-up tale.

Altogether, whatever else it may be, *Finnegans Wake* is not a great war novel. Considering Joyce's personal views on war (such as they were), one wonders, at first, why so much of the *Wake* as a whole, and III,3 in particular, has such a heavy overlay of martial imagery. The answer, I think, is complex: First, it is a depressing fact that one way of looking at history is that it is a chronicle of warfare, and a universal history, such as the *Wake* aims to be, must take cognizance of this fact. Secondly, the Viconian philosophy postulates warfare as a necessary preliminary to the *ricorso*. Thirdly, Joyce was fascinated by Bruno's eternal opposition of contraries, in which a condition of peace (on the historical level) is impossible. Finally, I believe that the *Wake* remains, like all the rest of the Joyce canon, a fundamentally autobiographical document. As such, it reflects the conflicts between an Irish husband and wife, among Irish brothers, and between Irish parents and children. From these domestic strains Joyce could not remain aloof, though they represented an aspect of reality that at times, with varying degrees of success, he tried to deny. Ultimately, if not resolved, they are at least sublimated in the tragi-comedy of the *Wake*.

Notes

1. *Letters* III, 145.
2. David Hayman, "From *Finnegans Wake*: A Sentence in Progress," *PMLA* LXXIII (March 1958), 136–154. The sentence in question is 449.26–450.2.

3. *Letters* I, 214.
4. Hayman, *A First-Draft Version*, 37–39.
5. Stanislaus Joyce, *Complete Dublin Diary*, 15–16.
6. On the subject of America in the *Wake*, see:
Bernard Benstock, "Americana in *Finnegans Wake*," *Bucknell Review*, XII, #1 March 1964), 64–81.
Stephen B. Bird, "Some American Notes to *Finnegans Wake*," *AWN*, III, #6 (December 1966), 119–124.
Clive Hart, *Structure and Motif in Finnegans Wake, passim*.
7. *Dubliners*, 178.
8. Stanislaus Joyce, *The Complete Dublin Diary*, 21–22.
9. Stanislaus Joyce, *My Brother's Keeper*, 140.
10. That it is leap-year and that the girls are pupils at "St. Bride's" (St. Bridget's) may have been suggested to Joyce by the following anecdote in Brewer:

> "St. Patrick, having 'driven the frogs out of the bogs,' was walking along the shores of Lough Neagh, when he was accosted by St. Bridget in tears, and was told that a mutiny had broken out in the nunnery over which she presided, the ladies claiming the right of 'popping the question.' St. Patrick said he would concede them the right every seventh year, when St. Bridget threw her arms round his neck, and exclaimed, 'Arrah, Pathrick, jewel, I daurn't go back to the girls wid such a proposal. Make it one year in four.' St. Patrick replied, 'Bridget, acushla, squeeze me that way agin, an' I'll give ye leap-year, the longest of the lot." St. Bridget, upon this, popped the question to St. Patrick himself, who, of course, could not marry, so he patched up the difficulty as best he could with a kiss and a silk gown." (Brewer, 738).

Joyce is known to have made frequent raids on Brewer's marvellous miscellany (see Arthur W. Blake, "Identifications from Brewer," *AWN* IV, #2 (April 1967), 38–39.). It does not seem that he could have passed this story up, particularly as it would foreshadow Yawn's role as St. Patrick.

11. The best account of the Four Masters is in O Hehir, 383–386.
12. Atherton, 145. See also Edward A. Kopper, Jr., *AWN* IV, #5 (October 1967), 85–94. Kopper's footnotes to this article provide a useful bibliography of earlier discussions of Patrick in the Wake. Adaline Glasheen, in the *Second Census*, has much useful information on Patrick.
13. J. B. Bury, 120–121.
14. Stokes, 45.
15. Campbell and Robinson, 298.
16. Vico, 306.
17. do.
18. Hayman, 238. (I have not been able to reproduce all of Hayman's critical indicators fully.)
19. The question of Parnell is a complicated one, and his role in the *Wake* even more so. Some critics hold the view that he was for Joyce the hero *par excellence*, but it is my opinion that Joyce thought him a weakling: certainly he is not treated with much respect in the *Wake*. (Query: who is?) On this point, the curious final note to *Exiles* invites discussion:

> "The relations between Mrs. O'Shea and Parnell are not of vital significance for Ireland—first, because Parnell was tongue-tied and secondly because she was an Englishwoman. The very points in his character which could have been of interest have been passed over in silence.

Her manner of writing is not Irish—nay, her manner of loving is not Irish. The character of O'Shea is much more typical of Ireland. The two greatest Irishmen of modern times—Swift and Parnell—broke their lives over women. And it was the adulterous wife of the King of Leinster who brought the first Saxon to the Irish coast." (*Exiles,* 127).

Joyce has his history wrong about Devorguilla, but one wonders whether he thought *her* manner of loving was Irish?
20. *Letters* I, 185.
21. *Letters* III, 16.
22. *Letters,* I, 357.
23. The translation is from Christiani, 14.
24. See Yeats, *Collected Poems,* New York, Macmillan, 1954, 449.
25. D'Alton, Vol. V. 69.
26. Patrick Weston Joyce, 27.
27. For an illustration, see Benstock, 265. Also Adaline Glasheen in *AWN* III #3, 65.
28. *Thom's* for 1891, 1805.
29. Brewer, 616.
30. Beckett, 178.
31. Tindall, 280.

Bibliography

I. Primary works:

Dubliners. Viking Critical Edition, R. Scholes and A. W. Litz, eds. New York, the Viking Press, 1969.
A Portrait of the Artist as a Young Man. Viking Critical Edition, C. G. Anderson, ed. New York, the Viking Press, 1968.
Exiles. Compass Edition. New York, the Viking Press, 1961.
Ulysses. (Old) Modern Library Edition. New York, Random House, 1942.
Finnegans Wake. London, Faber & Faber, 1964.
Letters. Volume I—Stuart Gilbert, ed. New York, the Viking Press, 1957.
  Volume II—Richard Ellmann, ed. London, Faber & Faber, 1966.
  Volume III—ditto.

II. Secondary works:

James S. Atherton, *The Books at the Wake,* New York, the Viking Press, 1960.
J. C. Beckett, *The Making of Modern Ireland.* London, Faber & Faber, 1966.
Bernard Benstock, *Joyce-again's Wake.* Seattle, University of Washington Press, 1965.
E. Cobham Brewer, *Dictionary of Phrase and Fable.* Philadelphia, Henry Altemus, 1898.
Frank Budgen, *James Joyce and the Making of Ulysses.* Indiana University Press, 1961.
J. B. Bury, *The Life of St. Patrick.* London, Macmillan, 1905.
Campbell and Robinson, *A Skeleton Key to Finnegans Wake.* New York, Harcourt Brace, 1944.

Dounia Bunis Christiani, *Scandinavian Elements of Finnegans Wake*. Northwestern University Press, 1965.

E. A. D'Alton, *History of Ireland*. London, Gresham, n.d.

Richard Ellmann, *James Joyce*. New York, Oxford University Press, 1959.

Adaline Glasheen, *A Second Census of Finnegans Wake*. Northwestern University Press, 1963.

Clive Hart, *Structure and Motif in Finnegans Wake*. Northwestern University Press, 1962.

David Hayman, *A First-Draft Version of Finnegans Wake*. University of Texas Press, 1963.

Patrick Weston Joyce, *Old Celtic Romances*. Dublin, the Talbot Press, 1966 (Reprint).

Stanislaus Joyce, *The Complete Dublin Diary*. George H. Healey, ed. Cornell University Press, 1971.

———, *My Brother's Keeper*. Richard Ellmann, ed. New York, the Viking Press, 1958.

Darcy O'Brien, *The Conscience of James Joyce*. Princeton University Press, 1968.

Brendan O Hehir, *A Gaelic Lexicon for Finnegans Wake*. University of California Press, 1967.

Whitley Stokes, (ed.) *The Tripartite Life of Patrick*. London, 1887 (Kraus Reprint, 1965).

Weldon Thorton, *Allusions in Ulysses*. University of North Carolina Press, 1968.

Thom's Official Directory. Dublin, 1891 and 1899.

William York Tindall, *A Reader's Guide to Finnegans Wake*. New York, Noonday, 1969.

Giambattista Vico, *The New Science*. Bergin and Fisch, eds. Cornell University Press, 1948.

12

The Porters: A Square Performance of Three Tiers in the Round

Book III

chapter iv

Margaret C. Solomon

The Porter chapter of *Finnegans Wake,* fourth watch of Shaun, is about watching. In chapter fifteen, the third watch corresponding to the Human subcycle within the larger Human cycle of the Viconian structure, time and space were expanded until the dreamer was made to perceive a four-dimensional universe.[1] From Yawn's inmost depths, he was given the breath-taking, mind-whirling apprehension of limitlessness. The vantage point of the perceiver was at the center of an extra-solar system admittedly inconceivable in terms of a finite individual's three-dimensional perception but certainly not beyond the mathematical capabilities of the human mind to construct in the abstract. When Shaun-Jaun-Yawn becomes "the people" in chapter sixteen, a sub-cycle Ricorso, the point of view is nearly reversed, so that the eyes of multiple watchers converge upon a stage within a cinema screen, or, later on, within a television picture-tube. Such a shift forces an impression that the ultimate achievements of the human, scientific age have already been recounted and that a shrinking of the humanistic world is in process.

Joyce's universe has expanded and contracted before, within the earlier sections of this novel; nevertheless, such a focal contrast at this particular stage in the Viconian structure of the book constitutes a statement about the outcome of scientific attainment: mind-expansion through abstraction in the Human cycle is eventually and inevitably reductive. In the last stage, abstraction has destroyed any real sense of meaning in everyday pursuits. Chapter sixteen represents, more than any other chapter in the book, the times we live in, when, according to Joyce, creativity is at a standstill. It is a period of sterility, when procreative sex is parodied in fun and games, in perversions, in voyeuristic stimulation; when conjugal duties substitute for love. Participation is surrendered to vicarious living—in spectator sports, in the passive watching of movies and television, in glazed-eyed assimilation of sensational news stories. Law, once a vital recreation of Logos, is a shell emptied of any remembered meaning, and the abstract nature of legal language has permeated all discourse. Empty laws, imposing curfews, blackouts, and other curtailments, need "watchmen" for enforcement, because guilt is a talked-about but no longer a controlling emotion. It is a period of no privacy, for when the spirit is gone, everyone needs spying upon. Yet there are ghosts of the old gods, goddesses, and heroes haunting the house and the park. People can still see personifications of them in the movies, can dream and fantasize about them, gossip about their exploits, and even hear their phantom voices at times. Sodom and Gomorrah cry for destruction, but when *that* drama has been played out, it will be time for the new day. The Porter chapter is as filled with anticipation as it is with degeneration.

Hence, the world of the dream in the Ricorso stage of the Human cycle is reduced once more to a specific time and a limited space. The park, with all its memories of "good old lousy days gone by" is the immediate environment; the setting for the drama of "the times we live in" is the house of the Porters, actordescendants of the great ones and representatives of the end of an era. The dreamer is in understandably foggy confusion in the first few lines, while the universe contracts and the dream changes levels;[2] thus the "now" and the "then" are mixed so that there are two merging layers of apprehension: While the "kinderwardens" keep watch over the nascent, about to emerge, twin-generation, their old counterparts, as sycamores, and the old paleologist ass watch the playing out of the age, listening for NEWS (North, East, West, South: "esker, newcsle, saggard, crumlin") of the dying out of the old generation and the birth of the new stars of the show. "Infantina Isobel" lies sleeping in her chamber as an unborn babe, soon to take part in a new cycle—virgin nun, nurse, bride, widow—while the archetypal Isobel rests as a leaf ("child of tree") among the trees. The old watchman patrols, picking up leaves and leavings ("leavethings") from the dying age. Old Kata dreams of telling the thousand treasures of the "real story" and in her dream sees once again the great, potent phallus of the mountain king. In their various quarters, the twelve jurymen sleep, dreaming again the confusing details of the famous "trial." In memory's gardens, the twenty-nine maggies sentimentally mourn the loss of their "nice topping-shaun."

Book III, chapter iv . . . Solomon / 203

And the ancient forebears, guilt-ridden "Nyanzer" and his victim, "Nyanza," their days long gone ("his mace of might mortified" and her "fur" hung on a nail) lie in their lake beds.

"A cry off" does not awaken *this* old pair. It is, at the same time, the "cry of Sodom and Gomorrah" (Genesis 18: 20–21) against the perversions of the inhabitants and the cry of a newborn babe which announces and generates the Porter film-drama. Both "saying" and "seeing" are quelled (558.34), as the dream shifts to a "reel" time and space.

The Porter family film is a production to be witnessed in three "closeup" acts and then viewed from a fourth, father-removed position. The HCE cube-house is now on a reel (circling the square) and is arranged thus: EHC.[3] The "position" referred to in the text may be the sexual position of the Porter parents in bed, but, more importantly, it is that of the HCE aspect of Shaun-the-dreamer—"*h*armony. *Say* [C]! *Eh*?" (559.21–22; italics mine)—watching, in line sequence, three positions of himself: Act One, CEH (*Say!* [C] *Eh? Ha!*"); Act II, EHC ("*Eh? Ha! C*heck"); and Act III, HCE. The first view, a tableau in the setting of the Porter parents' bedroom, is a "See" version without sound. A closeup of the picture is provided; then a move is called for by the second "Cry off" (559.30), which is at once a director's call for action and the call of a boy-child in the drama about to begin. The language describes the actors as if they were "men" on a chess or checkers board. The viewer, who seems, as the film progresses, to be one of a larger and larger audience, sees only the springing out of bed and to the door of the Porter parents, the nannygoat and her billy; then there is a blackout before the two actor-parents are shown climbing stairs—actually not moving in space, for the stairs and bedroom sink into the cavity below the stage, turning on a reel at the same time, so that the viewing level will not be changed for the audience. Such a move puts the old hamburg (H) on the bottom of the "reel" house, so that it is on its head ("dead").[4] Under the house, along with the old imperial noggin, are many other ghosts of personages the old Bluebeard has "fordone."

Now occurs the first interlude, the questioning of the four old gospelers by the audience. Matt conducts a tour of the upstairs, explaining that the actors, called in the film the Porters (door-keepers, carriers, pub-servers), are playing the parts of an old family with a grand musical history, written in keys from a to z (560.34; *Ton*-musical key [Germ.]). The "tourists" inspect the rooms upstairs of the babes in the wood—the children to be "saved." In olden days, bedroom arrangements were different. Now the pussy-daughter sleeps in Number One, masturbating in her sleep (561.26). The onlookers are tempted, as exhibitionists, to show her the "word in flesh," but the guide forbids it. She has a mirror-playmate, a doll to whom she is wont to talk.

On request, the guide, Matthew, moves to Number Two bedroom. Here, the Porter twins are shown about to be born, soon "to be eldering like those olders" who have been pictured in their downstairs bedroom. Kevin's senses are not yet awake, but he will very shortly "smell [and smile] sweetly" and will "hear a weird" (word). He is associated with sound, with music; he is "audorable." "But hush!" This is a tableau, for C-ing only (562.18; 563.19). The other twin, crying in his "foetal" sleep, will be more closely connected with images and writing. By breakfast time, both will "become yeastcake." Now "the hour of passings sembles quick with quelled"; it is neither-nor time, a moment of transition. Their birth will mean "soft adieu" to this nice present moment, and goodbye to the parents, too. Until tomorrow, then.

The film is started for the second act of the drama, corresponding to the second position: EHC. The twins (Gemini) are dreaming, while Mark now supervises the watching—and the listening—and interprets the dream which the audience is allowed to witness. What the twins envision is Phoenix Park as the rear end of their ancestral father—partly obscured because of the "feminine" ground-cover—and so attention is called to rear perversions as well as to incest, activities of the cities of the plain (564.28). Sound is added to the pantomime, "Say" (Ear) as well as "See" (564.21 and 34; 565.9, 15–17). In their dreams, Kevin seems to be dictating the description to Jerry, who finds the threat of *Gotterdamerung*, the twilight of the gods, to be too much ("to feel, you?" = *zu viel, ja?* [565.11]) for his presence of mind; his brain flinches. Thirsty to begin his own cycle, Jerry trembles with fear and timidity at the moving pictures of his dream, while Kevin scoffs that it is only a shadow show and that it must be told how death takes its toll. But a feminine voice is heard which puts them both to silence. Kevin says he has heard that voice before. Their ears, at least, are now open, and the scene becomes the part of the drama where one of the parents enters the room, although the father's presence is sensed by the melancholy baby. The mother tries to shoo away the phantoms of the nightmare and promises that she will slap father's bottomside to make it go away. There are whispers between the parents: Are they asleep? Sh—not very happily sleeping. What were those cries? Infant words. Sh.

The second interlude intervenes, while the movement of the film is temporarily arrested. An invitation is given to all to visit the Porters' pub, and everyone is called to witness the "still" of the mother kneeling by the sleeping twins while the father, wheeled about, shows his "drawn brand" to the daughter in her bedroom, the other corner of the stage. The sound returns to augment the vision ("*Here*in *see* ye fail not" [566.24]; italics mine). The mother's exclamation of caution to the father comes too late. The daughter, sitting up in bed, describes the entrancing vision. It is fitting that the boys should describe the rear view of the father with sodomistic language and that the daughter should witness the front view with penis-envy ("I fear lest we have lost ours" [566.31–32]). The conversation which ensues is in question-and-answer form. Perhaps the questions are from Mark or perhaps from the entire audience. Since the language is not typical of Issy, I suggest that the voyeurs are pressing the point and prophesying the future when "her liege of lateenth disguises shall come" and their wedding celebration shall be broadcast to all, while spectators come from far and wide. It is the promise of a new knight: "Arise, sir Pompkey Dompkey"; even while we "miss that horse elder," still the nightmare of *this* (k)night will be deposed and a new "Sire, great, big King" will set the bells ringing again (568.25 -569.5). Such a situation will be the reverse of this EHC position, "*C*all *h*alton *e*atwords" (569.29; italics mine). The music, shouting, and songs, will serve at the same time for a Wake celebration and an Awakening. The daughter is abjured to have patience (568.5); her doubts expressed about tomorrow's ever coming are answered in an appropriately circular way: "Well but remind to think, you where yestoday Ys Morganas war [tomorrow's 'was'] and that it is always tomorrow in toth's tother's place" (570.11–13; *toth-ball* = Gaelic for female genitals).

The composite audience, speaking as a single viewer, is enthusiastic, asks for "more soundpicture," for it makes "him" think. And he is more than ever curious about the Porter family—a curiosity in which his voyeuristic excitement is increasing. In fact, he follows Isobel and her mother to the outhouse, in his agitation having "to go" himself, and is only too willing to obey the guide who cautions him not to look back on the earlier sodomistic scene and turn to a pillar of salt, like Lot's wife (570.33-36). On the way, the guide indicates the streams, the trees, the leaves which appear to form Tristan spellings and Tantric spells (571.7-8). At the water-trysting chapel of "eases," where there is also a grave, the Porter daughter is heard weeping for the lost lover of her vision, lamenting "after that swollen one." The voices she hears in her urination are phantoms of HCE and ALP: "Horsehem coughs enough. Annshe lispes privily" (571.25-26).

The scene shifts back to the twins' room, where father and mother pause beside the bed to be sure the twins are asleep. Jerry is quieter now, but one of the twins (or both?) is talking in his sleep, muttering something about the advantages of legal marriage over sexual perversions (571.28-29). The mother and father are about to leave when another set of sleep-mutterings arrests their attention. They are waiting to listen to the rumblings of their own doom on the morrow. For, says the commentator, in the tombs of wombs, the "young-fries" in their "bridge" game plan the overthrow of and dig graves for their "fourinhand forebears" (572.2-5). On their way down the hall, the parents notice that the daughter's door is open, another sign that mama's door will be closed. Soon.

The third interlude is the longest one: the story of this end time—of "Plentifolks Mixymost." The chapter has already presented the period as a time of spectator entertainment, of plays, movies, broadcasts, of voyeurs who do not act but get their kicks from watching and listening. The Honuphrius "proposal"—a real poser—indicates that it is also a time of multiple perversions, when brotherly love is distorted into incest, homosexuality and illegitimacy abound, and conjugal rights are determined by a complex legal structure parodying those rules, imposed by the Roman Catholic Church, which were primarily devised to set man free from guilt; by extension, the law is a travesty of the original Word. The grotesqueness of the Honuphrius report is followed by the legal case, in this modern "umbrella history," which has to do with condoms (for the fun of the thing: 574.22-23), with sterility, with, in fact, a rubber "check" which means no cross-fertilization at all between the parties involved; despite the fact that "payment had been made," in "mutual obligation," it has been declared "invalid having been tendered to creditor under cover of a crossed cheque," DUD, 1132, resulting in "nine months . . . without issue" (575.12). The verdict in the case is worthless, for the original litigants are, for all practical purposes, dead, and "no property in law can exist in a corpse" (576.5). It is obviously time for the worn-out age to come to a close.

And so, back in the drama, the two Porter parents—alteregos (576.33) of the first parents (576.27)—prepare to descend, to hide themselves for a last act in *their* bed of trial. The commentator offers a prayer for this "end," when the parents will be brought down the ladder to the bottom rung to couple for the last time.

After hesitating, to be sure the stirring child is asleep, the Porters start downstairs. The commentator accompanies them all the way, waxing eloquent in his belated respect for their lineage; they do bear yet a resemblance to the mighty ones. He offers much proverbial advice, in admonitions which reflect present-day creature-comfort philosophy and show what the lofty aims and accomplishments of both science and art have actually come to in terms of the lives of ordinary human beings: apartment living (579.6–7); necessity for locked doors and watchdogs (579.8); *Readers' Digest* mental-feeding; illiteracy; quack ads, quick news and noise from the radio; Gideon Bibles and cults (579.9–10); showy doorplates and mail slots—and beggars kept outside (579.10–12); lazy grasping and ineffectual ecclesiastics, and a gospel which is deprived of power (579.12–14); collection agencies; militarism; propaganda (579.14–16); welfare; socialism; time payments (579.16–17); pop art; canned goods; colorless jobs (579.19–20); degeneration of language, especially in preaching (579.20–22); greed, full tables, dependence on the god of prosperity (579.22–24); in short, the degenerate practices of Sodom and Gomorrah (579.21–22). The Polonius-type gospeler wishes them well, praying that the "laws" which survive the original power and potency will "assist them and ease their fall!" (579.26). They have, after all, a long history of procreation, planting and building. They have made their mistakes, sure enough, never having "learned the first day's lesson" (579.35). They have not respected the environment, have been "responsible for congested districts" and the cutting down of too many trees; they built shipyards and struck oil, in the process using "Rachel's lea" and ramming "Dominics gap" (580.3–7). Yet after their multifarious deeds "they wend it back . . . to peekaboo durk the thicket of slumbwhere, till their hour with their scene be struck for ever and the book of the dates" (*Book of the Dead*) be closed (580.13–16). They approach the bottom of the stairs in the House that Jack Built.

In a fourth interlude, the four old sycophants and then the twelve jurymen talk together in reminiscence as they look on. Complex matters, they admit, usually end up as "pure form" (581.30), cliche. Their own language is full of abstract jargon: "stillandbutallyouknow that, insofarforth as . . . another like that alter but not quite such anander and stillandbut one not all the selfsame and butstillone just the main . . . till the latest up to date . . . have evertheless been allmade amenable?" (581.27–36). But they give thanks to these two and wish good luck to an act that will put the old pair in a position to turn deaf ears on this tired-out esperanto language. There is no way to have escaped their history, and the whole thing will repeat itself so long as every man is equipped with penis and testicles (582.11–12). One warning is given: "Bloody certainly have we got to see to it ere smellful demise surprends us on this concrete that down the gullies of the eras we may catch ourselves looking forward to what will in no time be staring you larrikins on the postface in that multimirror megaron of returningties, whirled without end to end" (582.16–21). It appears to be a good thing for the dreamer to have been able to look upon his own rear end, for he has been afforded a preview of the cyclical nature of the future.

The drama takes over again for the last act: HCE, seen by Shaun-the-people from a third position. The concord of harmony and discord (presumably described by Luke, although there is no specific mention of him as the commentator) is ironically a scene from the front of a rear entry (582.30), and *all* are called upon to gaze without shame. Even the man in the street can watch the shadows provided by Mrs. Porter's lamp, and the broadcast to the whole world is now available on television ("photoflashing it far to wide" [583.15–16]). Gamblers on the outcome are urged to peep and "pay up" (583.25). Why not? It is only a spectator-sport, told in the language of Cricket. At the rooster's crow, this "long past conquering cock" has only managed a score of 932, out of a possible 1132 (584.24–25).

The NEWS of these "weekreations" will appear in "widest circulation round the whole universe" (585.3), along with a call to each of us drones "that is still life with death inyeborn" to wake and do (585.17–21). For this particular case is adjourned. It is time for a new A.D. The performance, after all, has been as boring as each of these modern-day onlookers is to himself. Curfew laws and petty prohibitions are recited for the performers and audience alike. You never know who may be watching, so look behind before you undress, don't pee out the window, don't even divulge secrets in bed, for fear your own mate or your servants will give you away. For there isn't much secrecy any more: "Every ditcher's dastard in Dupling" is likely to know your most private affairs, financial as well as amorous. Outside, the police will see to it that blackout regulations are enforced. That is the way it is in this age of fear ("Fearhoure").

A gathering of the old-crony soldiers among the trees of the park witness to the shadow show and gossip again about the old publican's sins while they smoke cigarettes, do their Number One and Number Two business, and speculate about the weather. The same old trees which witnessed the original sins in the park tremble again to hear "the stop-press from domday's erewold" (588.33–34). The whole cycle is recapitulated in the way "one generation tells another," after the fall and the flood, and after the explosion which results in bankruptcy and deposition for our old king, Mr. Time. Gamblers who lost on the final event pay up, agreeing that "His reignbolt's shot" (590.10).

The final tableau, reported by non-synoptic John, the fourth commentator, is seen from a much greater distance than the first three. The film on the reel becomes the earth turning; the ringing down of the curtain on the Porter pair is the slipping of the old HCE under the far horizon. We can already glimpse the head of the new sun-son, appearing with the rumbling of a new day. And so we-the-people have been allowed to see three "tiers" in the round from a fourth position of "solution" and distance, through dream. We have circled the square, touching all four points.

Notes

1. For an interpretation of the fourth-dimensional nature of the Yawn inquest, see Margaret O. Solomon, "The Coach with the Sex Insides," *Eternal Geomater: The Sexual Universe of Finnegans Wake* (Carbondale: Southern Illinois University Press, 1969).

2. Clive Hart's chapter on "The Dream Structure," in *Structure and Motif,* has been extremely helpful in my understanding of the dream levels of the novel and in determining how Joyce's expansion-reduction plan works in III.4.

3. David Hayman, ed., *A First Draft Version of Finnegans Wake* (Austin: University of Texas Press, 1963), p. 252. Joyce penned in the margin this arrangement of letters, with additions as shown below, at the point in the manuscript corresponding to (559.20).

    HCE   CEH
      Sodomy EHC
            HCE

4. Joyce is playing with both circular and square images. The parents move up the "one square step" of "the chequered staircase" "tiltop double corner" (560.9–12). Thus one can imagine the medium as either film on a circular track or else drama played on a stage, the house itself. In either case, the viewer is in a fixed position *outside* of the scene, so that he is actually getting a two-dimensional view: he sees squares, not cubes, and sound-

pictures on a reel, not a sphere, even though both stage drama and film media give illusions of three dimensions.

There is also the suggestion that the "men" on the downstairs board are competing with ("stalemating") a backgammon game upstairs, played by the twins, no doubt (cf. "two pieces" for the two "tables" of backgammon and "spill playing"—spilling of dice (560.5–6). Whist is mentioned here, as well, and the youngsters also play "bridges", a game bridging generations, as we learn later on (572.2–6).

13

Looking Forward to a Brightening Day

Book IV

chapter i

Grace Eckley

The cloven world of East and West, rotating alternate faces to the single sun, declared early in history that the "the" of theology should be either immanent or transcendent. Where and when such philosophical differences occurred, and where "earopean end meets Ind" (598.15), becomes the subject of the *Wake*'s ricorso. In the same image by which the *Matsya Purana* presented the universe as the body of a giant sleeping god, resembling a mountain breaking out of the water,[1] the Hill of Hafid (Howth) gives relief to the Irish landscape "as he strauches his lamusong" (595.4) to comprise its geography expressed in dioceses (595.5–17). But in spite of obvious similarities, writes Joyce, "graced be Gad[2] and all giddy gadgets, in whose words were the beginnings, there are two signs to turn to, the yest and the ist, the wright side and the wronged side, feeling aslip and wauking up, so an, so farth" (597.9–12).

Joyce begins the last chapter of *Finnegans Wake* between a waking and sleeping, with theology from the Orient, at the moment when the sun strikes pre-Christian monuments of sun worship in a Christian country, or "the spearspid of dawnfire totouches ain the tablestoane ath the centre of the great circle of the macroliths" (594.21–22). After a long discussion in the Dublin pub, the focal place is Ireland's Eden and the focal person is Glendalough's spiritual mentor, Saint Kevin, who seeks for contemplation of baptism (the Church's rite of admission to new life) an island surrounded by the "circumfluent watercourses of Yshbafiena and Yshgafiuna" (605.19–20), just as the Liffey will circle the globe at the novel's ending; and here the "the" of philosophy and theology antecedes another beginning, of "The has goning at gone, the is coming to come" (598.9–10). Representing the divergence, also, are change and permanence, tree and stone, Muta and Juva who await the hour when Saint Patrick and the Archdruid will debate the structure of the universe through opposing perceptions of solar light. With its matins, the day brings a letter confessing frank enjoyment of the "secret workings of natures" (615.14) in which the "mahamayability" (597.28) of the East blends, through Anna's maternal instincts, in the forgiveness of the West. Finally, that "maya," symbolized by the changing appearances of flowing water, reaches its only approximation of yogic stillness through Anna Livia's objective viewpoint as expressed in the closing monologue. The sun, lotus of the day, touches her youthful daughter in the Wicklow hills (and the daughter is also herself) but in Dublin a soft rain falls (619.20), a lotus spray (594.14); and Anna Livia the river in Dublin's estuary remembers and asks to be remembered. Meanwhile, HCE, her giant manunknown (though she has lived a lifetime with him) sleeps at her side. The earth and her spouse, he-it "is just about to rolywholyover" (597.3), and she will presently awaken him.

Joyce explained the *Wake*'s last chapter with its four dramatic episodes—the baptism, the debate, the letter, the monologue—as a triptych and preferred to regard the letter and monologue as the central panel, with the three panels preceded and loosely bound by exposition. The first of these expository passages (593.1–599.25) presents in its opening paragraphs rousing eastern ("Sandyhas!")[3] and western ("Calling all downs") calls which blast the tranquility of the night. At 4:00 a.m. the phoenix, fabulous bird of the risen sun (593.4), plus the morning ablutions which dispense the night's grime (Piers' soap—593.9), and the wish to begin again after drunken stupor or fall ("let Billey Feghin be baallad out of his humuluation"—593.15), all stress the novel's theme of resurrection. But in the repetition of history, implied by the statement that HCE will rouse himself because "old human has godden up on othertimes to litanate the bonnamours," is the threat of repeated tension. Indeed, it will be necessary to announce "Confindention to churchen" that "Genghis is ghoon for you" (593.16–18); and once more the *Wake*'s famous Guinness as water of life and loosened tongues will generate the discussion in the pub ("Arcthuris comeing!"—594.2) where Tom-Tim, the mysterious clerk-bartender of philosophical proportions[4] serves a powerful brew ("Take Tamotimo's topical"—599.23).

The discussion preamble, in many ways the profoundest of the *Wake's* searches into primal causes, begins in the Word of God, creation itself ("A hand from the cloud emerges, holding a chart expanded"—

593.19), which is parodied in all the religious books of the world and even in the newspapers which, at dawn, announce the events of the created world ("Tass, Patt, Staff, Woff, Havv, Bluvv and Rutter"— 593.6). The paragraph which follows (593.20–24) concisely parodies *The Egyptian Book of the Dead,* a book which assures reawakening in Heliopolis[5] (594.8), the city of the Sun, through "Hymns to Ra at Rising" and the chapters "Of Coming Forth by Day." Carried throughout the nocturnal or death sleep, the "Word" implies that which of the gods;[6] the words to which the scribe Thoth reduced divine will the self-created god Nu uttered in making his names the company for creation of the universe and which later gave Osiris power to vanquish his foes, reconstitute his body, and become god of the dead; and the words of *The Book of Dead* itself. Nut, the sky goddess and wife of Seb, the earth god, gave birth each morning to the child Sun; the sky itself, across which he travelled daily was the mother's body or an inverted rectangular iron pot.[7] Joyce writes in summary, "after the night of the carrying of the word of Nuahs and the night of making Mehs to cuddle up in a coddlepot . . . tohp triumphant, speaketh" (593.21–24).[8] "Triumphant," now familiar as the resurrected Christ's triumph over death, resounds often through ancient Egyptian theology, where it signifies the power of the word; "triumphant" means "he whose voice is right and true."

Because Egyptian theocracy sired both Indian and Hebraic theology, it sparks the discussion, which questions the exact time in space the East-West dichotomy occurred, how its philosophical differences may be resolved, and a principle of unity be found. Joyce's Egyptian-Hebrew-Christian "toph" then offers in Sanskrit his rousing hymn of praise to the sun with the magical word of creation "Be!" (594.2). The symbolic washing (as the sun descended into the sea at night) could be achieved in warful Ireland "if soomone felched a twoel and soomonelses warmet watter" (594.9–10); and the sun, with its element, fire, unifies the entire speech, through which the mystical "om" of Hindu affirmation reverberates to unite the gods of the Orient with the Celtic sun god Lugh of the long rays (594.19, 595.9) and those of the Scandinavian Hel (594.23). The dog of darkness[9] should be, admittedly, loping off at dawn, "But why pit the cur afore the noxe?" (594.26–28); for this is the hour of crowing fowl (594.30–31), or "So an inedible yellowmeat [the sun, not its edible symbol, a bird] turns out the invasable blackth" (594.32–33).

Such a long speech, and comments on it (594.1–595.29), concludes with another cock crow, through which HCE sleeps ("Svap"—595.32). Yet the friarbird (the four o'clock bird) crows a message recapitulating the history of all religions through a god-like hero. He is typically born as a child, with name unknown or secret ("aya! aya!"—595.34), kidnapped (Moses abandoned in the bulrushes, for example, or Oedipus), or he conjured himself, as did many gods of creation;[10] he rises to manhood, returns to his community after a fall or death, to reside in mountain, suburb, Stonehenge (596.11, 596.13), cave, or sky (596.28-29). He may be a "dark stranger" ("one of the two or three forefivest fellows a bloke could in holiday crowd encounter"—15-17), or represented as a World Tree ("Jambudvispa Vipra"—29), or celebrated as a god of springtime in the maypole rituals (.21). He may be a fish god ("roache"—.18), or bull god ("oxmaster"—.18), or thigh god ("the thick of your thigh"—.20).[11] He may be likened to the devil ("the Diggins"—.12, "sorensplit"—.31)[12] or even a toilet ("hygiennic contrivance"—.19) when maligned by an editor. His varied names include Dagda ("doghis"—.2), Finn ("fincarnate"—.4) and "fum in his mow"—.6), Odin-Wodin (.13), Gunnar (there are two Gunnars in *The Poetic Edda*—.15). He is white-haired (.26) but an everyoung paladin (.25); true to himself ("atman as evars"—.24);[13] all colors (.21) and vaguely colorless (.27). Certainly he is idealized by others ("paddypatched"—.31) and not real ("synthetical"—.31), and his vigor parodies omnipotence ("sure, straight, slim"). He is the unmoved ("serene"—.33) mover; his swiftness, like that of thought, parodies omnipresence; and he arches over the flat pan of this earth like a huge "keddle" (596.29).

Not exhausted by any means in this survey, the topic of the god-hero intrudes in the ensuing discussion to perplex the questions of the nature of matter and of existence; often matter, even symbolic matter, mars the hero's existence: "You have eaden fruit. You have snakked mid a fish" (597.35-36),[14] or "There is something supernocturnal about whatever you called him it" (598.17-18). Further, a hero may become outdated, or "Mildew, murk, leak and yarn now want the bad that they lied on" (598.22-23),[15] but prayers in his name, and to many gods, elevate "towards joyance" in the *Wake*'s reiterated resurrection (598.23-25).

A long speech (596.34-597.22) repeatedly seeking the "Why" of "twein adjacencies" (597.13) or divergences in a single world suggests an imperative heart throb of the universe, a "systomy dystomy" (597.21) of pulsating life. At this moment, as if to counteract sleep ("howpsadrowsay"—597.23) with wakefulness, a sunbeam lances the cold dawn, bringing "infinitesimally fevers" (597.25) among which the temperatures of debate and climate perceptibly rise. The philosophy of George Berkeley ("Gam on Gearge!"—599.18) becomes a part of the discussion (see "Every those personal place objects if nonthings were soevers"—598.1) and anticipates the later debate between Saint Patrick and the Archdruid. If the philosophical cruxes, space and time, matter and spirit, may be resolved in terms of perceptions of objects as mind, not matter, the perceived sunbeam triggers the question, "Where did thots come from?" (597.25). What arouses consciousness, or "sleeper awakening, in the smalls of one's back presentiment" (597.26–27)? From the East the summation of existence is not the heart throb but the lifebreath of the Immortal Gander; and creation began when Vishnu stirred the primordial waters to produce Sound, from which arose wind. Joyce tells this creation story in combination with that of Genesis as "a flash from a future of maybe mahamayability through the windr of a wondr in a wildr is a weltr as a wirble of a warbl is a world" (597.28–29).[16] The pranayama, exercises which enable the yogi to hear the song of the inner gander through the rhythm of his breath, which is also the breathing of the Highest Being, then may be represented in the West's "comparative accoustomology" (598.23) of prayer. Further, when the chime of a western clock represents "exactlyso fewer hours by so many minutes of the ope of the diurn of the sennight of the maaned of the yere of the age of the madamanvantora" (598.31–33),[17] European end has met India. These waters of Eastern existence and the Western god-the-father ("oura vatars that arred in Himmal"—599.5) inspire a glorious summation of the history of the universe and the unity of all diverse philosophies (599.9–18), but the hearers greet the speech with discordant jeers (599.18–22) in this "tavarn in the tarn" (599.22), basically because the unavoidable dualities of time and space, male and female (600.2–3)[18] persist.

In fact, one duality is that of politics and religion. Politically, Ireland has just emerged from the dark night of the nineteenth century, dominated by the unshared splendor of Queen Victoria's Jubilee, but for the Irish "an Allburt unend, scarce endurable" (598.6–17); and the twentieth century dawns[19] hopefully out of that "stumbletumbling night." While the light clouds over Ireland drift toward the Nile with its two lakes named for Victoria and Albert (598.6), attention focuses on Glendalough, the "Valley of the Two Lakes," which was visited in 1849 by the Queen (declared Empress of India) and her consort (600.12–13). Famed for its Edenic beauty and its early monastic remains, and for the inaccessibility of holy Kevin's cliff hermitage, Glendalough nevertheless hears a history of human malignity; it is a "booty spotch" (600.16). Joyce acknowledges its possibilities geographically, astrologically,[20] theologically, romantically, and politically; but he freights each possibility with bitter satire. "The kongdomain of the Alieni" (600.10–11) reflects England's attitude toward the Irish, an ape-like (King Kong), insane (alien in the sense of mentally deranged) pirated ("accorsaired"—600.11) race, an outpost of humanity (the patriot Michael O'Dwyer's "outstretcheds"—600.18) with any present amenities haunted by the "blunterbusted pikehead which his had hewn in hers" (600.19). The Tree and Stone exist here, symbolic of Life and Death; but the elm tree is "scainted to Vitalba" (600.22), a reference to England's plunder, and the stones are "slab slobs, immermemorial" (600.26). This "shame rock" and that "whispy planter" remind romantic couples that religions disapprove of love (600.30–34); and celebration of the holy mystery requires celibacy ("celibrate"—600.35). Such a "spotch," certainly, is the legend of romantic Cathlin, pushed to her death by the outraged Kevin, a fiction which celebrates celibacy but makes nonsense of Christian love, for which was erected the chapel called "Kevin's Kitchen" (see "Kathlins is kitchin"—600.32). The isolated spot becomes popular for pilgrims from "Mainylands beatend."

Combining East-West attitudes, Kevin as a "nake yogpriest" clothes his loins in Adamic "frondest leoves" (601.1–2) while the twenty-nine girls of lunar time, cathedral names (601.21–28), and seven colors (the seven notes of the keyboard correspond with seven colors; see "vantads by octettes"—601.14) dance their rainbow arc between heaven and earth, their number minus one necessary for a trinity of decades ("ayand decadendecads by a lunary with last a lone"— 601.14–15). The imperfect hymn (601.31–36) they raise to heaven in honoring Kevin ("Keavn!"—601.18) rouses him from his slumber in a hollowed trunk (601.32) and stresses the importance of his horoscope ("Soros cast"—601.33; "austrologer"—601.34); but here intrudes a survey of attitudes about the ideal man (602.1–5), "someone imparticular," who will, hopefully, "somewherise for the whole anyhow" (602.7–8). Certainly Kevin, with his assumed saintliness ("Is his moraltack still his best of weapons?"—602.10) and his detrimental history (being announced once more in the morning papers—

602.16–27) cannot be such a man. Yet just as Glendalough-Eden holds all possibilities for perfection and the fall, or night and day comprise one unit of time, so the imperfect public man Shaun may be reawakened-reborn in the innocence of Kevin. And just as the arc of the rainbow unites the animal and the spiritual, the rainbow and leapyear girls (leapyear adjusts lunar and solar time) have consistently believed good things of Shaun. In the Shaun-Kevin panel of Joyce's triptych may be seen the *Wake*'s central message.

But first, the old Shaun, not an ideal "someone imparticular," as a resumé of his specific characteristics shows. He has been consistently, as now,[21] associated with the stone ("Rowlin's tun he gadder no must"—602.11), with Butt (602.27, 603.13), with food (602.36), with lechery (603.14, 603.28), and with the ass (602.14–15). (Joyce knew from reading J. Lewis McIntyre's *Giordano Bruno* that "The attitude of mind which formed the ideal of the Church for its members Bruno typified frequently enough by the Ass," and that "Asinity is in the sphere of practice as submission to authority in that of speculation, or pedantry in that of teaching,"[22] all of which make the Ass an appropriate symbol for Shaun's character.) He is round like a stone or the sun (602.12) and has prominent lips (603.1–2). He repeatedly asks the time (603.15),[23] and he is known especially by his feet (603.24), which indicate his immovability of viewpoint and his closeness to the earth (as opposed to the high intellect of the artist Shem). His asinity, or perhaps his lechery and saintliness together, mean that the hyacinth-heliotrollops for him constitute "a lable iction on the porte of the cuthulic church and summum most atole for it" (603.29–30). Nevertheless, the colors of the girls represent those of the stained glass ("vitroils"—603.35), church windows which depict the saint's legend when lighted by the sun ("Let Phosphoron proclaim!"—603.36).

A son of the soil and flower of the bog ("which puckerooed the posy"—604.3), his Irish craftiness denies his innocence ("Man shall sharp run do a get him"—604.1). At his time (d.619?) Ireland has already blossomed from the vine of legendary Heremon and Heber (Irish Cain-Abel prototypes) but remains blissfully unaware of future events (recorded by eighteenth and nineteenth century writers such as "Higgins, Cairns, and Egan"—604.6), of dire productions of overpopulation (Malthus—604.7), and of inventions such as jolting railways (604.12) and blaring radios. The "free state on the air" (604.23) should indicate the unity of all nations, except that "Western and

Osthern Approaches" expose Ireland's susceptibility to invasion and should blow a Gael warning for sailor Kevin in his bathtub; but sailor Popeye's song of the twentieth century ("Oyes! . . . I yam as I yam"—604.22-23) survives the intermittent devastation by flood and fire.

As forerunner of Shaun, Kevin is a "filial fearer" (604.27) of the Lord Creator, a "springy heeler" (604.29), "fond of stones" (605.1) and of food ("friend of gnewgnawns bones"—605.1). Shaun earlier in the *Wake* has committed the sins of pride, covetousness, lust, anger, gluttony, envy, sloth (all of them, in fact, may be seen in the night bird passage—448.34-451.7); but now Shaun-Kevin will demonstrate his virtues as he retires to an island in one of the lakes of Glendalough with his one piece of equipment, the *"altare cum balnea,"* which serves as altar when erect but as boat or tub when inverted.

As a son of the Christian God, Kevin's experience reflects Chrisian symbolism. The arc of the blue sky has been called an "arkypelican" (601.34) and the place an "yrish archipelgao" (605.5) to recall the folklore of the pelican as a symbol of Christ.[24] The seven sacraments are represented (baptism—606.11, penance—605.11, eucharist—605.31, confirmation—605.35, matrimony—605.9, holy orders—605.15, and extreme unction—605.22); as well as nine stages toward beatification (Kevin is "poor"—605.7, "pious"—605.13, "powerful"—605.18, "holy"—605.22, "most holy"—605.25, "venerable"—605.27, "most venerable"—605.33, "blessed"—605.36, "most blessed"—606.3; the Trinity in "trishagion"—605.14); the three days of Passion in "third morn hour"—605.23); the Celestial Hierarchy in seraphim (606.10), cherubim (606.6), thrones (606.3), archangels (605.11), angels (605.6); the Ecclesiastical Hierarchy of minor orders in porter (606.8), lector (605.33), exorcists (605.36), acolyte (605.24), and the major orders of subdiaconal (605.21), diaconal (605.15), and priest (605.7); the office of cardinal (605.25); ascension of the spiritual path through guidance (605.11), prayer (605.22), praise (605.14), penitence (605.23), fortitude (604.24), counsel (605.28), obedience (605.29) to perfection (605.36) with the intellectual virtues confirmed in meditation, memory, intellect and ardor (606.8-10); his repetition of a good act, filling the bathtub-altar "seven several times" confirms him in natural virtue. Kevin represents the first order of men with solemn vows, his holy sister water represents the second order of women with solemn vows (605.36-606.2), and Shaun belongs to the third order of those without solemn vows.

Disconcerting levity, however, infuses the grave Christian elements. The bathtubaltar never stands erect as an altar; Kevin's reiterated isolation (he is "lone"—605.15, "anchorite"—605.27, "recluse"—606.9) assures that, while devoting his life to the holy sacrament of baptism, he will have no one to baptise; he completes a reverse creation ("letting there be water where was theretofore dry land"—605.33-34); and his seeking yogic transcendance concludes with a Johnsonian refutation of Berkeley as he exclaims "Yee" upon contact with the cold water and thereby interrupts his proclaimed meditation (606.10-12). Clearly, as Joyce indicated about the Saint Patrick and the Archdruid episode, "much more is intended." A universality, then, surrounds the particular Christian elements and includes Kevin's position as center of the universe, his Orientation, the water and the baptism, the day's work, the numbers three, seven, and nine, the stages of creation, and the colors.

The soul in its spiritual ascension, among neoplatonists and gnostics, passed through the seven planetary spheres; with improved science, these spheres were later recognized as nine, and nine to the Hebrews meant truth, to others a mystical resurrection (in that when multiplied it reproduces itself, or that its square root is three). Kevin takes his position in the center of an island (in Glendalough) in a lake in an island (Ireland) or "an enysled lakelet yslanding a lacustrine yslet" (605.20), in a beehivehut he builds, in a cavity of the earth, in water in a tub of water. Joyce emphasizes this central position through circles within circles ("midmost"—605.11, "amiddle"—605.12, "amidships"—605.14, "centripetally"—605.15, "midway" and "ventrifugal"—605.16, "epicentric"—605.16, "centre"—605.19, and "concentric"—606.3). Kevin travels from the West (605.10) and genuflects toward the East (605.29), which is celebrated in Islamic thought as the focal point of spiritual light, just as devout wisemen followed the Christian star, and rose windows of churches face the East. He begins his work at matin (605.9), works through "sextnoon" (605.30), and concludes "when violet vesper vailed" (606.4). Water is the maternal liquid which began life in every creation mythology known, with its powers of renewal confirmed in purification rituals of baptism. Writing of the Mesopotamian god, Enki ("God of the House of Water"), Joseph Campbell adds, "there is surely more than a coincidence to be seen in the fact that in the work of a late Babylonian priest Berossos, who wrote in Greek, c. 280 B.C., the name given him was Oannes: compare the Greek *Ioannes,* Latin *Johannes,* Hebrew *Yohanan,* English *John*:

John the Baptist and the idea of rebirth through water (John 3:5)."[25] (And the Irish Shaun.)

The universal trinity (Heaven, Earth, Man; Creation, Preservation, Destruction; past, present, future; father, mother, son) contains positive and negative powers symbolized by the trident of Poseidon-Neptune, Shiva, and of Satan, and the cross. Seven means perfect order of a completed period or cycle, such as in the days of the week, the planetary spheres, the musical notes, the sum of the ternary and quarnary or the triangle and the square, the "Yoga Vasistha's" seven steps to transcendence. Kevin advances through stages of "regeneration (606.11); he is "precreated" (605.5), "postcreated" (605.18), "concreated" (605.35), and "recreated" (607.7), which reflect Vico's cycles, India's decline of dharma, and Ovid's Ages. Kevin's colors include white (605.6) for purity and spiritual illumination; gold (605.1) from the sun; green or "'vert" (605.11) for growth; red or "rubric" (605.23) for passion, penitence, and blood; violet (606.4) for nostalgia and memory, appropriate to the evening. Kevin does not follow the alchemical path of spiritual ascension (black—white—red—gold) but exemplifies the cycle of a nature god such as Osiris in traveling from the west to rise in the east in the golden sun of the dawn and declining to the darkness of black or "sable" (606.5) at sunset. The leapyear girls praise the coming forth of the city of Isis (601.5); as dairy maids (601.8) in association with Shaun-Kevin's butter (603.7) they suggest the Christian Good Shepherd and milk of kindness, the folklore of the Milky Way, the stories of sacred or heroic cows (often sired by bull gods) in Egypt, Greece, Ireland, with the epiphanic Butter placed on altars by the Hindus.[26] Joyce's repetition of the initial Letter M implies the maya-mare-mem-Mary sequence, and of the initial Y (as in "yslet") recalls not only Kevin as "yogpriest" but also the sacred Y as Three-in-One.

The passage of discussion-exposition (606.13–609.23) which follows the Saint Kevin episode explains Glendalough's beehive huts ("They were erected in a purvious century, as a hen fine coops"—606.16) and round towers ("Whether they were franklings by name also has not been fully probed") and Kevin's Kitchen ("Their design is a whosold word") as male and female symbols (domed hut and phallic tower) for Shaun-Kevin and all humanity: "*O ferax cupla!* Ah, fairy-pair!" (606.23) with the inevitable fall ("monster tiral"); the complete history of heaven-reaching and earth-confined humanity is the god-like All exemplified in the fallen and the reformed, or "What will not arky paper, anticidingly inked with penmark, push, per sample prof, kuvertly falted, when style, stink and stigmataphoron are of one sum in the same person?" (606.25-28). No one is without imperfection, or "We veriters verity notefew demmed lustres priorly magistrite maximollient in ludubility learned" (607.1-3). Shaun-Kevin's history is that of the Earwicker family; "Great sinner, good sonner, is in effect the motto of the MacCowell family" (607.4-5). Evil ("the gloved fist"—607.5) "was intraduced into their socerdatal tree before the fourth of the twelfth" (607.5-6) or before 1175.

Joseph Campbell, in explaining the *Wake's* reiterated number 1132, recalls Leopold Bloom's musing on the number 32 as "the number of feet things fall 'per sec. per sec.,' the number, therefore of the Fall; whereas 11 is the number of the renewal of the decade, and so, of Restoration." Campbell traces the message in "Paul's Epistle to the Romans, Chapter 11, Verse 32, which reads: *'For God has consigned all men to disobedience that he may have mercy upon all,'* " and he adds that this is the message of *O felix culpa,* "repeated by the priestly celebrant of the Roman Catholic ritual of the blessing of the Paschal candle on Holy Saturday: the dark, dark night of Christ's body lying in the tomb, between Good Friday and Easter Sunday."[27] But, as Campbell warns:

> between Joyce's and the Roman Catholic clergy's ways of interpreting Christian symbols there is a world of difference. The artist reads them in the universally known old Greco-Roman, Celto-Germanic, Hindu-Buddhist-Taoist, Neoplatonic way, as referring to an experience of the mystery beyond theology that is immanent in all things, including gods, demons, and flies. The priests, on the other hand, are insisting on the absolute finality of their Old Testament concept of a personal creator God "out there," who though omnipresent, omniscient, and omni-everything-else is ontologically distinct from the living substance of his world—and a ponderously humorless, revengefully self-centered cruel old Nobodaddy, to boot.[28]

Accordingly, since time began, writes Joyce, "It is even a little odd all four horolodgeries [religions which measure time] still gonging restage Jakob van der Bethel, smolking behing his pipe, with Essav of Messagepostumia, lentling out his borrowed chafingdish, before cymbaloosing the apostles at every hours of changeover" (607.10).

Shaun has all the qualities of the Cad with the Pipe (35.11); he is throughout the *Wake* identified with Jacob while Shem is Esau, and here represents with Esau the taking and the giving, the exonerated and the denigrated, the sinning and the sinned against. This duality, a necessary degeneration-regeneration or fall and rise, is "the first and last rittlerattle of the anniverse" (607.11); it is represented cosmologically in night and day, in the cycling year marked by the twelve months of twelve apostles,[29] and in the birth and death of successive generations. The path of life itself, writes Joyce, is a "Heroes' Highway where our fleshers leave their bonings and every bob and joan [boy and girl] to fill the bumper fair" (607.12–13). Yeats wrote "Make him fill the cradles right" but Joyce implies the constant abuse of growing flesh, or its momentum toward a fall. It is the song and dance of life itself (607.14–22); or man seems to be in the grip of a huge cosmic game— the yearly cycles and his successive rebirths in familiar patterns (607.24–33), so that the newspapers plead for a rest (607.34–36). The *Wake*'s mysterious sin is now attributed to ourselves and our brothers (608.7–11). The mother is still awakening (608.15) and sleepgarbled speech (608.22) responds to the view of humanity dimly realized on the landscape (608.22–32). One must apologize for mixing all humanity, "like so many unprobables in their poor suit of the improssable" (609.5–6) through Viconian cycles adapted to the Orient and the Four Gospels (609.6–8), but such is inevitable.

Such plain statements would appear to leave nothing to be said, but in moving to the opposite side of the "staneglass" (609.15) Joyce moves from Kevin to Patrick, from recluse to missionary, from native on to invader, from the topic of immaterial soul to that of material universe, from lonely meditation to public debate.

Muta and Juva introduce saint Patrick and the Archdruid, with Muta demonstrating Shaun characteristics and Juva those of Shem. Muta, the orthodox Catholic, speaks the Church's Latin and defends the "high host," perceives through the morning's fog the "tall chap" Saint Patrick (also a Shaun type) who is "theosophagusted" (food and theology) and exclaims in stone terminology "Petrificationisbus!" (610.3); and he observes that Patrick, like himself, has "rugular lips" (610.10). Muta borrows from Shem-Juva his pen, and Juva recognizes Shaun-Muta's patriotism in calling him an "Erinmonker" (610.32). The symbolic "Shoot" then echoes that in which Shaun-Butt, like one wearing ecclesiastical garments, shot the Russian General ("I shuttm, missus, like a wide sleever!" [352.14–15]), follows a reference to the

"Eurasian Generalissimo" (610.13), and foreshadows Patrick's defeat of the Archdruid. For his part, Shem-Juva answers Muta's questions; counters Muta's stone with his own tree image ("Beleave filmly, beleave!"—610.5); identifies the Archdruid who, in the terms of George Berkeley's *Siris* (which provides an example of the *Wake*'s motto for the city of Dublin—610.7-8),[30] drinks tar water ("Wartar wartar!"—610.20, and see 613.5); and views holy wars ("Piabelle et Purabelle"—610.21 or Vico's phrase *Pia et pura bella*) as a stage in Vico's cycles. Muta summarizes these cycles—unification, diversity, combat, the spirit of appeasement (610.23-27), and Juva confirms this view in a view of the immanent-transcendent god who is in all and on high ("By the light of the bright reason which daysends to us from the high"—610.28-29), an appeasement appropriate to the *Wake*'s *ricorso* and its sun symbol. The excessive politeness of Muta's request for Juva's pen which he uses as a blunderbuss ("hordwanderbaffle"—610.30) makes the act of shooting a symbolic gesture of all four cycles.

Just as Muta-Juva represent the eternal brother conflicts, though temporarily resolved in the harmless gesture, so Saint Patrick and the Archdruid represent cultural, political, and philosophical differences while discussing the nature of a common material universe. Through the conversation, Joyce represents two cultures through language—the "pidgin speech" of the Archdruid and the "Nippon English" of Saint Patrick—and represents the development of picture writing, in which a letter stands for an entire word, through a term which implies idea and object, color and unity ("pan") and manifestation of spirit ("epiphanal"). The term "furniture" of this "hueful panepiphanal world" (611.13) progresses into Chinese picture-shorthand as it telescopes parenthetically to "furnit of heupanepi world" (611.10) to "part of fur of heupanwor" (611.18-19) to all objects "of panepiwor" (611.22) to "obs of epiwo" (611.24). The neighborly countries at philosophical and political war, a continent and an island, provide also an Oriental parallel for England and Ireland. Both have engaged in what Joseph Campbell calls "mythic enthnology"—the certainty that beyond the pale are barbarians, not quite human, whom it is one nation's cosmic mission to control[31]—and so church and state blend in a common purpose to subdue another culture. Their common cause, ironically overlooked, obtrudes in the discussion.

Between writing the first draft in 1923 and the revision in 1938, Joyce brought the characterizations of Saint Patrick and the Archdruid in line with those being developed for Shem and Shaun throughout the seventeen years of "Work in Progress," and changed Berkeley from towering over Saint Patrick to the one being towered over. Shaun, as should be expected from his gross appetite, has gross proportions (see "He was immense, topping swell"—405.21); "bullocky vampas tappany bobs" (611.4) repeats his role as the bull-god Dionysus, the emphasis on the feet, and his roundness ("bobs") while the pipe he taps has been appropriated from the Chinese, a Joss-stick ("My tappropinquish"—612.24), and his membership in the "greysfriary family" recalls the Dwyergray Ass (see 602.14–15, 609.9–10). He wears white ("alb"—611.8), as do the Shinto priests (with black headdress and shoes). The Archdruid, "pidgin fella Balkelly" (611.5), wears a mantle of seven colors and discusses perception of objects in the spectrum of solar light as willed by the Universal Mind which is immanent in all things (611.11–15), with each object distinguished by the "one photoreflection of the several iridals gradationes of solar light" which it had shown itself "unable to absorbere" (611.19). Believing nothing exists separate from Universal Mind, Berkeley dismissed "things as they are"; Patrick therefore defends "the Ding hvad in idself id est" (611.21) and maintains the six colors ("sextuple gloria of light"—611.23) and *retained* inside objects. For the Archdruid Berkeley, matter is impossible if unperceived and therefore cannot be named ("tomorrow till recover will not"—611.12); Patrick's certainty of a universe separate from God enables him to project a future of things, even though they do not exist in mind until tomorrow ("tomorrow recover thing even is not"—611.26). The Chinese philosophers of the Han dynasty (202 B.C.–220 A.D.) developed a system in which five colors corresponded to directions, seasons, virtues, gods and emperors, and sound (the Pentatonic scale);[32] and therefore Joyce could regard Berkeley's theories of light and color as basically Oriental.[33]

Since Patrick, as Shaun, drinks up color in the same way he drinks up words ("vision so throughsighty"—611.32), High King Leary's *red* hair appears in edible "herbgreen" (611.34), his "*saffron* pettikilt" like "boiled spinasses" (611.36), his *gold* torc like "curlicabbis" (612.2), his *green* hat like "laurel leaves" (612.5), his *blue* ("bulopent") eyes like "choppy upon parsley" (612.7), the *indigo* gem on his finger like an "olive lentil" (612.10), and his *violet* ("violaceous") contusions in "sennacassia" (612.15), so that he is "tinged uniformly" (612.15) in the color of Patrick's shamrock, the vegetal intermediary color between black (mineral life) and red (blood and animal life) or between the blood of life and the decomposition of death. Patrick has been preparing his rebuttal while pretending to listen ("speeching, yeh not speeching noh man liberty is"—611.10–11) and, unable to understand ("no catch all that preachy-book"—611.25), simply gobbles up the Archdruid, first, by attributing his own black-and-white garments to the "Bigseer,"[34] whom he calls a "pore shiroskuro blackinwhitepaddynger"—612.18), and second, by adopting his terminology; in this way Christendom has generally spread by absorbing pagan cultures. "Tripeness to call thing and to call if say is good," announces Patrick (612.17); and, because Berkeley claimed that causality, too, is the activity of conscious spirit, Patrick gives an example of an activity and its relationship to things: "as My tappropinquish to Me wipenmeselps gnosegates a handcaughtscheaf of synthetic shammyrag to hims hers" (612.14–15). In other words, "as my tapping myself is to my wiping myself" represents tactual consciousness; "so a handerkerchief is to an it" ("hims hers") represents visual consciousness, two modes of perception Berkeley believed connected only by the will of the Universal Mind. By the power of his rhetoric, his faith, and his ego, Patrick claims "such four three two agreement" (the year of his arrival in Ireland) a sweeping demonstration of "heart to be might" (612.26). He kneels dramatically three times to the common symbol, the rainbow ("Balenoarch") while flagrantly plagiarizing Berkeley under the guise of reverence for "the Father, the Son, and the Holy Ghost." As Berkeley believed nature is conscious experience (visible in the rainbow) and forms the sign or symbol of a divine, universal intelligence and will, Patrick speaks of "the sound sense sympol in a weedwayedwold of the firethere the sun in his halo cast" (612.30). Since the rainbow cannot be perceived or experienced without the sun, it serves "aposterio-prismically" (612.19) to realize divine mind; religions, however, argue *a priori*, or so Noah and his followers believed they understood the intentions of Jehovah before the rainbow appeared in the sky. The Archdruid can only shake his head (612.34–35) at such defiance of Locke and Juva's "bright reason," but the "heliots" (613.1) or sunflower girls break forth in praise of the sun and God our Father ("comdoom doominoom noonstroom"—613.3) to confirm Juva's "Dies is Dorminus master" (609.28) and the Day is Lord over Sleep.[35] The "firethere" and the girls' triumphant song celebrate Patrick's successful lighting of the Paschal fire in spite of druidic orders that all fires must be quenched,[36] a demonstration of the mythic ethnology and opposing views of a single sun. As a further example of opposition to Catholicism, a protestant Archbishop named Bulkeley destroyed the convent, school and chapel at Saint Francis' Church (Adam and Eve's) on Saint Stephen's Day in 1629; Bulkeley (not Buckley) no doubt contributes to the variations of "Bilkilly-Belkelly-Balkally" for the Archdruid-Berkeley.

The discussion passage which follows Saint Patrick's triumph gives additional evidences of the Viconian cycles as representative of the history of humanity (one of these recalls the symbolic sun-egg in terms of the creative animal world, "eggburst, eggblend, eggburial and hatch-as-hatch-can"—614.32–33), a continual fall and rise, and stresses the importance of washing (614.1–13), a material baptism. The topics in this passage (613.7–615.11) introduce Anna Livia's views as expressed in letter and monologue.

As Joyce intended, Saint Lawrence O'Toole adumbrates the central panel.[37] Second only to Kevin in the history of Glendalough, he was abbot there from 1153 to 1162; and, as brother-in-law of Dermot III (MacMurrough) of Leinster, in that period of half-Irish half-Norse rule of Dublin, he became Archbishop through the efforts of High-king Muirchertach MacLochlainn. In him can be seen the twelfth century blend of druidic-Protestant-Catholic faith and the Irish-Norse-Danish-English rule, a blend surviving in the family at Howth up to 1909 when the last Earl ("at Lucan"—620.8) died and the estates passed to another name, a history represented in "Tomothy and Lorcan, the bucket Toolers, both are Timsons now they've changed their characticuls during their blackout" (617.12–14). But for fine traditions of hospitality, Anna Livia commends to Saint Laurens her best wishes (616.33) and praises the Old Lord on Howth as a model for HCE (623.4–11). In keeping with the optimism of the ricorso and the new day, the sun of Ireland rises in his name over its past history: "Lo, the laud of laurens now orielising benedictively when saint and sage have said their say" (613.15–16).

Remaining to have her say is the procreative force of the universe, the female principle of water, Anna Livia Plurabelle. Joyce had acknowledged through Stephen of *Ulysses* that fatherhood may be a legal fiction (*U* 207) and therefore disguised in virgin births (*U* 391), but bowed to paternity in the character of Leopold Bloom in his bath (*U* 86), where his genitals recall the lotus of the universe which stems from the navel of Vishnu, the "very lotust" (620.3) which Anna Livia desires of Earwicker. Anna Livia, of course, knows all the facts of life—rumored and verified—and accomplishes stylistically a startling transformation from the multiple syllables of Saint Patrick (modified only by the discussion in the pub) to her own monosyllables with which she reduces the most abstract philosophies to the practicalities of "nonsery reams" (619.18). Flowing through all of life, she insists on rising up whenever her husband, or anyone else, is put down; as the river which circles the globe she combines the maya of the East (617.29), which knows no Fall, with the forgiveness of the West, which provides for the Fall in the blessing of baptism and resurrection. She admits that great books record only the past ("the book of the depth is. Closed"—621.3) and, urging continuation ("Come! Step out of your shell! Hold up your free fing!"—621.3-4), she confines her written expression to a gossipy letter which, together with the monologue, affirms HCE's innocence, confirms the Viconian cycles, and embraces—through the maternal means of folk tales, folk medicine, and nursery rhymes—the entirety of the micromacrocosm.

Anna Livia's primary concern, her husband, reveals the national extent of his role as Adam, "our former first Finnlatter and our grocerest churcher" (619.5), whose store not only provides the country with food (he "never put a dramn in the swags but milk from a national cowse"—615.26-27) but also involves the plunder and graft and "clerical fands" (617.30-31) of national politics, of which she maintains his innocence of all but the best intentions. A "great civilian" (618.26), who is "gently as a mushroom," he has had storekeeping difficulties with Sully; and although Anna believes "Stringstly is it forbidden by the honorary tenth commendmant to shall not bare full sweetness against a neighbor's wiles" (615.32-33), she realizes lodging a complaint would mean Sully's "health would be constably broken" (618.32) and refrains. In considering Earwicker's funeral, she writes, "Has now stuffed last podding" (617.19).

This, his professional role, sustains him in her good opinion through the exaltation of her love for him and the disappointment of his admitted failings. In the former capacity, associated with their romance, she remembers him as avatar, both Christian and nature gods. She broke off writing her other, legendary, letter when she heard his voice and "left it to lie till a kissmiss coming" (624.6); she expects at the last he will bear down on her "under whitespread wings like he'd come from Arkangels" (628.10); and as "grocerest churcher" he provides a "crossmess parzel" (619.5). "If I knew who you are!" she exclaims, and remembers "When that hark from the air said it was Captain

Finsen makes cumhulments and was mayit pressing for his suit I said are you there here's nobody here only me. But I near fell off the pile of samples" (624.27–30). In the same image, as her virile nature god, his onrushing spirit in wind and cold takes her breath away (625.8–9, 626.4–7, 626.23–26); his piercing her "rawly," an "invision of Indelond" (626.28), results in three children.[38] As folk hero, representative of the god-hero described in the pub (595.34–596.33), she recognizes him among her mother's store of nursery rhymes and tales such as the *Thousand and One Nights* (627.15–16) : Robinson Crusoe (619.24), Old King Cole (619.27), Sinbad the Sailor (620.7), Neptune-Poseidon with his trident of terrible prongs (628.5), Gulliver (620.13), Uncle Tom (622.7), David with his slingshot (622.18), the king of Asia-Ayesha (625.4), Finn McCool (625.16), the Colossus of Rhodes (625.22), Puss in Boots (621.24–26), the Duke of Wellington (620.9), Masterbuilder Solness (625.11). His current political aspirations resemble those of Dick Whittington (625.35–36), and Anna promises him "Next peaters poll you will be elicted or I'm not your elicitous bribe" (622.1–2). Many such tales, however, popularize nature myths. Of these principally Humpty Dumpty (624.13, 628.11) derives from a myth of the sun-egg, pulled by its forty horses, and the fear that, having set, it may not rise again. Little Red Ridinghood (suggested by several beast images) records the Scandinavian representation of the setting sun as swallowed by a wolf. Jack and the Beanstalk (615.25) preserves the heaven-arching World Tree such as Yggdrasil. Bluebeard (617.21) may be associated with the sacrificial deaths of spouses as found in pyramid tombs, evidence of belief in resurrection.

In application, Anna Livia finds in such tales the archetypes of human life, her relationship with Earwicker, her tenderness, and her fears. At the store he may be "hairy of chest, hamps and eyebags in pursuance to salesladies' affectionate company" (616.14) ; but Beauty and the Beast (which derives from Cupid and Psyche) celebrates love surpassing physical appearances: "Draw back your glave. Hot and hairy, hugon, is your hand! Here's where the falskin begins. Smoos as an infams" (621.24–26). Earwicker's giant strides as Anna imagines a long walk with him calls forth her protest: "Not such big strides, huddy foddy!" (622.9–10). As Finn McCool who could straddle a valley with a foot on either mountain, she cautions him, "Steadyon. Cooloosus! Mind your stride or you'll knock" (625.21–22). His colossal height and his stride contrast with her water level, "dodging the dustbins" (625.23) in her "cubarola glide" (618.22) and leisure paces, a "gentle motion all around" (622.12–23). As Little Goody Twoshoes (622.10) she protests damage to her "antilopes"; she contrasts his fierce battles as Brian Boru and the Russian General (625.17–19) with the tenderness of "A Real Princess" (625.23–25) and empathy for the Babes in the Wood (625.25). His climbing as Masterbuilder Solness opposes her wandering as Little Bo Peep (624.9–10); and she matches his high accomplishments with mere yearning for the olympic heights of Jove (624.10). The heroism of Earwicker's "national cowse," in the terms of Snow White, "was the prick of the spindle to me that gave me the keys to dreamland" (615.28), while Peter who counted numerous pickles (616.11) could judge how much of a man would be left after "private shootings" for slander. This Punch and Judy show of life (620.23–26) at one point elicits a disgusted "Enough of that horner corner. And old mutther-goosip" (623.3–4) but seriously includes tales of its end, dominated by the death goddess who Hansel and Gretel (618.2–3) narrowly escaped and whom Anna anticipates in "the stormies" (627.31) of the sea. Meanwhile, Earwicker's failure to make her a Cinderella ("I thought you were all glittering with the noblest of carriage. You're only a bumpkin"—627.21–22) reflects his "graundplotting and the little it brought" (624.12–13); nevertheless optimism is "in the castles air" (623.19) and the dream survives for her in her "Saltarella" (627.5) daughter.

In scintillating mischief Anna exposes serious national and religious themes in terms of her intimacies with Earwicker. *O felix culpa* becomes "O felicious coolpose!" [*Kolpos,* Greek for vagina]" (618.1); an Alice-in-Wonderland innocence ("beaux to my alce"—618.4). The motto of Sinn Fein recalls a romantic "Ourselves, oursouls alone" (623.28), and the rocky road to Dublin (623.24) provides erotic memories of "Giving Shaughnessy's mare the hillymount of her life" (623.22–23). Lord Lawrence of Howth's famed hospitality means "His door always open. For a newera's day. Much as your own is" (623.5–7). The folk medicine of Anna Livia's earlier "Peeld gold of waxwork" (206.36) reappears with "Pale bellies our mild cure" (618.12–16), cures for genital infections. She suggests another for Earwicker on the morning walk, "the helpyourselftoastrool cure's easy." (622.13).

Surrounded by betrayal and fault, and surviving the threat of McGrath as a snake in the grass, Anna finds something good to publish about everyone; for even Lily "became the wife of Mr. Sneakers for her good name" (618.4–5) and "Sully is a thug from all he drunk through he is a rattling fine bootmaker in his profession" (618.29–30). In the monologue she resolves "The Kinsella woman's man will never reduce me" (622.3–4); and having flowed through all the *Wake*'s motifs, such as the Guinness brewery (621.8), the Lawrences of Howth (623.5–7), the Kerss tailors (623.11), the Vamhomrighs (623.16),[39] the prankquean and Grace O'Malley (623.14), and the unenlightening Four Old Men who sit in pubs talking about writing a "kingly work in progress" (625.2–14), she responds to the knowledge of evil in men with the statement "We'll lave it. So" (621.33)—wash it clean and leave it—and to evil in women, "Allgearls is wea. At times" (626.3).

The washing theme, developed in the Anna Livia Plurabelle chapter, acquired permanence on the landscape when the telling and asking washerwomen were transformed into the tree and the stone, washed by time's waters. They are the brothers Shem and Shaun, whom Anna speculates may have been influenced by "those two old crony aunts . . . Queer Mrs Quickenough [the tree] and odd Miss Doddpebble [the stone]." She adds, in her staunch disapproval of scandalous gossip, "And when them two has had a good few there isn't much more dirty clothes to publish" (620.18–21). She sees spanking new clothes, like his erect posture, important for Earwicker's character, "second to nill" (620.3) and imagines his enemies in swankier suits (629.9–11). She plans for herself a new girdle to improve the portion of her aging body that has "slooped its line" (621.17–20); she cherishes her one decoration, a floating leaf (619.34–35) and wants to be called "Leafiest" (624.22) to remember her association with the vanishing shore. The appearance of clothing is the character of the earth itself, and washing is a perpetual baptism in Anna's waters. The men in the pub have realized the importance of this cosmic renewal: "Mopsus or Gracchus, all your horodities will incessantlament be coming back from the Annone Washwashwhose . . . blanches bountifully and nightsend made up, every article lathering leaving several rinsings so as each rinse results with a dapperent rolle" (614.1–6). Such recurrent "Ardor vigor forders order" (614.0) to find expression in the washerwomen" "Anna was, Livia is, Plurabelle's to be" (215.24) and the men's "Since ancient was our living is in possible to be" (614.10).

The vigor of life means continual strife, which Anna finds Earwicker-like in her twin but differing sons: "Them boys is so contrairy. The Head does be worrying himself. Heel trouble [Shaun] and heal travel [Shem]" (620.12–13), or "One chap googling the holyboy's thingabib [Shaun] and this lad wetting his widdle [Shem]" (620.22–23).

She wishes her daughter "had only more matcher's wit" and fears her gay and youthful irresponsibility (620.29–30); but she and Earwicker rejoice in the children, knowing "He's for thee what she's for me" (620.33), and she consoles herself with accepting all the tides of life, "What will be is" (620.32).

Demonstrating Viconian cycles, Anna's letter (actually three letters) approaches its first close with urging the "mitigation of the king's evils" (619.29) and reiterates the necessity to proceed in spite of defeat or to nullify the terror of death: "Once you are balladproof you are unperceable to haily, icy and missilethroes" (616.31–32). Saint Lawrence as venerated city father exemplifies this theme so that the letter closes hoping for him "all in the best" (616.33–34), signed "Moral"—the writer's name and viewpoint. The first postscript addresses "Mrs Stores Humphreys" (616.36) and anticipates the neutral position of the "Certified reformed peoples" of the close who are quite agreeably deaf; they are those who recognize that a "quiet stinkingplaster zeal" would smother the cause of many a slander on war. The neutrality of "good in even" rather than the particularized faith fosters another beginning (617.5), just as Anna accepts the wrongs of the past and continues in spite of them: "my check is a compleet bleenk. Plub. Meaning: one two four" (617.1–2). With the same counting-rhyme plurality Anna later meets the oncoming waves ("Onetwo moremens more"— 628.5–6) and now closes the letter, "Whereapon our best again to a hundred and eleven ploose one thousand and one other blessings" (617.4–5); but the conclusion "to your great kindness" (617.4) doubles as the second beginning, where "well" (617.13) introduces another newsy letter (617.6–29). This one speaks of funeral arrangements as if the funeral, attended with "earnestly conceived hopes" (617.28) is indeed a phoenix pyre. The letter concludes, "So help us to witness to this day to hand in sleep," signed "From of Mayasdaysed most duteoused" (617.29). Then, to balance men's work, defined by the "Wolkmans Cumsensation Act" (616.25), the third letter (617.30–619.19) concentrates on the "Married Womens Impropery Act" (617.34–35). As such, it disapproves Lily's conduct and corrects rumors about the present household: "Item, we never were chained to a chair, and bitem, no widower whother soever followed us about with a fork on Yankskilling Day" (618.24–26). The letter's third beginning, "Well, here's lettering you erronymously" (617.30) implies the Fall can be a misprint but cites improvement: "Well, our talks are coming to be resumed by more polite conversation with a huntered persent human" (618.35–619.1). Ending on a note of renewal, "for my daily comfreshenall, a wee one woos" (619.16) means "Fostering Mother of Earth and Water and the Beautiful Many." Still typically reluctant to end, the letter's postscript goes on, about life and love, its "Worns out" signalling Anna's admitted weariness.

Not unaffected by the dirt of the world through which she flows, "those slimes up the cavern door around you" (615.34), Anna in a sense welcomes the oblivion of the sea: "All me life I have been lived among them but now they are becoming lothed to me. And I am lothing their little warm tricks. And lothing their mean cosy turns. And all the greedy gushes out through their small souls. And all the lazy leaks down over their brash bodies" (627.16–19). The sequence of her thought surprises her into the realization that she still does not know the reason for her husband's fall: "One time you told you'd been burnt in ice. And one time it was chemicalled after you taking a lifeness. Maybe that's why you hold your hodd as if. And people thinks you missed the scaffold. Of fell design" (621.26–29). She prefers, mother-like, to imagine her giant Earwicker not a general on a white horses but a child beside a toy horse, "a weenywhite steed" (621.31); or so youth preserves an ideal.

The mystery of the letter, the mystery of life itself, now appears in sexual duality, for there are two. Anna imagines joining Earwicker "At the site of salvocean" to "watch would the letter you're wanting be coming may be. And cast ashore" (623.30–31). It merges into Joyce's comment on his own letter, the present book: "Scratching it and patching at with a prompt from a primer. And what scrips of nutsnolleges I pecked up me meself." She alludes to its obscurity, its many languages, its writer's hope for fame: "Every letter is a hard but yours sure is the hardest crux ever. Hack an axe, hook an oxe, hath an an, heth hith ences. But once done, dealt and delivered, tattat, you're on the map" (623.33–35). Womanlike, she abandoned writing her own letter when she heard Earwicker's god-like voice and surrendered her future to him (624.4–6), burying it in the soil of her past, but she consoles him with hope for the letter of the future: "When the waves give up yours the soil may for me" (624.3).

Anna's position in the last paragraph of the novel enforces the neutrality from which may arise a "newera's day"—the gathering together of the elements of lapsed civilization in the *ricorso,* heralding the new cycle. With silence and humility ("humbly dumbly"—628.11), except for the natural creative sounds of moving water ("Lff!"—628.7),

Anna positions herself at the novel's nine closing lines in the center of a series of polarities: "Carry me" (628.8) versus "bearing down on me" (628.9), the commercial ("toy fair"—628.9) versus the spiritual ("Arkangels"—628.10), "die down" (628.11) versus "washup" (628.11), going ("We pass"—628.12) versus "coming" (628.13), an inhalation or water ("Lff!"—628.7) versus an exhalation or wind ("Whish!"—628.13), "There" (628.12) versus "here" (628.13), "hush" (628.12) versus "calls" (628.13), "First" (628.13) versus "last" (628.15), "Take" (628.14) versus "Given" (628.15). Her position, essentially one of weariness, disillusionment, acceptance, neutrality, wakefulness, waifulness, at the dawn of the day, befitting the void before creation, is latent with possibilities for the beginning of life and letters: neither a yes nor a no but a the.

Just as Indian art and mythology (the latter in the Ramayana) represents the Descent of the Ganges from heaven to earth, so also on this softest of Dublin mornings (621.8–9), independent of particular theologies, Anna Livia embraces the world and her spouse in lifegiving fluid. He-it turns toward the brightening day (626.36) which diffuses a white light from Arkangels, transcendent-immanent, to appear golden in her distant hair (619.29–30). The combination of sunlight in Wicklow and rain in Dublin promises a rainbow arc of cosmic love.

Notes

1. See Heinrich Zimmer, *Myths and Symbols in Indian Art and Civilization*, ed. Joseph Cambell (New York: Harper, 1962), p. 35.
2. Gad is a Semitic god of fortune. See Adaline Glasheen, *A Second Census*, p. 92.
3. For translation of "Sandhyas," a prayer recited at dawn, and other Sanskrit terms in the *Wake*'s last chapter, see Campbell and Robinson, *A Skeleton Key*, pp. 340–46.
4. The discussion in the pub, for example, shows Tim being called (598.27) and then thanked for a drink: "Much obliged Time-o'-Thay. But wherth, O Clerk?" (599.3). For his role as clerk in Earwicker's store, see 617.12–14. Mrs. Glasheen has observed that Old Tom is a strong gin. The Egyptian god Tem, chief god of Heliopolis and later joined with Ra, is the Arabic idol Tim. See E. A. Wallis Budge, *The Gods of the Egyptians*, II (London: Methuen, 1904), p. 289. Also Tom is a Greek transcription of Themat-Hert, one of the gods of the Dekan. See *Ibid.*, p. 304. Tum was the great god of Annu, representing the evening or night sun. See Budge, *The Egyptian Book of the Dead* (New York: Dover, 1967), p. cx, a reprint of the 1895 edition of *The Papyrus of Ani*. These variations account in part for the varied vowels of Tim-Tom. See also Edward L. Epstein, "Tom and Tim," *JJQ*, 6 (No. 2), 158–162.

5. Budge writes, "The home and centre of the worship of Ra in Egypt during dynastic times was the city called Annu, or An by the Egyptians, On by the Hebrews, and Heliopolis by the Greeks; its site is marked by the village of Matariyeh, which lies about five miles to the north-east of Cairo." Ra, like Saint Kevin, bathed there each day at sunrise in a lake or pool. See *The Gods of the Egyptians,* I, p. 328.

6. *Ibid.,* p. 134. Since most mythologies depict a sky father overreaching a prone earth mother, Joyce's "old man of the sea and the old woman in the sky" (599.34–35) refers to the Egyptian theogony.

7. See Budge, *The Egyptian Book of the Dead,* p. ciii.

8. "Toph" signifies the Hebrew borrowings from the Egyptian underworld of Tuat in which the power of the sun-engulfing water serpent Apep was destroyed in effigy by fire; the Hebrew abode of the damned, Ge Hinnom or Gehenna, included the place Topheth where sacrifices were burnt. See Budge, *The Gods of the Egyptians,* I, pp. 2/0–2/3.

9. Many mythologies include a dog (for example, Garm in *The Poetic Edda,* Cerberus in the *Aeneid,* Anubis the dog-like jackal of *The Book of the Dead*) who guards the entrance to the afterworld, partly because of the folklore that a dog could see in darkness. For a comparative study, see Maria Leach, *God Had a Dog* (New Brunswick, New Jersey: Rutgers Univeristy Press, 1961).

10. "conjured himself from seight by slide at hand" may imply creation by masturbation, attributed in one version of *The Book of the Dead* to Tem and to Khepera. See *The Gods of the Egyptians,* I, p. 297.

11. Fish gods include Finn; thigh gods are "golden thighed Pythagoras," Jacob of the shrunken thigh, or Set, represented in the northern sky by his "Thigh," the Great Bear constellation; bull gods include Dionysus and the Egyptian Unas. Joyce notes these cosmic bull gods at Glendalough were "a teamdiggingharrow turned the first sod" (600.13–14). Campbell explains "The bull—who not only sired the milk-yielding cows, but also drew the plow, which in that early period simultaneously broke and seeded the earth . . . the horned moon . . . was equated with the bull; so that the animal became a cosmological symbol, uniting the fields and laws of sky and earth." See Joseph Campbell, *Oriental Mythology* (New York: Viking, 1962), p. 41.

12. "Søren" a Scandinavian euphemism for Satan; the devil is "split" or has a cloven hoof, in contrast with God, which is Unity or the One.

13. *Atman* is Sanskrit for the Self, "the Highest Being, of unlimited consciousness and existence" (see Heinrich Zimmer, *Myths and Symbols in Indian Art and Civilization,* ed. Joseph Campbell (New York: Harper, 1962), p. 50) and compares linguistically with the German *atmen,* to breathe, linking the soul with the Breath of Life.

14. The fruit of Eden and the fish of Finn are generalized in world mythology (compare the apple awarded by Paris; the apples of immortality stolen from Ithun in Asgarth; the fisher King myths and the Christian fast day of fishes).

15. "Mildew, murk, leak and yarn" as parody of the nursery rhyme, "Matthew, Mark, Luke and John,/Bless the bed that I lie on" implies many *Wake* themes. This rhyme, write William and Cecil Baring-Gould, was "in the country districts of England, the best-known prayer . . . as the "White Paternoster," it was a night spell; as the "Black Paternoster," a distorted version of it was used as an enchantment by witches. . . . it may be half Celtic magic and half Christian ritual." See *The Annotated Mother Goose* (New York: Bramhall House, 1962), p. 221. With "leak" Joyce implies the

Wake's creation-micturition theme, a Shem-artist theme, as in "This lad wetting his widdle" (620.22). The four terms here summarize the creation process: the minute fungi (mildew) growing in darkness or in the refuse of fruit (murk) combined with fluid (leak), from which are spun the thread of life (yarn) of the literature of cosmogony. In the Eastern process, the world began when Vishnu stirred the water (dew), space began in a tiny cleft (leak) in which wind strove violently so that its friction produced fire which dried up much of the water, so that from the navel of Vishnu springs the lotus—a lengthy yarn.

16. Spirit is often represented as wind and portrayed as birds, which move with outspread wings to catch the air; in "mahamayability" Joyce combines "maya" with Mahayana, a branch of Buddhism. See also 628.10.

17. One thousand mayayugas (4,320,000,000 years) constitute one kalpa, or a single day of brahma; every kalpa is subdivided into fourteen manvantaras. See Zimmer, p. 16. Joyce combines "manvantara" with his madam, "Littlelady" or Anna Livia as universal mother (598.33–36).

18. "Father Times and Mother Spacies boil their kettle with their crutch" (600.2–3) repeats the male and female, cup and lance, symbols known to the Grail myths, as described in Jesse Weston's *From Ritual to Romance*.

19. Hugh Kenner notes MCM (1900) in the sequence "my cold father, my cold mad father, my cold mad feary father" (628.1–2). Since 1900 represents the nineteen centuries as summation of the magical numbers three, seven, and nine, the year should inaugurate a new and better century. See *AWN*, 9 (No. 3), 38.

20. Between February 20 and December 1, "atween Deltas Piscium" or the last sin of the Zodiac with its parallel fishes symbolizing water and mysticism, looking one to the past and one to the future (evolution and involution), and "Sagittariastrion" (600.6), cosmic symbol of the complete man whose animal and spiritual qualities link heaven and earth in the sign of the rainbow.

21. I maintain that Shem and Shaun never "merge" in the *Wake*. Simple characteristics of Shem (he is the artist, partially blind, the tree, fond of words, the hawk or eagle, characterized by the head, condemned as obscene) distinguish him consistently from Shaun (he is the public man, partially deaf, the stone, fond of food, the hen or partridge, characterized by the feet, exonerated as saint).

22. J. Lewis McIntyre, *Giordano Bruno* (London: Macmillan, 1903), p. 257.

23. Since Shaun as stone should represent permanence, I believe the explanation of his asking the time is in *Ulysses*, where Bloom considers magnetism: "Earth for instance pulling this and being pulled. That causes movement. And time? Well that's the time the movement takes. Then if one thing stopped the whole ghesabo would stop bit by bit" (*U* 374).

24. The pelican was thought to feed its young of its own blood from its wounded breast, actually a pouch in which it stored food for its young, and so became a symbol of Christ who shed his blood for mankind.

25. *Oriental Mythology*, p. 101.

26. Campbell discussed this in connection with the "dreamery creamery butter" of the Circe episode of *Ulysses*. See "Contransmagnificandjewbangtantiality," *Studies in the Literary Imagination* 3 (No. 2), 3–18.

27. *Creative Mythology* (New York: Viking, 1968), pp. 259–60.

28. *Ibid.*, pp. 260–61.

29. In solar symbolism, the twelve months of the year have a common center, the sun, represented in twelve disciples with Christ, twelve Knights

of the Round Table with Arthur, the twelve tribes with Levi in the Hebraic Genesis.

30. James Atherton, p. 99.
31. *Oriental Mythology,* pp. 383–84.
32. *Ibid.,* p. 432.
33. Atherton, *Books,* p. 47, pp. 98–99.
34. Shem as Joycean-partially blind artist has a black eyepatch. See also Taff as a "blackseer" (340.13).
35. *Letters,* I, p. 406.
36. *Letters,* III, pp. 345–46.
37. *Letters,* I, p. 406.
38. These passages refer to the drying of the Liffey in 1452, the freezing of the Liffey in 1338, and the "big wind" of 1576 or January 6, 1839.
39. Anna Livia plans a visit to Lord Lawrence of Howth, for his possible patronage of Earwicker, a pattern perhaps provided by Miss Vanhomrigh, Swift's Vanessa, who left Berkeley half her property.